Trafalgar in History

Trafalgar in History

A Battle and its Afterlife

Edited by
David Cannadine

First published 2006 by
PALGRAVE MACMILLAN
Houndmills, Basingstoke, Hampshire RG21 6XS and
175 Fifth Avenue, New York, N.Y. 10010
Companies and representatives throughout the world

PALGRAVE MACMILLAN is the global academic imprint of the
Palgrave Macmillan division of St Martin's Press LLC and of
Palgrave Macmillan Ltd.
Macmillan® is a registered trademark in the United States,
United Kingdom and other countries. Palgrave is a registered
trademark in the European Union and other countries.

ISBN-13: 978-0-230-00900-4 hardback
ISBN-10: 0-230-00900-X hardback

This book is printed on paper suitable for recycling and
made from fully managed and sustained forest sources.

A catalogue record for this book is available from the British Library.

A catalogue record for this book is available from the Library of Congress.

Printed and bound in Great Britain by
Antony Rowe Ltd, Chippenham and Eastbourne

Contents

List of Plates

The plates appear between pp. 120 and 121.

Notes on Contributors

Simon Burrows is Senior Lecturer in Modern European History at Leeds University. His books include *French Exile Journalism and European Politics, 1792–1814* and (jointly with Hannah Barker) an edited collection on *Press, Politics and the Public Sphere in Europe and North America, 1760–1820.*

David Cannadine is Queen Elizabeth the Queen Mother Professor of British History at the Institute of Historical Research, University of London, and Chairman of the Trustees of the National Portrait Gallery. Among his many publications are *The Decline and Fall of the British Aristocracy*; *G.M. Trevelyan: A Life in History*; *Class in Britain*; and *Ornamentalism: How the British Saw their Empire.*

François Crouzet is Emeritus Professor of History at the Université de Paris-Sorbonne. His books include *L'économie britannique et le blocus continental, 1806–1813*; *Britain Ascendant: Comparative Studies in Franco-British Economic History*; *Britain, France and International Commerce*; and *A History of the European Economy, 1000–2000.*

Marianne Czisnik trained and practised as a lawyer in Germany before completing a PhD at the University of Edinburgh on aspects of Nelson's life, image and iconography. She has published on a wide range of subjects related to Nelson. Her book, *Horatio Nelson: A Controversial Hero* will be published in autumn 2006.

Martin Daunton is Professor of Economic History at the University of Cambridge, and Master of Trinity Hall. His most recent work has been on the politics of taxation in Britain since 1799, which resulted in two books: *Trusting Leviathan: The Politics of Taxation in Britain 1799–1914* and *Just Taxes: The Politics of Taxation in Britain 1914–1979.*

Paul Kennedy is the J. Richardson Dilworth Professor of History and Director of International Security Studies at Yale University. He is the author and editor of 14 books, including *The Rise of the Anglo-German Antagonism*; *The War Plans of the Great Powers*; *The Realities Behind Diplomacy*; *The Rise and Fall of the Great Powers* and *Preparing for the Twenty-First Century.*

Roger Knight spent most of his career in the National Maritime Museum, leaving as Deputy Director in 2000. Since then he has been Visiting Professor of Naval History at the Greenwich Maritime Institute at the University of Greenwich, where he wrote *The Pursuit of Victory: The Life and Achievement of Horatio Nelson*.

Andrew Lambert is Laughton Professor of Naval History in the Department of War Studies, King's College, London. He is the author of *The Crimean War: British Grand Strategy against Russia 1853–1856*; *The Last Sailing Battle-fleet: Maintaining Naval Mastery 1815–1850*; *The Foundations of Naval History*; *John Knox Laughton, the Royal Navy and the Historical Profession* and *Nelson: Britannia's God of War*.

Mark Philp is a member of the Department of Politics and International Relations, University of Oxford, and is a Fellow and Tutor in Politics at Oriel College. He is the author of *Godwin's Political Justice*, and *Paine*, and has edited collections of the works of both Godwin and Paine. His most recent work includes *Napoleon and the Invasion of Britain*, co-authored with Alexandra Franklin, and a forthcoming edited volume of essays, *Resisting Napoleon 1797–1815*.

Geoffrey Quilley is Curator of Maritime Art at the National Maritime Museum, Greenwich. He is the co-editor of *An Economy of Colour: Visual Culture and the Atlantic World, 1660–1830* and co-convened the major conference 'Art and the British Empire' at Tate Britain in 2001. He was curator of the international exhibition 'William Hodges 1744–1797: The Art of Exploration' and co-editor of the exhibition catalogue.

N.A.M. Rodger is Professor of Naval History at the University of Exeter. The first two volumes of his *Naval History of Britain* have now been published: *The Safeguard of the Sea, 660–1649* and *The Command of the Ocean, 1649–1815*, and he is currently at work on the final volume.

Introduction

The Battle of Trafalgar was the greatest and most enduring naval victory that the British ever won, and there has been nothing to compare with it, before or since, in the annals of a nation that often claimed to rule the waves, and for the best part of two centuries actually did so. The Armada was seen off without a formal, set piece encounter between the English and Spanish fighting ships. During the seventeenth and eighteenth centuries, there were many naval battles between the British and the French, from the Saints to St Vincent, but none ever attained the iconic significance of Trafalgar. During the nineteenth century, Britain's naval supremacy and global hegemony were never tested by a major engagement on the high seas between rival fleets. And during the twentieth century, the Battle of Jutland was at best a strategic success but a tactical disappointment; there was no great confrontation between the Royal Navy and the enemy battle ships in the Second World War; and the Battle of the Atlantic was a very different sort of encounter, between destroyers and submarines, rather than ships of the line or dreadnoughts, and lasted for years rather than hours. It is, then, scarcely surprising that the bicentennial of the Battle of Trafalgar in 2005 prompted an unprecedented display of retrospection – at least in Britain, although less so in France, where Napoleon's smashing victory at Austerlitz was an understandably more appealing commemoration.

But much of this British retrospection was necessarily ephemeral: the naval review off the Isle of Wight, the thanksgiving service at St Paul's Cathedral, the observances in Trafalgar Square, and the re-enactment of Nelson's funeral procession on the Thames. And most of the enduring publications of 2005 were more concerned to re-examine Nelson's life and death than to re-evaluate the battle which had brought him both mortality and immortality, or to set it in a broader contemporary context or a longer historical perspective. Yet Trafalgar was not only the end point in Nelson's extraordinary biography: it was the culminating encounter in a century-long struggle between the British and the French for what they believed would be global dominion; it was a battle whose significance at the time was varyingly evaluated and whose subsequent meaning has often been mis-understood; it cast an influential and often distorted shadow on British naval thinking and practice during the nineteenth and early twentieth centuries; and across the last 200 years, Trafalgar has been as much a patriotic memory, national myth and invented tradition as an authentic, originating historical event. What was the relative strength of the British and the French economies, and why were the British so much more successful than the French in financing the wars they fought? What was the margin of the British victory at Trafalgar, and how much did it matter in terms of the subsequent history of the Napoleonic Wars? What was Trafalgar's afterlife, in popular culture and naval thinking? And how does the battle look when situated in the longer perspective of British maritime history and the global struggle between great powers? These are some of the questions that are raised and addressed in this book.

In the long run, as Paul Kennedy famously argued in *The Rise and Fall of the Great Powers*, strong economies tend to overwhelm weak economies, not only in terms of wealth and production and output, but also in terms of relative military strength and success. According to François Crouzet, Britain was the most advanced and the richest country in the world in 1805, and its economy was significantly more developed than that of France. To be sure, the pioneering industrial transformation that the nation was undergoing was more evolutionary than revolutionary: but this transformation continued throughout the conflict, and it helped make possible ultimate victory. But wealth has to be mobilized for war, deliberately, directly and effectively, and there, too, the British were superior to the French. Martin Daunton's chapter shows how the British government taxed more efficiently and raised more revenue, and how they floated loans more successfully, and at lower rates of interest, than the French were able to do. Unlike France, the British state never defaulted on its debts, and it was this fiscal strength and robustness which underpinned the British Navy's success at Trafalgar. Only in the realm of propaganda were the French ahead. For as Simon Burrows points out, Napoleon was not only a skilled general, but he was also a master propagandist, who sought to control the public agenda of his empire. Despite the relatively limited resources available, he was remarkably successful in this endeavour, and the British were obliged to increase their own propaganda efforts in response to his.

But while the British nation boasted a stronger and more advanced economy, and also a more efficient and effective way of raising money, there was nothing 'inevitable' about Nelson's extraordinary victory at Trafalgar. Economic strength and sound government revenue may be necessary conditions for military success, but they are not sufficient conditions for it: battles have to be fought – and won. As Roger Knight explains, the British ships were operationally superior to the French in that they fired more frequently, but in numerical terms, there were only just enough of them to fight at Trafalgar. Under the wrongheaded administration of Lord St Vincent, the morale and resources of the British Navy had been much reduced, and his successor, Lord Melville, repaired the damage just in time: by the late summer of 1805. Albeit for different reasons, Trafalgar, like Waterloo, was a close run thing. But where these two battles markedly differed was that Waterloo was a land battle that ended the Napoleonic Wars, whereas Trafalgar was a sea battle that didn't. In this sense, as N.A.M. Rodger explains, it was less significant in influencing the course of the war than its prominent place in British historical memory and myth might suggest. It neither saved Britain from invasion (Napoleon's plans and schemes had already effectively collapsed), nor did it assure ultimate victory (there were ten more years of fighting before that). Thus regarded, the British triumph at Trafalgar was no more decisive than it was inevitable.

Yet the scale of the victory, and the death and glory of Nelson, did give Trafalgar an iconic status which meant that, with appropriate management and manipulation, and also in response to (fluctuating) public and political demand, the battle subsequently took on a life of its own in the nation's consciousness. As such, Trafalgar had not only an historical context, but also an historical afterlife. According to Mark Philp, songs about Nelson had become increasingly common during his day, as one victory followed another; but it was after Trafalgar that they became an integral and long-lasting element of the nation's popular culture. In the same way, and as Geoffrey Quilley explains, the battle was immediately seized upon by artists in Britain, as the ideal subject for modern, national history painting: but as Turner would discover, when he completed his vast canvas in 1824, any extended visual re-creation of Trafalgar was also deeply controversial. Across the nineteenth century, the battle and the death of Nelson were both commemorated annually in a variety of places and forms. But as Marianne Czisnik points out, it was in the late nineteenth and early twentieth century that these occasions reached their climax: partly as the centenary of 1805 drew on, but also because of the growing naval rivalry between Britain and Germany. For most Britons, the hundredth anniversary of Trafalgar was an occasion to proclaim their sense of national identity; but for the Navy League it was an occasion to argue for an increase in spending and in ships.

Where, exactly, did the authentic historic Nelson fit in all this turn-of-the-century junketing and lobbying? The answer, Andrew Lambert insists, is nowhere very obvious. For he argues that it was not only the British people to whom his victory at Trafalgar had become a myth: it was also to the Admiralty and to the politicians who ran it. All of them were bewitched by Nelson's triumph in 1805: but they were bewitched by the wrong version of men and of events. They believed that they had created a modern navy, evolved operational and tactical systems, and promoted commanders, all in Nelson's image, which they were convinced would result in another Trafalgar-like triumph. But all this led to was to Jellicoe and to Jutland. Thus was Trafalgar, by turns, mythologized, mis-remembered, manipulated and mis-understood, and invested with a range of meanings and of expectations which the historical reality could not realistically sustain. But the result, as Paul Kennedy explains in the concluding chapter, was that Trafalgar did become, in its afterlife more than it had been at the time, a world-historical event, a key turning-point in the eternal struggle for power between states and nations and empires.

As these chapters make plain, there are (and were) many Trafalgars, and it is (and was) a battle with many faces and facets. Some of them, but by no means all, are on display here, and as such, this book opens up a subject, but makes no claim to be definitive. The chapters that follow were all originally delivered as lectures at a three-day international conference entitled 'Europe at War: The Trafalgar Campaign in Context', which took place in London in mid July 2005, and which was jointly sponsored by the National Maritime Museum, the Institute of Historical Research, and the Maritime Institute of the University of Greenwich. I am especially grateful to Nigel Rigby, Margarette Lincoln, Sarah Palmer, Roger Knight and Colin White for their work in organizing the conference, and to Janet Norton, Felicity Jones and Richard Butler for running it so smoothly. The ten authors have shown patience, professionalism and promptness in admirable abundance, in getting their chapters in to a very tight deadline. And once again, it has been a pleasure to work with Michael Strang and the staff of Palgrave, and with Ray Addicott and his production team. I thank them all. Now let the Battle of Trafalgar once again be joined!

David Cannadine
National Humanities Research Center,
Research Triangle Park,
North Carolina

15 January 2006

Part One:
The Battle in Context

1
The British Economy at the Time of Trafalgar: Strengths and Weaknesses

François Crouzet

From one very significant perspective, the wars between Britain and France that extended across the whole of the 'long' eighteenth century were wars of rival economies and of relative resources; and this was a conflict which, like the Battle of Trafalgar itself, the British eventually and conclusively won. Accordingly, this chapter seeks to survey the British economy at the beginning of the nineteenth century, for it was Britain's economic strength which underlay the Royal Navy's power. What exactly was the nature of that economic strength, and how did it enable the British to bear the costs of fighting Napoleon? But this was not the only such issue between the two nations during the Napoleonic Wars. For after Trafalgar had been lost, the only weapon which the French could use against Britain was economic: an attack on her trade and finances. And it was just such an attack which Napoleon launched 13 months later when he promulgated the Berlin decree of 21 November 1806, which inaugurated what became known as the Continental Blockade: a blockade not of the Continent by Britain, but of Britain by the (increasingly French-controlled) Continent. Given not only the strengths, but also the weaknesses, of the British economy in the early nineteenth century, it is pertinent to ask how far the nation was vulnerable to the threat embodied in that blockade to close European markets to British exports.

I

In 1805, Britain's economy could be described as being both rich and advanced, but this statement needs some qualifications. She was a rich country by the standards of the time: in 1800, her gross domestic product per capita was about 2,000 dollars at 1990 values, which to us no doubt seems rather low. But at the beginning of the nineteenth century, Britain was the richest country in the world: only the Netherlands approached it, while gross domestic product per capita in France was 30 or 40 per cent below the British level. These figures, like many others I shall quote, are guess-estimates, but they do provide useful, though rough, orders of magnitude.[1] Moreover, Britain was also the most advanced country in the world, as she was already in the throes of the Industrial Revolution, which had hardly started elsewhere. To be sure, this is a concept, and an historical phenomenon, which must be handled carefully, and which some economic historians have called a misnomer. A revolution is a sudden and brutal change – a *coup de Trafalgar*, according to an old French expression. But recent research has shown that the British industrial revolution was slow and gradual. Nevertheless, there was significant and substantial change in the British economy, in a way that was not true of France during the same period.

For some developments, which were truly revolutionary, had been taking place, at a fast pace, since the 1770s, in narrow sectors of British industry. This was especially so in the case of cotton spinning, which had become mechanized and increasingly concentrated in factories, which were often powered by steam. At the same time, the printing of cottons and the throwing of silk had also been mechanized. On the other hand, the weaving of cottons and other fabrics was undertaken by handloom weavers. Another sector which had greatly changed was the primary iron industry; and an engineering industry had also emerged. As for the rest of industry, from brewing to candle-making, it remained largely traditional in its modes of production, even though some innovations had begun to emerge here and there. But outwork and putting out, rather than factory production, were still the most widespread forms of organization. Technological change was thus confined to a narrow sector, and that most revolutionary of recent inventions, the steam-engine, only played a minor role. Indeed, it has been estimated that the social savings due to all steam engines at work in 1800 were only 0.2 per cent of Britain's national income.[2]

Structural change in the British economy was more pronounced; but it had been going on for such a long time – since the seventeenth century – that it was hardly revolutionary. For a long time, agriculture had been releasing labour and other resources, which went into industry and services. Here again, Britain was far ahead of all other countries – including France. Estimates vary, but not too much. In 1801, agriculture employed just under 40 per cent of the labour force, industry about 30 per cent, and services another 30 per cent. As for the contribution of each sector to the national income, they were one third from agriculture, 20 to 25 per cent from industry, and over 40 per cent from services. Britain had industrialized for over a century, but she was not yet an industrial nation (nor an urban nation: only one third of her population lived in large towns).[3] Agriculture was a large sector and a prosperous one during the war, and this had an effect upon the economy as a whole. It also dominated most of Britain, industry being concentrated in small 'manufacturing districts' – islands amidst a sea of rurality. However, if a serious depression struck the branches of industry which were large-scale exporters, great numbers of people would be unemployed and miserable (1 million people may have been employed in exporting industries).

A major conclusion of recent research about British economic growth between 1780 and 1820 is that it was much slower than earlier writers had estimated; a sustained rate of growth of national output of 2 per cent per year was attained only in the 1820s.[4] Admittedly, the few 'glamour' industries, which benefited from decisive technological progress, enjoyed a very fast growth indeed. Between 1790 and 1801, both the cotton and the iron industry grew at 7 per cent per year (the latter was stimulated by the war). But they were exceptions and all other industries grew much more slowly. As a consequence total industrial output grew far less than these most advanced sectors (Table 1.1).[5]

Table 1.1 Rates of growth per year of real output

Industry	Period	Rate of growth (%)
Cotton	1790–1801	6.7
Iron	1790–1801	6.5
Total industrial output	*1790–1801*	*1.8*
Agriculture	1780–1801	0.75
Commodity output	1780–1801	1.35
National product	1780–1801	1.32
National product per capita	1780–1801	0.35
GDP at constant prices*	1788/92–1798/1802	1.4

* Figure from P. O'Brien, unpublished PhD.

Productivity also grew very slowly, except in the handful of glamour industries already mentioned, and it has recently been calculated that the total factor productivity of the British economy grew at a rate of 0.2 per cent per year between 1760 and 1800.[6] In fact, by 1805, Britain was evolving into a two-sector economy. One was undergoing rapid technological progress and productivity growth, but it included only a few industries and it was relatively small (the contribution of the cotton industry to national product was about 5 per cent). The other sector was much larger, but growing and changing slowly. Such a model implies that rapid change in the economy as a whole was a mathematical impossibility,[7] although some economic historians have argued that sharp dividing lines between the traditional and the modern sectors are inappropriate, because of many interactions between these two ostensibly separate sectors, and also because of improvements in techniques in the traditional sector.[8]

Several writers have seen this slow growth during the late eighteenth and early nineteenth centuries as abnormal, and argue that it may be explained by the low level of capital formation resulting from the costs and consequences of fighting the wars against France. According to this interpretation, the enormous loans which the British government issued to finance its war effort absorbed a large share of the nation's savings and deprived the private sector of much-needed capital. As a result, productive investment in industry was kept below the level it would have reached had Britain been at peace: it was 'crowded out' by the government's borrowing to finance war. And there are statistics to support this interpretation: Jeffrey Williamson estimated the rate of capital formation in Britain from 1791 to 1801 to be only 9 or 10 per cent of national income; N.F.R. Crafts puts the ratio of gross domestic investment in 1800 and 1801 at only 8 per cent of gross national product.[9]

But other economic historians have dismissed the 'crowding out' thesis. They argue that there was no inverse relationship between government loans and capital formation, for *both* peaked during the late 1790s, thanks to a rise in total private savings. Well-to-do Britons were encouraged by the Jacobin threat to save more, and to lend to the British government to finance the defence of the realm and thus of their own property. Moreover, the younger William Pitt and his successors practised virtuous fiscal and monetary policies from 1797 onwards: borrowing was kept under control, and popular consumption was restricted, as a result of which private capital formation was encouraged. And throughout the war, nominal interest rates were not markedly higher than in peacetime, which suggests that there was no tension on the capital market between the demands of industry and the demands of government.[10] Such criticisms of the 'crowding out' thesis are valid, but it has not been entirely destroyed. For the enormous drainage of funds towards the Exchequer, which went on for over 20 years, must have had some negative impact upon private investment, especially in industry; but this investment was restrained and not crowded out, and the growth of Britain's productivity and of its gross domestic product was also restrained.[11]

II

An important feature of the British economy at the time of Trafalgar was that it was an open economy, with a large foreign trade; and it was this export sector which Napoleon sought to target. British exports had grown rapidly during the 1780s, there had been a slowdown after war broke out with France in 1793, but then a sharp increase from 1798 to 1802. During these years, trade grew thanks to the technological progress of the Industrial Revolution, which made British cotton yarn and goods cheaper relatively to other textiles, so that they were exported to Europe and the United States of America in unprecedented quantities. At the same time, re-exports of foreign and colonial goods had grown specially fast during the 1790s, thanks to the ruin of San Domingo and to the occupation of enemy colonies (Table 1.2).[12]

Table 1.2   Mean rates of growth in exports per year

	Exports (%)	Re-exports (%)	Total exports (%)
Volume			
1781–1792	7	5	7
1792–1802	4	11	6
Computed values			
1784/86–1804/06	6	5	6

But Britain's exports reached a peak in 1802, during the peace of Amiens, they fell back sharply in 1803 when war was resumed, and they did not recover much in 1804 or in 1805. This set-back resulted from a fall in exports to Europe, even though only part of the Continent was then under French control. This in turn suggests that British exports were vulnerable to the closing of European markets. However, during previous conflicts, British trade had had to adapt and reorient, according to the vicissitudes of war. Experience had shown that indirect routes could be found to go round obstacles to British trade; the art of smuggling had developed in countries subject to France, even though war caused rises in transaction costs.

A crucial problem is to try to determine how far the British economy at the time 'depended' upon foreign trade. The very idea that it did so is anathema to most economists, who consider that resources which are devoted to producing goods for export can be reallocated to make substitutes for imports, so that 'even on the absurd premise of no foreign trade at all, Britain's loss would have been small'. But it has also been conceded that 'had Britain suddenly be denied all trade by strike or edict, the immediate effects would have been larger' – which is precisely what happened as a result of Napoleon's Continental Blockade.[13]

So it is worth trying to find out how far Britain was 'dependent' upon foreign trade on the eve of the Blockade. It has recently been calculated that the ratio of exports (re-exports excluded) to national output had increased from 9 per cent in 1780 to 16 per cent in 1801; while the ratio of exports to gross industrial output had risen from 22 per cent in 1780 to 34 per cent – a full third – in 1801.[14] But the export ratio varied widely between industries, as is shown in Table 1.3.[15]

Table 1.3   Export ratios in selected industries

1801	Cotton	Woollens and worsteds	Iron and steel
Proportions of gross output sold abroad (%)	62	35	24
Shares of exports in total exports (%)	40	17	9

During the late 1790s, the cotton industry had become the leading exporter, overtaking the venerable woollen and worsted industry (although that continued to maintain significant exports, nonetheless). The secondary metal trades of Birmingham and Sheffield were responsible for most of the metal exports (which included exports of raw or wrought non-ferrous metals). As for the rest of British industry, its role in the export trade was small and its exports-ratio was quite low.

The distribution of British exports between their main overseas markets must also be considered, and they can be divided into three major groups. The first was Continental Europe, which was liable to fall, in part or in toto, under Napoleon's domination. The second was the United States of America, which was the leading neutral power, but also for Britain a potential enemy, because of a number of differences between the two English-speaking nations. (Indeed, in April 1806, the United States Congress would vote a non-importation act against British goods, an omen of a succession of hostile measures which eventually resulted in the Anglo-American War of 1812.) The third was the rest of the world, which consisted mainly of British possessions (Ireland, the British West Indies, British North America, and India), and eventually, from 1808 onwards, the Portuguese and Spanish colonies as well. I shall describe this rather motley group as the zone of British influence. Table 1.4 shows the distribution of British exports between these three markets, in the year of Trafalgar.[16]

Table 1.4   Distribution of British exports, current values in 1805

	Exports (%)	Re-exports (%)	Total exports (%)
Continental Europe	33	68	40
USA	27	4	22
Zone of British influence	40	28	38

Most of Britain's trade with the Continent was with Northern Europe – mainly with the North Sea ports of Germany. Exports to countries around the Baltic and to Southern Europe were much smaller. A complete closure of the Continent to British goods by France was a pipedream, but a partial closure could have serious effects for British industry – or at least for the cotton and wool industries – especially if it coincided with a closure of the American market. British trade with the United States had grown very rapidly since the end of the war between the two countries in 1783 and it had played a decisive role in the overall expansion of British exports, with the result that newly-independent America had become Britain's most important single customer. So the major danger for Britain in the aftermath of Trafalgar was a simultaneous closing of both the Continental and the American markets, which together took in 1805 over 60 per cent of total British exports. Britain's cotton industry was especially dependent upon Europe and the United States, which together received over seventy per cent of its exports, and these two markets also took two thirds of woollen and worsted exports. By contrast, the rest of the world took about 40 per cent of Britain's exports, the main markets being Ireland and the West Indies. This trade was safe, because it was under the protection of the Royal Navy; but the matter was not that simple (or that comforting), for the purchasing power of the colonies depended partially upon re-exports of colonial produce from Britain to the Continent.

As an open economy, Britain was not only a large exporter, but also a big importer. Imports were made up first of raw materials for industry. All cotton came of course from abroad, mainly from the United States, as well as raw silk (partly from Italy, partly from the East Indies); and home production in wool, flax and tallow had to be completed by imports from Europe.[17] But imports also consisted of naval stores and grain. The former were indispensable for building and maintaining ships. Britain had a shortage of timber, especially of masts; she also needed hemp, pitch, and tar. The main source of naval stores was Northern Europe – Russia, Prussia, Sweden, Norway: all countries which might join the Continental Blockade. Still, dockyards had reserves of stores and enormous potential reserves of timber stood in the forests of British North America.[18] As for grain: during the second half of the eighteenth century, despite much technical progress in farming, Britain's food production had lagged behind population growth, and except in years of bumper crops, the country had a deficit and imported grain in increasing quantities. On average, imports covered one tenth of the nation's wheat consumption, but they were much larger if the harvest failed. Moreover, three quarters of grain imports came – like naval stores – from Northern Europe. Serious difficulties could therefore emerge, as in 1799 and 1800, when two consecutive bad harvests, and the action of the League of Neutrals, threatened grain supplies, and caused a panic. Wheat prices increased three-fold from November 1798 to April 1801; the cost of living went up by 57 per cent from 1798 to 1800, real earnings fell by 30 per cent, and for a time riots threatened public order. This partly explains why the British government decided to open negotiations with France. A similar combination of bad weather and blockade might happen again.[19]

On the other hand, if we do not consider accidents like those of 1795, 1799–1800, but averages of several years, then wage earners' real incomes, which strongly recovered after bad years, appear stable to the optimist, or stagnant to the pessimist. In fact, the prevalent view is that the workers' standards of living neither improved nor deteriorated during the Industrial Revolution. And it was as a result of this strong performance by the British economy that the wars with France, despite some sharp fluctuations in earnings and the pressures of military expenditure, did not depress the standards of living of the workers, and real private consumption per capita, for long. In any case, in 1800, private consumption was only 77 per cent of Britain's national expenditure. One must therefore stress not only the heavy burden of the war but also the capacity of the British economy to bear this burden.[20]

III

This leads us to finances. Britain's banking system was more developed and sophisticated than in any other country. It consisted of three tiers: the Bank of England, the London private banks, and country banks by the hundreds (Scotland had a special regime). The Bank of England

and the country banks issued banknotes, which had been convertible into gold up to the crisis which broke out in February 1797. Because of a combination of circumstances, the Bank of England had been losing gold in large quantities. The news of a small French landing in South Wales had been the last straw and, on 26 February, an Order-in-Council authorized the Bank to suspend its payments in specie. However, this was not the disaster which some expected. There was no collapse of public credit and confidence was soon restored. It was decided that the suspension of cash payments would continue up to the peace, and this was a major advantage for Britain, which was lucky to have suffered this crisis early in the war, for the simple reason that it could not happen a second time. Whatever economic and political upheavals took place, the Bank of England's cash reserves could not be suddenly drained away. The nation's currency and credit were no longer at the mercy of a panic; borrowing by government, and a liberal credit policy by the banks were made easier.[21]

However, the pound was vulnerable to inflationary supply shocks as in 1799–1801, when the balance of payments had also been in heavy deficit because of grain imports and on account of military and political expenditures abroad. As a result, the pound fell on foreign exchange markets, a premium appeared on precious metals (reaching 18 per cent on silver in 1801), and at the same time, the circulation of banknotes sharply increased. But this crisis did not persist, and it was succeeded by several years of monetary stability, from 1803 to 1807. Prices fell, rates of exchange were close to par, the premium on gold was only 5 per cent in 1805, the depreciation of the pound was slight and public opinion ignored it.[22] Still, this stability was fragile, and depended on favourable circumstances: foreign trade prospered, while the government did not undertake heavy expenditures abroad. If circumstances changed, the situation might well deteriorate. And there were two more direct threats. First: the danger of excessive money creation, which was built into the banking system. The men who ran the Bank of England had the power to control the volume of credit and money, and they ignored this danger. They never refused any advance to the government, and they discounted any good bill of exchange. The second threat was the balance of payments, which would fall into deficit if there was a fall in exports, an increase of heavy grain imports, or the sudden incurring of large expenditures abroad by government, as in late 1805, when the modest subsidies Britain sent to Austria and Russia resulted in a fall of foreign exchanges. The British pound was at risk of depreciating, and that was a risk which the Continental Blockade would make worse. It was also exposed to inflationary pressures, but there was no danger of run-away inflation. The paper pound was not the *assignat*. [23]

On the other hand, and despite these weaknesses, Britain's monetary and banking system was a source of strength, and a formidable weapon in the fight against France. Credit facilities to industry and trade supported activity in case of recession; they also made it easier for government to finance the war effort. The French might consider the British credit system as a house of cards, but in fact it was a major asset to Britain. Still, a weak balance of payments and a serious depreciation of the pound could hamper Britain's operations on the Continent and limit the financial help she could make available to her allies.

IV

To sum up, the British economy in the year of Trafalgar did indeed have some weak points. Its major industries depended largely for their overseas markets upon exports to Europe and to the United States. The country needed naval stores and grain which came from Northern Europe. There were also weaknesses in the balance of payments and in the position of the pound. Napoleon's blockade plus a quarrel with the USA could create much unemployment, plus shortages and inflation. On the other hand, Britain's economy was advanced, flexible, powerful, and resilient. Thanks to the agricultural revolution, a growing population was fed, most of the time, from home sources. Entrepreneurship and dynamism prevailed among businessmen. And neither the ruling oligarchy nor the business middle classes were in the least disposed to accept defeat.[24] The 'crowding out' thesis maintained that Britain did not have enough resources for both industrializing and waging large-scale and protracted wars. Actually she had – or almost. I am reminded of a cartoon of the 1960s, when the Liberal Party was holding a conference. A crowd of young Liberals were carrying placards with the usual slogan: 'Make love, not war'. Two old Liberals were looking and one said: 'But Lloyd George made both!' In the same way, Britain went on with her industrial revolution (though likely at a slower pace), and the war was eventually won, while standards of living were roughly maintained. This was a remarkable achievement.

Notes

1. Angus Maddison, *L'économie mondiale: une perspective millénaire* (Paris, 2001), p. 264, table B-13; Angus Maddison, *L'économie mondiale. Statistiques historiques* (Paris, 2003), pp. 62–3, t. 1 c; Roderick Floud and Paul Johnson, *The Cambridge*

Economic History of Modern Britain, Vol. I (Cambridge, 2004), pp. 456, 463, t. 16.4 and 16.6.

2. Quoted in Floud and Johnson, *Cambridge Economic History of Modern Britain*, p. 144.
3. N.F.R. Crafts, *British Economic Growth during the Industrial Revolution* (Oxford, 1985), pp. 15, t. 2.2, 14, 62–3, t. 3.6.
4. Ibid., pp. 2, 47; Joel Mokyr in Floud and Johnson, *Cambridge Economic History of Modern Britain*, p. 1.
5. Crafts, *British Economic Growth*, pp. 23, t. 2.4, 26, t. 2.6, 32, t. 2.7, 42, t. 2.10, 45, t. 2.11, 46, t. 2.12; François Crouzet, *L'économie britannique et le Blocus Continental* (Paris, 1987, 2nd edition), pp. xlvii–xlviii.
6. Crafts, *British Economic Growth*, p. 159, t. 8.1.
7. Mokyr in Floud and Johnson, *Cambridge Economic History of Modern Britain*, p. 5.
8. Maxine Berg and Pat Hudson, 'Rehabilitating the Industrial Revolution', *Economic History Review* 45, 1 (February 1992): 24–50.
9. Jeffrey G. Williamson, 'Why was British Growth so Slow during the Industrial Revolution?', *Journal of Economic History* 14, 3 (1984): 687–712; Crafts, *British Economic Growth*, p. 73, t. 4.1; Crouzet, *L'économie britannique*, pp. li–lii.
10. Patrick Karl O'Brien, 'The Impact of the Revolutionary and Napoleonic Wars, 1793–1815, on the Long-Run Growth of the British Economy', *Review. Fernand Braudel Center* 12, 3 (summer 1989): 345 sqq.
11. Crouzet, *L'économie britannique*, pp. liii–liv, lvi–lxi; H.V. Bowen, *War and British society, 1688–1815* (Cambridge, 1998), pp. 63–5.
12. B.R. Mitchell, *British Historical Statistics* (Cambridge, 1988), pp. 450, 452; F. Crouzet, 'The Impact of the French Wars on the British Economy', in H.T. Dickinson (ed.), *Britain and the French Revolution* (Basingstoke, 1989), p. 191, t. 1.
13. In Floud and Johnson, *Cambridge Economic History of Modern Britain*, pp. 191–2, 194–5.
14. Crafts, *British Economic Growth*, pp. 131–2, t. 6.6 and 6.7.
15. Ibid., p. 143, t. 7.2 and 7.3.
16. Table based on Crouzet, *L'économie britannique*, p. 884, t. 2; also Mitchell, *British Historical Statistics*, p. 498.
17. Crouzet, *L'économie britannique*, pp. lxxxv, 84, 86.
18. Ibid., p. 90.
19. C.H. Feinstein, 'Pessimism perpetuated. Real wages and the standard of living in Britain during and after the industrial revolution', *Journal of Economic History* 58 (1998): 640, t. 2, 648, t. 5, 652–3, t. 1.
20. Ibid., pp. 642, 649, 652; Crafts, *British Economic Growth*, p. 63, t. 3.6; Crouzet, *L'économie britannique*, pp. lxxiv–lxxxvii.
21. Crouzet, *L'économie britannique*, pp. 105–6; Floud and Johnson, *Cambridge Economic History of Modern Britain*, pp. 156, 162.
22. Crouzet, *L'économie britannique*, p. 109.
23. Ibid., pp. 111–15, 117, 119; Crouzet in Dickinson, *Britain and the French Revolution*, p. 196.
24. Crouzet, *L'économie britannique*, pp. 203–4.

2
The Fiscal-Military State and the Napoleonic Wars: Britain and France Compared

Martin Daunton

General rule: one can raise higher taxes, in proportion to the liberty of the subjects; and one is forced to moderate them to the degree that servitude increases. This has always been, and will always remain so. It is a rule drawn from nature, which does not vary at all; one finds it in all countries, in England, in Holland, and in all States in which liberty becomes degraded, right down to Turkey.

Charles Montesquieu, *De l'esprit des lois*, *III*, 1748, ch. 7[1]

It might be expected that in France a revenue of thirty millions might be levied for the support of the state with as little inconveniency as a revenue of ten millions is in Great Britain. In 1765 and 1766, the whole revenue paid into the treasury of France … did not amount to fifteen millions sterling…. The people of France, however, it is generally acknowledged, are much more oppressed by taxes than the people of Great Britain.

Adam Smith, *The Wealth of Nations*, 1776, book 1, 2, p. 47[2]

These two great representatives of the French and Scottish enlightenment realized that the finances of their two nations had taken very different paths. Despite the larger population of France and its great resources, it could raise much less revenue than Britain – yet the French people believed that their burdens were greater. Louis XIV's finance minister, Jean-Baptiste Colbert (1619–1683), put the matter more graphically in his reputed remark that 'the art of taxation consists in so plucking the goose as to obtain the largest possible amount of feathers with the smallest possible amount of hissing'.[3] The British goose was plucked more skilfully than its French counterpart. Apart from riots against the malt tax in Scotland in 1725, fuelled by Jacobite and nationalist sentiments against a supposed breach of the terms of Union in 1707, and the 'excise crisis' of 1733–34, taxes in Britain achieved a remarkably high level of consent and compliance.[4] The British state in the eighteenth century was able to extract more revenue from its subjects with fewer political difficulties. In 1700–25, the English paid something over twice the French level of taxes per capita, and by the 1780s the discrepancy had widened to 2.7 times.[5] The contrast was still more obvious in the French financial and political crisis of 1788/89 when a much smaller financial burden than in Britain started the chain of events leading to Revolution and – in due course – Trafalgar. The weakness of French finances contributed to the demise of the *ancien régime*, and the strength of British finances underpinned military and naval success.

I

Military spending formed a very high proportion of total government expenditure in England/Britain, amounting to 74 per cent in the War of Austrian Succession between 1689 and 1697, 71 per cent in the Seven Years War of 1756–63, and 61 per cent in the American War of Independence between 1775 and 1783. The navy was usually the single largest component of government spending. In 1765, the new first-rate man of war, HMS *Victory*, cost £63,174 to build – a vast sum compared with the investment in a cotton mill at around £5,000. The cost of keeping a first-rate ship seaworthy was around £26,000 a year. The naval dockyards were amongst the largest industrial plant of the eighteenth century, involving massive investments. At the end of the Seven Years War, £680,000 was spent on improvements at Portsmouth and Plymouth. Provisioning the navy was a major task, for the ship-board population of 40,000 in the middle of the eighteenth century exceeded the population of any British city except London. In the year of Trafalgar, net spending on the navy was £17.0m.[6] Such a level of spending was only possible because the legitimacy of the taxation system of Britain far outstripped that of France, and the efficiency of the market for government loans in London was far superior to that in Paris. Contemporaries such as Montesquieu and Smith were well aware of the differences, as were politicians and officials in France who realized that they lacked the financial clout of their enemy.

In the early modern period, European states more or less successfully transformed themselves from 'domain states' which relied on the landed estates of rulers for their finance, and the provision of goods and services by dependants. Elements of the domain state survived into the nineteenth century in some parts of Europe, such as Prussia with its state mines, forests and railways. However, the costs of warfare forced most European states to turn to taxes for revenue, which led to conflict over the surplus available in economies with little spare capacity. The state's demand for taxes conflicted with the landlords' desire for rent, the churches' claim for tithes, and the peasants' livelihood or subsistence. These conflicting demands were resolved (as far as that was possible) through negotiation and alliances between the crown and various interests. Consent to taxation might be achieved by giving exemptions to particular groups, such as nobles and the church. The crown might form a mutually beneficial alliance with aristocratic landlords to erode the position of small peasants – or the crown might side with the peasantry against the landlords. In Reformation Europe, the crown might confiscate church land and remove the exemption of the clergy, unlike in Counter-Reformation Europe where the position of the church was usually strengthened. In some states, consent was achieved through regular meetings of assemblies or parliaments; in other states, the crown managed without representative assemblies or estates. Where assemblies controlled direct taxes, the crown might opt instead for indirect taxes to preserve its autonomy. In some cases, the crown secured the right to tax without future meetings of assemblies or estates, so creating problems when fundamental reform of the tax system was needed which would require the consent of taxpayers. The estates could be side-lined by turning to other methods of raising revenue, such as the sale of offices. The process of transformation from a domain to a tax state took very different forms in European states, and not least between Britain and France.[7]

Prior to 1688, taxes in England were usually in the range of 1.3 to 4.4 per cent of national income, a relatively low level compared with France. The accession of William III and wars with France between 1689 and 1697 took the level of taxation/spending to between 7.3 and 9.5 per cent of national income, and it remained at around 8 to 10 per cent until the outbreak of the French revolutionary wars. Between 1790 and 1810, total government expenditure in Britain rose from 12 per cent of GNP to 23 per cent. Britain made a further transformation from a tax state into a 'fiscal state' or, more precisely, a 'fiscal-military state' – the only such state in Europe by 1815. In a fiscal state, a steady and secure flow of tax revenues formed the basis for large-scale borrowing without the threat of default and hence the need for the state to pay high interest rates to obtain funds. The level of expenditure during a war far exceeds the annual flow of income from taxation, so that success in battle depends not only on the prowess of soldiers and sailors but on the ability to raise loans on favourable terms to provide them with munitions, pay and provisions, as well as making large investments in ships and fortifications. Warfare needs both taxes *and* loans. By the end of the war against Napoleon, about 55 per cent of the gross expenditure of the central government went in interest payments on these loans or servicing the national debt.[8] The British government was able to sustain payments of interest on the national debt and to avoid defaulting on its loans. The next section considers why Britain was able to extract taxes at a higher level and with less resentment than in France.

II

Why was the British state able to extract taxes much more easily than the French state in the course of the long eighteenth century? The answer was partly a matter of timing. In the seventeenth century, the French were heavily involved in large-scale European land warfare and needed to find large sums of money in excess of the annual flow of tax revenues.[9] The solution was to sell offices and to 'farm' taxes. In both cases, the purchaser of the office or tax farm made a down-payment in return for the future income from an office or the collection of taxes. Colbert consolidated the collection of most excise duties in one tax farm, the Farmers General – a drive for efficiency that gave the farmers more control over the fiscal system. By the second half of the eighteenth century, the Farmers General employed 35,000 men, of whom 20,000 comprised a paramilitary force. In the 1780s, the Farmers General collected 150m livres a year of which about 30m livres were paid to officials, and 100m livres were handed over to the Hotel de Ville in Paris for direct payment to debt holders; only 18m livres went to the crown.[10]

The sale of offices offered another way of raising large sums of money. The crown sold offices in return for a capital sum, and also levied continuing payments to allow the right to sell or inherit the office; in return it paid a salary or *gage* to the office-holder to give a return on the investment. In the seventeenth and early eighteenth centuries, the crown received a large income from the sale of offices; the contribution of venality to revenues fell by the middle of the eighteenth century, and probably contributed only 5 per cent of the cost of the Seven Years War. The original justification of venality had been lost: as William Doyle remarks, 'What remained was the swollen bulk of the legacy, now largely there because it was there – too expensive, and extensive, even to dream of abolishing.'[11] By contrast, seventeenth-century England was much less involved in European land wars and so did not need to engage in tax farming or the sale of offices on anything like the scale of France. Indeed, tax farming was generally ended in the later seventeenth century: the farms of customs, excise and hearth tax were abolished in 1671, 1683 and 1684 respectively. The relatively low number of offices sold meant that the English state escaped from France's curse of 'a sprawling, tentacular state apparatus made up of venal office holders'.[12]

French reliance on the sale of offices and tax farming contributed to the lack of consent to taxation in the eighteenth century. The sale of offices meant that the bureaucracy was large, unaccountable, and exempt from taxes. Office-holders took their fees and salaries, and left the work to paid deputies. Why would taxpayers wish to pay in order to support a venal system of administration? Why would they willingly hand over their taxes to a 'farmer' who retained the difference between the actual revenue and what he promised to pay the state? Tax exemptions extended to the church and to the nobility, so that the payment of taxes was perceived as biased and partial. French taxes might be lower than in Britain, but they lacked consent and legitimacy.

The contrast was reinforced by the process of negotiating taxes with the subjects of the crown. In France, representative institutions were much weaker than in England and Britain, and there was no political forum for negotiating changes in the system of taxation. The Estates General – an assembly of the three estates of clergy, nobility, and commoners – did not develop in the same way as the English parliament with control over finances, legislative authority and the ability to initiate policies. The Estates General were called by the king to provide advice, and had no legislative power which rested entirely with the crown. By the second half of the seventeenth century, after an attempt by the Estates to assert their control, the monarch had established the right to impose taxes on his own authority. Indeed, the Estates General were not called at any time between 1614/15 and 1789 when the decision marked a political crisis that soon escalated into revolution.[13]

Provincial Estates General with limited powers did survive in the *pays d'états* such as Brittany, Burgundy and Provence. In Britain, separate Scottish and Irish parliaments were abolished at the time of Union so that there was one unified representative body which minimized (though it did not entirely remove) opposition to taxation. The survival of provincial Estates in France created fiscal complexities, for they had a variety of exemptions (such as Brittany's exemption from the salt tax), and each might challenge the power of the crown to levy taxes without consent. The closest similarity is with the revolt of the Thirteen Colonies from British rule. The assembly in Massachusetts opposed the imposition of taxes by Britain to which it had not consented, leading to revolt and ultimate independence. In the case of France, similar tensions existed within the domestic sphere.[14]

In the absence of the Estates General, the only real counter to royal power came from the *parlement* of Paris and the provincial *parlements* in a number of other cities around France. The Paris *parlement* differed from the British parliament which passed legislation and took an active role in shaping policy. Its initial role was judicial rather than representative, with political influence as a result of registering royal edicts and hence providing at least a veneer of legitimacy. Although *parlement* had the right to remonstrate at any breach of tradition, the king could impose his will by summoning the *parlement* to his presence or by issuing an order that they obey. The difficulties were apparent to Nicholas de Maupeou, the royal chancellor between 1768 and 1774, who had been president of the *parlement* from 1763 to 1768. In his new royal position, he soon realized that *parlement* could resist change and defend privileges without making any positive proposals for reform. Maupeou concluded that the only way forward was through royal imposition of reform from above. In 1771, Louis XV abolished the Paris *parlement* and replaced it with a new judicial court without the power of opposition. Not surprisingly, the result was highly unpopular and Maupeou's attempt to force through financial reform soon failed. In 1774, Louis XVI restored *parlement* and tensions reappeared. The ability to raise taxes meant either a wider political participation as in Britain or the adoption of a more absolutist policy as in 1771–74, but the crown was not firmly committed to either approach.[15]

Jacques Turgot, as controller general or minister of finance between 1774 and 1776, tried to reduce government spending and increase revenue by stimulating private enterprise and overturning Colbert's policy of state-sponsored industries which he believed were inefficient and uncompetitive. He soon ran into problems as the cost of involvement in the American War of Independence mounted. His abolition of controls on the trade in grain in 1775 coincided with crop failures and led to food riots which were put down with considerable force. His popularity fell still further in 1776 when he removed the *corvée* or peasants' labour service to the state and introduced a tax on property which outraged landowners. Turgot pressed ahead with his policies by means of royal decrees rather than consultation, but in 1776 he lost royal favour and was removed from power. His successor, Jacques Necker, was a disciple of Colbert and reversed most of Turgot's reforms. Rather than raising revenues through economic growth, he relied on short-term loans – a strategy which secured immediate popularity at the cost of potential bankruptcy. He lost power in 1781, and his successors, Alexandre de Calonne and Etienne Charles de Lomenie de Brienne, had no more success in restoring order to French finances. Despite their personal animosity, both wished to introduce a new land tax which met with opposition from the *parlement* of Paris in 1787. Brienne sent the *parlement* of Paris into exile, and their stand-off came to a conclusion in 1788 when the *parlement* resolved on its dissolution, on condition that the Estates General were called to deal with the imminent bankruptcy of the French state.[16]

III

Turgot's attempt to reform the tax system relied on imposition from above through decrees, and Brienne's proposals collided with the *parlement* of Paris with eventually disastrous consequences. France lacked a political forum for negotiating changes in the system of taxation, unlike in England/Britain where acceptance of taxes was secured in parliament which met every year after 1688. In contrast with France, parliament controlled the taxing powers of the state. In France, spending was determined by the monarch and his officials who were themselves exempt from direct taxes. *Parlement* could then seek to block the authority to tax to meet the crown's expenditure. In England/Britain, spending and the authority to tax to meet the expenditure were integrated. In 1697, parliament granted the crown a 'civil list' for its upkeep and for the salaries and pensions of judges, officials and courtiers. Parliament did not grant a permanent revenue to the king for additional expenditure, above all on war, which was voted on an annual basis.[17]

Parliament was therefore a forum for negotiating an acceptable level of spending and the composition of taxes in Britain. Constraint on the central executive resulted in a high level of consent, and resistance to taxation was limited. Of course, the distribution of seats in the Commons bore little relationship to the population, with many 'pocket boroughs' and control by large aristocratic landowners. One outcome, as we shall see, was a fall in the contribution of landowners to the revenues of the state. Nevertheless, commercial interests were represented either through purchasing seats or by ensuring that local landowners expressed their views through lobbying and bargaining at election time. Any changes in the structure of taxes or adjustment in duties were negotiated between different interests, whether North European merchants protesting against preference to timber from North America, woollen textile producers seeking to limit competition from Indian cotton cloth, or West Indian planters eager to secure markets for their sugar against East India Co. pressure for a free trade in sugar and a monopoly for their China tea.[18] The balance of custom and excise duties on different commodities was negotiated rather than imposed, and in the process economic interest groups were incorporated into the political system. Parliament was deeply jealous of its fiscal powers, as was apparent in the excise crisis of 1733–34. Robert Walpole's proposed extension of the excise duties led to a fear that he intended to introduce a general excise on all commodities and hence to free the executive from parliamentary control and to overturn the constitutional settlement of 1697. The country gentry, with their dread of a powerful central executive, united with commercial interests in opposition to the proposals.[19] Strict limits were set to the independence of the central executive from parliamentary control.

The ability of parliament to control the executive and monitor spending rested on the availability of reasonably accurate accounts supplied to parliament by the Treasury Commissioners. Britain was the first European state to compile a full statement of its financial position, which meant that its operations were visible. Representatives in parliament could challenge waste, so that taxpayers had some confidence that their payments were being used for the intended purpose. Similarly, the state's creditors had confidence that the state was solvent and honest. The same could not be said of France, where accounts simply did not exist – and when Necker did attempt to produce a financial statement in his *Compte Rendu* of 1781, the result was scepticism rather than confidence.[20]

Whereas the costs of the American War of Independence resulted in crisis in France, in Britain it led to 'economical reform' or a concern for administrative efficiency. The Association movement and others demanded an end to sinecures, a reduction in the costs of government and the court, and constraints on the excessive power of the executive. Politicians at Westminster responded by taking steps to improve the efficiency of financial administration, by controlling expenditure and preventing waste through the work of the Commission for Examining the Public Accounts of 1780 and parliamentary committees to examine expenditure and accounting methods in 1782, 1786 and 1792. The work was continued by William Pitt who took steps to reduce the national debt and to adjust the level of duties in order to increase their yield, and to remove sinecures from the Customs service. By taking action, ministers aimed to separate demands for economical reform from pressure for parliamentary reform and attacks on the crown. The government's desire for efficiency in order to protect the credit-worthiness of the state coincided with the demands of the critics. The Association movement was in part a 'country' critique of court and the great magnates – but it was also a demand for professionalism and commercial probity in the affairs of the state.[21]

Parliamentary scrutiny of spending meant that the British state was more public and accountable, and hence 'stronger rather than weaker, more effective rather than more impotent. Public scrutiny reduced peculation, parliamentary consent lent greater legitimacy to government action. Limited in scope, the state's powers were nevertheless exercised with telling effect.'[22] The seemingly absolutist French state was in reality weaker than the constitutional monarchy of Britain. Its revenues were 'owned' by others – the tax farmers and office-holders – with many exemptions and privileges. Although the need for reform was obvious to finance ministers, action was extremely difficult for they lacked representative institutions to simplify and standardize taxation across the country. A more effective tax system would provide the holders of French government bonds with greater security against default, but change proved impossible within the existing institutional structure. The power of the crown in France was severely limited in practice by bodies with the power to resist without responsibility; and the crown was not willing to adopt the British solution of a more formal constraint on its power in order to achieve greater effectiveness. The preferred solution was to turn to more direct and unfettered rule without the ability to follow through its implications. By the time the Estates General were finally called in 1789, reform was too late.[23]

IV

The method of collecting taxes was crucial to the relationship between subjects and the state. In France, collection was highly problematical as a result of tax farming, exemptions and regional variations, and the difficulties were intensified by reliance on internal customs barriers and the need for a paramilitary presence in internal trade. Many opportunities occurred for resistance and hostility between taxpayer and tax collector. In Britain, tensions were reduced. There were no exemptions for nobles and clergy, no internal customs barriers and hence fewer tax officials to intervene in the trade of the country.[24] Consent to taxation was increased by using the taxpayers themselves to assess and collect some taxes. Not only did local élites validate taxes through parliament; they were also the local magistracy and commissioners for the land tax. The commissioners were not paid and were not officials of the crown; they were members of the landowning or urban élites serving in the same way as they did as justices of the peace. The British system did have problems, for the land tax was granted by a parliament of landowners in return for control over the finances of the crown and was administered by them in the localities. Consent was achieved but adjustment to the land tax proved difficult. In theory, the land tax was levied at one of four rates, from 1s to 4s in the £. In reality, the rates were stereotyped to produce a yield of £500,000 to £2m, with no adjustment to take account of the rising value of land in the later eighteenth century or the differential growth of regions of the country at a time of major structural change. The agreement on the land tax of 1689 survived until 1799 when the pressures of the revolutionary war led William Pitt to introduce a new income tax. The landowners' contribution to the finances of the state fell over the eighteenth century (see Table 2.1).[25]

Table 2.1   Direct and indirect taxes as a share of total tax revenues in Britain (%)

	Direct taxes on wealth and income (land and assessed)	Indirect taxes on commodities			
		Customs	Excise	Total	Other
1711–15	31.1	26.4	35.9	62.3	11.1
1791–95	16.0	20.9	47.3	68.2	15.8
1811–15	29.2*	19.2	37.7	56.9	13.9
1831–35	10.0	36.6	34.7	71.3	18.7

* including income tax.
Source: B.R. Mitchell and P. Deane, *Abstract of British Historical Statistics* (Cambridge, 1962), pp. 386–8, 392–3.

The lack of buoyancy in the land tax meant that the government turned to other sources of revenue. Assessed taxes were imposed on conspicuous signs of wealth such as male servants, hair powder and riding horses. They were designed to fall on the rich, and were administered by the same local commissioners as the land tax. The result was a degree of tax evasion and a fair degree of consent and legitimacy. As we shall see, the commissioners administered the income tax between 1799 and 1816 with much the same trade-off between evasion and acceptance. By the early 1790s, the land and assessed taxes taken together had fallen to barely half their share of total taxation at the start of the eighteenth century. Landowners and the wealthy controlled parliament and failed to maintain their proportion of the tax burden, yet without the serious problems of financial collapse experienced by France.

Customs duties were a major source of revenue at the start of the eighteenth century, but fell by the end of the century. The customs service was an inefficient part of the state. Officials were appointed by the Treasury, often with more concern for political patronage than efficiency, and many had a life interest in the position. They were paid a modest salary and drew fees from the office, leaving the work to paid deputies who might supplement their income by offering advice to merchants on their payment of duties. The high level of duties on goods resulted in smuggling and evasion which was extremely difficult to police around the British coastline. Clearly, particular taxes in Britain provoked resistance, though usually at the level of smuggling brandy or tea past customs officials rather than tax revolts and a collapse of revenues. Unlike in France, there were no internal tariff barriers within Britain after the union with Scotland in 1707 so that tensions between the population and officers were mainly confined to the coastal areas and ports. Britain did not have a highly visible and deeply resented *milice financière* with a presence throughout the country. Revenue from customs duties failed to keep pace with the growth in British trade in the eighteenth century. Tariffs were higher on manufactures than on food and raw materials, on goods from foreign countries than from the empire, and on luxuries than on necessities. In the eighteenth century, imports of food and raw materials grew more rapidly than manufactures, trade with the empire more rapidly than with foreigners, and necessities more than luxuries. Reforming the structure of duties was difficult, both for strategic reasons and because change would provoke outcry from vested interests.[26]

The major source of additional finance in the eighteenth century was the excise (see Table 2.1), where the mode of collection differed from both the local commissioners and the customs service in Britain, and from the fiscal system of France. Officials or Gaugers were appointed for their competence which was ensured by a career ladder with promotion by merit and a pension on retirement. They were paid a salary rather than fees, so that they had an incentive to create efficient methods in order to reduce their work load, in contrast to customs officials who were paid fees and had an incentive to maintain existing procedures. The producers of excisable goods such as salt, glass and beer made monthly returns of their output to the Gaugers who checked the figures for accuracy; the

Gaugers were in turn monitored by Surveyors. In the case of large plants, such as in the glass industry, an officer was permanently assigned to monitor production. The excise duty on glass was high, at around twice the cost of production. The firms and excise officials were in constant negotiation over allowances for waste, which could on occasion result in a breakdown of relations. However, in most cases they worked together within acceptable bounds. Most producers preferred to work with officials to ensure that competitors were not taking an unfair advantage; and the task of administration was much easier if the excise officers could rely on the producers. In some cases, excise officers did face hostility. Small-scale distillers of whisky in Scotland were fiercely hostile to paying duties, and compliance depended on the emergence of larger concerns with an interest in a national market. In 1824, the first excise licence in Glenlivet was issued to Smiths, much to the annoyance of other distillers who realized that it would bring excise officials into the glen. The example of Scottish distillers illustrates a general point: larger commercial producers were more likely to comply and even to inform on competitors who avoided paying duties to gain a competitive advantage. Above all, the excise officials dealt with producers rather than the general public, and consequently tension did not permeate society.[27]

The British state was therefore able to extract more revenue from the population with fewer political difficulties than in France. A steady and secure stream of revenue partly explains the ability of the British government to borrow and to avoid defaulting as in France. The next section explores other reasons for the contrast between the politics of borrowing in Britain and France.

V

The secure basis of tax revenues meant that the British state was able to borrow money on generous terms, at around 2 per cent lower interest rate than in France between 1746 and 1793. In France, the state paid a 'default premium' throughout the eighteenth century and, in the words of Velde and Weir, 'the financial market was the economic conscience of the Old Regime'.[28] The British state never defaulted on its debts, so that the risks of lending were much lower than in France with its high risk of default. Neither did the British state attempt to escape from its debt though currency debasement and inflation – a temptation which many other countries did not resist. Creditors had justified suspicion of the security of loans to the French state, with partial defaults in 1720, 1759, 1770, 1788 and 1797. Although Louis XVI resolved not to default when he came to the throne in 1774, he had difficulties sustaining his policy given the lack of tax revenues to service the debt. His opposition to default provides the context for his calling of the Estates General, for in 1788 he suspended payments with the promise that they would be made good in the future, once the Estates General created new taxes to honour the debts. The decision set in motion the chain of events leading to his execution. By rejecting default, he brought the *ancien régime* to its final crisis.[29] Borrowing rose to new levels, and between 1751 and 1787 debt service rose from 28 per cent of total expenditure to 49.3 per cent – still much lower than in Britain.[30] It was not that financial markets failed to develop in France, for the rate of interest on private loans was similar to the level in Britain.[31] The problem was that the French state did not have the confidence of creditors, or in the words of economists, it could not offer them a credible commitment to meet their claims. Risk was therefore discounted through higher interest rates. How is the difference in the security of loans and the credibility of the commitment of the two states to honour their obligations to be explained?

The answer is, in part, the different financial strategies of the two states. The French state resorted to a number of stratagems which merely intensified the problem and avoided the creation of a credible commitment. One was to borrow indirectly from the holders of venal offices. By withholding *gages* to the officers, threatening to create more offices which would reduce the value of the existing posts, or demanding lump-sum payments for the right to inherit or sell offices, the crown could force office-holders to provide additional capital. The office-holders formed corporations to ensure that each office-holder paid their share and to borrow the money at cheaper rates than they could as individuals. Hence the *secretaries de roi* of the Grande Chancellerie in Paris mortgaged their offices and raised 6.37m livres for the crown in 1701–07. The crown welcomed these corporations for they could borrow on much better terms than the crown; their creditors could sue the corporations for failure to pay whereas they were powerless when the crown defaulted. The office-holders were obliged to repay their creditors on pains of surrendering their office; they had little recourse against the crown if their *gages* were suspended. Consequently, the lack of a credible commitment by the crown to honour its debts was passed from the private lenders to the office-holders, a way of side-stepping rather than resolving the risk of default.[32]

Another strategy was to turn to the provincial Estates. The Estates of Burgundy, for example, issued loans at lower rates than the crown, at a maximum of 5.5 per cent compared with 7 to 8 per cent on loans to the crown. In the Seven Years War, the Estates of Burgundy borrowed 5.6m livres and passed 4.8m to the crown. The crown granted the right to collect duties on the river Saone, which were converted into a large capital sum much as with the sale of offices. These duties increased over time, and at least in theory the crown could alter the terms of the grant to secure some of the revenue. However, the Estates were in a stronger position than office-holders in dealing with the crown, and were able to resist attempts to regain part of the duties. The crown was therefore securing loans on more favourable terms at the expense of a loss of prospective revenue.[33] Again, the stratagem marked a lack of a credible commitment and did nothing positive to change market sentiment towards the crown.

French government loans took a very different form from British government loans which were dominated in the second half of the eighteenth century by Consols – consolidated stock – introduced in 1754. The bonds were in a single issue, so that the credit of the British state was easily assessed and on public display through accounts presented to parliament. The Consols were long-term loans without a redemption date, paying interest indefinitely. A holder of a bond who wished to secure the capital sum needed an active market on which the bond could be sold and the right to interest transferred. Here was the basis of the London Stock Exchange. Potential state creditors were more likely to accept a lower interest rate if the market for bonds was active and liquid. The British state relied on consolidated, long-term and traded loans.[34]

France did not adopt any of these practices. Loans were short-term rather than perpetual; they were not traded; and they took many different forms with divergent terms and security. A tabulation of 1789 listed 38 different loans, each with their own terms and collateral. A number of problems emerged. Potential investors were reluctant to accept long-term loans as a result of their justified concern about the credibility of the state's commitment to maintain interest payments in the future. Short-term loans reduced the creditors' risk but required the state to make capital repayments which placed additional strain on finances. The wide range of different short-term loans forced up the cost of borrowing, for assessing the risks of each issue was difficult, not least in the absence of government accounts. [35]

The situation was made still worse by the growing reliance on life annuities. England experimented with annuities in the 1690s, but soon abandoned them. In France, annuities became ever more important from the 1720s and surpassed term loans from 1771. Men and women loaned money to the government in return for an income or annuity during their life – they were purchasing a pension for their retirement. The market for pensions was stable and relatively modest; the bulk of annuities were issued on the lives of third parties, and they were purchased above all by parents to provide for their children. Annuities were popular and attracted large sums of money to the state, and in view of the risk of default similar rates were needed as for other forms of loans. However, there were serious problems. The main concern of pensioners was to secure a decent income in old age; whether the return was good or bad depended on how long they lived which was a gamble worth taking. If they lived for many years, they had a good return; if they died in a few years, their rate of return was scarcely a major consideration. An annuity on the life of a child was a different matter at a time of high levels of mortality. An early death would result in a large loss of capital with little return, so that investors demanded a very high rate. In 1757, the government introduced life annuities at a flat rate of 10 per cent which was very attractive – and high rates of interest were always a prime target for default. After all, the predominantly middle-class holders of the earlier *tontines* were sacrificed in 1770, and they had little reason to believe that they could protect their interests. Annuities were even worse than term loans in creating an active market. The holder of an annuity might wish to convert the flow of income into a lump sum; the return to any purchaser depended on the holder's life expectancy which was difficult to predict, and resulted in low valuations.[36]

These differences between British and French borrowing strategies suggest to James Macdonald that 'the high cost of French borrowing was partly the result of the mistaken policies of its finance ministers'.[37] In reality, ministers had very little room for manoeuvre within the existing political system. Velde and Weir argue that the problems were structural, owing more to 'institutional, even constitutional flaws than to errors by individuals'.

> Persistent deficits were not the result of bad planning, court extravagance, economic weakness, or even an administration built on venal office holders. Cleverer or more honest administrators could not have eliminated them. They arose from a political system that completely separated the privilege of spending from the obligation to pay taxes and at the same time left the public enough political power to resist taxation.[38]

The different strategies adopted to secure loans were a response to the underlying factors which gave the ministers little freedom for action. A large part of the divergence was the result of Britain's possessing a more efficient fiscal system to provide security for the payment of interest. It was not the full explanation, for there was always the possibility that taxpayers (who were in the majority) could take advantage of creditors (who were in a minority) by defaulting. In the mid eighteenth century, there were around 50,000 to 60,000 creditors in an electorate of around 300,000, and the willingness of electors to maintain interest payments cannot be taken for granted.[39]

In the first half of the eighteenth century, some landowners and old-fashioned merchants were fiercely hostile to the loan contractors and financiers on the grounds that they were subverting 'republican virtue'. Landowners had the leisure and liberty for the disinterested pursuit of public affairs and to bear arms in defence of the state, unlike the narrow, self-interested moneyed power. 'The landed interest', remarked Bolingbroke in 1749, 'are the true owners of our political vessel, the moneyed men as such, are no more than passengers in it.'[40] Moneyed power was criticized as self-interested, corrupting political life for their own ends – not least because many of the great loans contractors from Samson Gideon to Nathan Rothschild were foreigners and Jewish. Political economists shared the concern at the size of the debt and its effect on the economy and politics. David Hume feared that the size of the debt might lead to 'grievous despotism' through the dominance of financiers and the destruction of an 'independent magistracy'. He advocated a voluntary declaration of state bankruptcy to clear the debt. Although he accepted the possibility of a more harmonious relationship between land and finance, Adam Smith had similar reservations about the debt and proposed that the costs be shared by the colonies through the creation of estates general for the British empire.[41] Why was the promise of the state to service the debt sustained in the face of these concerns?

An obvious answer is that Britain had representative political institutions in contrast to France, and that a credible commitment was guaranteed by constitutional checks and balances which prevented taxpayers from taking advantage of lenders. David Stasavage is sceptical, arguing that checks and balances cannot prevent power falling into the hands of interests in favour of default. In his view, the answer is the nature of political divisions and the existence of parties. Where a society has 'multiple political cleavages', and the choice of party affiliations was determined by non-economic issues, the division between creditors and taxpayers was buried within a wider coalition of interests and opinions. In France, parties did not exist so that any conflict between creditors and taxpayers was not contained within a wider coalition, and at times of financial crisis, opinions could polarize around this one issue. In Stasavage's opinion, the greater likelihood of default in France reflected the absence of cross-cutting political alliances.[42]

Stasavage exaggerates the role of parties in preventing default compared with representative institutions. Can parties be separated from the existence of the representative institutions they were seeking to control? Parties are not so likely in the world of court politics at Versailles as in the parliament of Westminster. Representative institutions were also important in underpinning consent to taxation which provided the flow of income for servicing loans. The absence of any serious possibility of default, and the implausibility of a sharp divide between creditors and taxpayers, can be explained by other factors than the existence of parties.

Edmund Burke, in his *Reflections on the Revolution in France*, noted one major difference between the British and French systems of finance. The strength of British finance rested on a 'miscible' collaboration of landed and moneyed interests in a patriotic alliance.[43] In chemistry, two liquids are miscible if they dissolve completely in each other, whatever their proportions, and Burke believed that the same happened with financiers and landowners. Stasavage is right to point to the lack of a clear political divide on the single fault line of creditors and taxpayers, but the explanation is not only to be found in the existence of parties. The complaints of Bolingbroke were submerged by a different view, that loans and the moneyed interest sustained British liberties and prosperity by defeating French Catholicism and winning new markets in the colonies. 'The *national Debt*', in the opinion of a supporter of loans, 'was contracted in Defence of our *Liberties* and *Properties*, and for the Preservation of our most excellent *Constitution* from *Popery* and *Slavery*.' Although financiers and the debt were potential threats to republican liberty, the solution was to contain them within a parliamentary system of close scrutiny of accounts and spending, in order to defend British liberties and Protestantism against external threat.[44] Many landowners were themselves beneficiaries of the fiscal-military state, and not only through positions in the army and navy or engagement in the empire.

The commitment of the British state to pay its debts was linked with the credibility of any creditor in paying his debt – a serious consideration in such a highly commercialized society as Britain. Many taxpayers – merchants, industrialists and traders – were not likely to support default given their own reliance on credit. They had a general concern to maintain the sanctity of credit, and a very immediate fear that a loss of income might lead bond-holders to default on their own obligations and so threaten the entire, fragile, system of interlocking claims. Landowners shared their concerns, for they were deeply involved in the financial world through their use of mortgages. They could borrow on the security of their estates in order to carry out improvements, to cover the costs of enclosure, to purchase the land of smaller neighbours, or to construct large country houses. Land and finance were 'miscible' as a result of the willingness of great landowners to borrow – not through financial pressure but to improve their economic position. At the same time, the composition of bond-holders shifted in the second half of the eighteenth century so that their ranks were no longer dominated to the same degree by foreigners and London moneyed interests. Most politicians and office-holders were bond-holders, so that default would harm their own interests. Bonds were held by insurance companies which dealt with a large number of policy-holders; charities purchased bonds as a secure investment; and so did widows. A concern for the stability of government loans was widespread.[45]

VI

During the revolutionary and Napoleonic wars, the British fiscal system continued to evolve to cope with the increasing demands for taxes and loans. Borrowing fell as a proportion of the costs of the war. In the American War of Independence, borrowing covered 82 per cent of the total costs, and the level was still higher in the revolutionary wars with France between 1793 and 1797, at 89 per cent. The proportion then fell in the Napoleonic Wars of 1798–1815, to 49 per cent. In the Seven Years War, government borrowing was 10.6 per cent of national income and in the American War of Independence 10.0 per cent. During the first phase of the wars against revolutionary and Napoleonic France, the figure rose to 11.6 per cent, but fell back to 4.3 per cent in 1802–10 and 9.0 per cent in 1811–15.[46] The impact on the British economy is the subject of debate between historians who believe that industrial investment was 'crowded out' by the costs of war, and those who argue that an efficient capital market served to 'crowd in' investment. The most likely outcome was that the 'financial revolution' produced additional savings, but that government spending at around the same level as other, private, investment led to some diversion of savings from peacetime uses, especially in the form of social overhead capital. Certainly, there was no crisis of state finance as in France: the real interest rate actually fell and the credit-worthiness of the government remained strong.[47]

Taxes formed a larger share of the costs of the Napoleonic Wars than at any time in the eighteenth century. The additional taxation came in large part from increases in the rates of existing taxes (55 per cent of the additional tax revenue 1793–1815), with 36 per cent from new taxes and above all the income tax introduced in 1799. The land tax and assessed taxes had fallen as a proportion of tax revenues, and Pitt introduced the income tax as a way of increasing the contribution from landowners and wealthy members of society. He imposed a rate of 2s in the £ (10 per cent) on incomes above £200, with abatements for incomes down to £60. The tax was seen as an exceptional wartime duty: it was abolished with the Treaty of Amiens in 1802, reinstated in 1803 on a somewhat different basis, and abandoned again in 1816. Initially, Pitt tried to collect the tax by aggregating an individual's income from all sources – an intrusive and complex process. After 1803, the tax was collected on each source or schedule in a way that minimized the intrusion of the state: tax was deduced automatically at source by the person paying rent or interest and dividends; and income from the profits of trade or business were assessed by local commissioners rather than by state officials. The commissioners were crucial to the legitimacy of the tax, and when they were suspended in the City of London in 1814, the outcry contributed to the post-war demise of the tax as a threat to liberties.[48] Of course, payment of the income tax was not universally popular, yet it did produce a considerable revenue and did increase the proportion of revenue from direct taxes (see Table 2.1). Britain was the most heavily taxed state in Europe: in terms of the amount of wheat purchased, the per capita taxation in Britain between 1803 and 1812 was almost three times that of France.[49]

Napoleon deeply distrusted debt, and applied the principles of prudent family finances to the state. He was, in the words of Louis Bergeron, 'more concerned with not falling into the mistakes of a recent past than with seeing solutions for the future'. He thought that Britain's reliance on loans would be its downfall, a 'gnawing worm' which would lead to disaster.[50] He was wrong, for France's failure to become a 'fiscal state' contributed to his downfall. In 1789, the National Assembly (the successor to the Estates General) resolved to continue collecting the existing taxes 'although illegally established and collected'. Not surprisingly, the result was resistance rather than legitimation. Tax reform was confused with tax cuts, and the Assembly abolished indirect taxes. The worsening financial situation meant that new direct taxes were introduced in 1790: the *contribution foncière* (a tax on the revenue from land and buildings), *contribution mobilière et personelle* (a tax on external signs of affluence on movable property) and the *patente* (a form of licence on trade and industry according to the type of trade, its size and location). These taxes amounted to a major reform of the fiscal system, and they continued to form the basis of French revenues in the nineteenth century. They were the equivalent of the land, assessed and income taxes in Britain. Indeed, the abandonment of the income tax in Britain in 1816 meant that France had a higher proportion of direct taxes and arguably a more equitable system of taxation. In 1840, direct taxes were 37.9 per cent of central government revenues in France compared with only 7.9 per cent in Britain. The reforms of 1790 marked a breakthrough in the longer term, but during the Napoleonic Wars difficulties of administration meant that the yield was disappointing and the deficit continued to mount under the massive burden of Napoleon's ambitions.[51]

The solution had two, interconnected, elements: the introduction of *assignats* in 1790 and war. The *assignats* were paper money based on the expected proceeds of the sale of church land, but the government issued far more than the security offered by sales of land. The *assignats* were the main way of financing war after 1792, accounting for 82.4 per cent of the cost compared with 5.4 per cent from taxes and 1.9 per cent from land sales. *Assignats* paid for war and war was a means of forcing occupied territories to accept *assignats* and obliging them to provide money to sustain French armies. The demands on the occupied territories were massive, amounting to perhaps a quarter of the revenue of France by the late 1790s. The policy proved a disaster, for the value of the *assignats* fell to less than 1 per cent of their face value by 1796. The issue of large amounts of paper money resulted in inflation which became the major form of 'taxation' by reducing the real level of debts and eroding the value of savings and incomes in a deeply disruptive way. Exploitation of the occupied territories led to resistance and revolt.[52]

VII

The French fiscal system was put on a more secure basis from 1797 when the revenue from direct taxes increased, indirect taxes revived, and the cost of servicing the debt fell as a result of another partial default. But exploitation of the occupied territories remained crucial. In 1798, for example, the Dutch were forced to introduce an income tax; by 1803, their per capita taxation was over four times the level of France. When Napoleon came to power, he rejected the use of paper money and stabilized the currency – in contrast with the British who abandoned the gold standard in 1797, introduced paper money and adopted inflationary finance in contrast to the previous policy. Britain's ability to adopt more flexible policies was a result of its accumulated credibility; Napoleon had to adopt conservative monetary policies because of the lack of credibility.

Furthermore, Napoleon had an aversion to loans and embarked on a reduction of the national debt. Financiers were, he remarked, 'the scourges, the lepers of the nation'. Of course, the default of 1797 meant that the credit of the French state was very poor and borrowing would have been difficult and expensive. Although taxation was more secure, the costs of war continued to mount: on one estimate, spending almost doubled from 549.6m francs in 1801 to a billion in 1811.[53]

Napoleon's policy was to wage war to support war, and the largest source of revenue continued to be impositions on the occupied territories. Napoleon's campaign in Italy in 1796–97 was financial as well as military: he levied a war contribution of 20m lire on Lombardy, as well as confiscating bank deposits; the pope had to pay 21m lire as well as surrendering art works. Pressure on Italy continued, with forced loans and huge levies which Napoleon believed, with scant concern for reality, that the Italian economy could bear. Similarly, the Austrians were forced to pay 40m florins to the French after their defeat at Austerlitz at the end of 1805. Precise calculations are difficult, but on one estimate, half of the military expenses between 1804 and 1814 were paid by the occupied territories. Clearly, fiscal problems arose as the French armies were expelled from the conquered territories and tax had to increase at home.[54]

The fiscal systems of the satellite and annexed territories were reformed in order to produce the revenue needed by the French. In Italy, for example, the demands of Napoleon forced Guiseppe Prina to reform the structures of taxes and the efficiency of collection so that revenues rose by 74 per cent between 1802 and 1812. Nevertheless, the deficit mounted in order to meet the French demands. In 1809, the accumulated deficit was 7.4m lire; the budget was balanced in 1810 by the sale of bonds, before deficits reappeared in 1811 (5m lire) and 1812 (4m lire). Prina pleaded with Napoleon for a reduction in demands, with no success. By 1813, the finances of the kingdom of Italy were in deep crisis and demands for forced loans and increased taxes led to a collapse of political and social stability. Prina created an efficient tax system to meet Napoleon's demands, at the expense of alienating the population. The outcome for Prina was tragic: in 1814, he was beaten to death in the 'battle of the umbrellas'.[55]

VIII

Britain out-taxed, out-borrowed and out-gunned the French during the wars. The real problem for Britain came after the war. The failure to renew the income tax in 1816, and the continued rigidity in the land tax, meant that the proportion of revenue from indirect taxes rose (see Table 2.1). After the war, the French tax system was more balanced and equitable as a result of the reforms of 1790. By contrast, the legitimacy of taxation in Britain was under strain until the 1840s. A high proportion of revenue went on the service of the national debt, so that it was easy to argue that the fiscal system was a device to take money from the poor and industrious members of society and to transfer it to idle *rentiers* and the hangers-on at court and office. The external enemy was defeated, and in the view of many radicals the main threat to liberty came from within. The reconstruction of the legitimacy of British taxation was reasserted with the reintroduction of the income tax in 1842, a reduction in customs and excise duties, and retrenchment. Success meant that Britain was able to embark on high levels of spending on naval warfare in the years leading up to the First World War. The fiscal-military state of the eighteenth century sustained Nelson's fleet at Trafalgar; the renewed fiscal state of the later nineteenth century paid for *Dreadnought*.

Notes

1. Quoted in J. Macdonald, *A Free Nation Deep in Debt: The Financial Roots of Democracy* (New York, 2003), p. 255.
2. Quoted in Macdonald, *Free Nation Deep in Debt*, p. 253.
3. The phrase is widely cited in books of quotations and the web; it is also attributed to Cardinal Mazarin.
4. J. Brewer, *The Sinews of Power: War, Money and the English State, 1688–1783* (London, 1989), p. 132; P. Langford, *The Excise Crisis: Society and Politics in the Age of Walpole* (Oxford, 1975).
5. Brewer, *Sinews of Power*, p. 89; for a pioneering comparative account see P. Mathias and P. O'Brien, 'Taxation in Britain and France, 1715–1810: A Comparison of the Social and Economic Incidence of Taxes Collected for the Central Governments', *Journal of European Economic History* 5 (1976): 601–50, especially pp. 610–11 and tables 7 and 8.
6. Brewer, *Sinews of Power*, pp. 34, 35, 36, 40; N.A.M. Rodger, *The Command of the Ocean: A Naval History of Britain, 1649–1815* (London, 2004), pp. 579, 642–5.
7. The concepts of domain and tax states were established by Joseph Schumpeter, 'The Crisis of the Tax State', reprinted in A.T. Peacock, R. Turvey, W. Stolper and E. Henderson (eds), *International Economic Papers*, no. 4 (London and New York, 1954), pp. 5–38; a detailed historical analysis of the process of transformation is contained in R. Bonney (ed.), *Economic Systems and State Finance* (Oxford, 1995) and R. Bonney (ed.), *The Rise of the Fiscal State in Europe, c1200–1815* (Oxford, 1999); for a conceptual model see R. Bonney and W.M. Ormrod, 'Introduction: Crises, Revolutions and Self-Sustained Growth: Towards a Conceptual Model of Change in Fiscal History', in W.M. Ormrod, M.M. Bonney and R.J. Bonney (eds), *Crises, Revolutions and Self-*

Sustained Growth: Essays in European Fiscal History, 1130–1830 (Stamford, 1999), pp. 1–21. On the tensions over the allocation of the surplus, see the controversial analysis in R. Brenner, 'Agrarian Class Structure and Economic Development in Pre-Industrial Europe', *Past and Present* 70 (1976): 47–75.

8.   The level of taxation is discussed in Mathias and O'Brien, 'Taxation in Britain and France', pp. 603–11; P. O'Brien and P.A. Hunt, 'The Rise of the Fiscal State in England, 1485–1815', *Historical Research* 66 (1993): 158–60 and appendix 3, tables 3 and 4; O'Brien and Hunt, 'England, 1485–1815', in Bonney (ed.), *Rise of the Fiscal State*, pp. 54–8; R. Middleton, *Government versus the Market: The Growth of the Public Sector, Economic Management and British Economic Performance, c.1890–1979* (Cheltenham, 1996), tables 3.1 and 3.2. On Britain as the first fiscal state, see Bonney, 'Introduction', in Bonney (ed.), *Rise of the Fiscal State*, pp. 13–14; for the concept of the fiscal-military state, see Brewer, *Sinews of Power*. On the emergence of government loans, see P.G.M. Dickson, *The Financial Revolution in England: A Study in the Development of Public Credit, 1688–1756* (London, 1967).

9.   Brewer, *Sinews of Power*, pp. 7–14, 24.

10. Macdonald, *A Free Nation Deep in Debt*, pp. 181, 196–8, 258–9; F.R. Velde and D.R. Weir, 'The Financial Market and Government Debt Policy in France, 1746–1793', *Journal of Economic History* 52 (1992): 7–8.

11. For a good account of the sale of offices, see W. Doyle, *Venality: The Sale of Offices in Eighteenth-Century France* (Oxford, 1996); the contribution in 1688–1715 is discussed on pp. 30–1, and later contributions on pp. 99–100.

12. Brewer, *Sinews of Power*, pp. 14–21, 23, 92–3.

13. For a summary of the Estates General, see the on-line *Columbia Encyclopedia* (6th edn, 2001–05) at <http://www.bartleby.com/65/st/StatesGe.html>; W. Doyle, *The Oxford History of the French Revolution* (Oxford, 1989), ch. 4.

14. Bonney, 'Revenues', in Bonney (ed.), *Economic Systems and State Finance*, pp. 494–5; Brewer, *Sinews of Power*, p. 132.

15. J.H. Shennan, *The Parlement of Paris* (London, 1968), ch. 9 on *parlement* and taxes in the eighteenth century; see pp. 317–19 on the conflict with Maupeou; W. Doyle, 'The Parlements of France and the Breakdown of the Ancien Regime, 1770–88', *French Historical Studies* 6 (1970); Velde and Weir, 'Financial Market and Government Debt Policy in France', p. 7.

16. These events are covered in many general histories of France: see, for example, Doyle, *Oxford History of the French Revolution,* see also F. Aftalion, *The French Revolution: An Economic Interpretation* (Cambridge, 1990), ch. 1 and Bonney, 'France', in Bonney (ed.), *Rise of the Fiscal State*, pp. 135–8. For a favourable assessment of Necker, see R.D. Harris, *Necker: Reform Statesman of the Ancien Regime* (Berkeley, 1979) and a critique of Colonne, J.F. Bosher, *French Finances, 1770–1795: From Business to Bureaucracy* (Cambridge, 1970).

17. E.A. Reitan, 'From Revenue to Civil List, 1688–1702: The Revolution Settlement and the "Mixed and Balanced" Constitution', *Historical Journal* 13 (1970); Velde and Weir, 'Financial Market and Government Debt Policy', p. 6.

18. For one case study, see P. O'Brien, T. Griffiths and P. Hunt, 'Political Components of the Industrial Revolution: Parliament and the English Cotton Textile Industry, 1660–1774', *Economic History Review* 44 (1991);

P. Langford, *Public Life and the Propertied Englishman, 1689–1798* (Oxford, 1991); on lobbying by Midland industrialists see E. Robinson, 'Matthew Boulton and the Art of Parliamentary Lobbying', *Historical Journal* 7 (1964).

19. Langford, *Excise Crisis*.
20. Brewer, *Sinews of Power*, pp. 129, 131; J.E.D. Binney, *British Public Finances and Administration, 1774–92* (Oxford, 1958); on the *Compte Rendu*, see Aftalion, *French Revolution*, pp. 24–5.
21. Brewer, *Sinews of Power*, pp. 85–7; J. Torrance, 'Social Class and Bureaucratic Innovation: The Commissioners for Examining the Public Accounts, 1780–87', *Past and Present* 78 (1978); E.A. Reitan, 'Edmund Burke and Economical Reform, 1779–83', *Studies in Eighteenth Century Culture* 14 (1985).
22. Brewer, *Sinews of Power*, pp. xix.
23. Macdonald, *Free Nation Deep in Debt*, pp. 258–9, 260–1.
24. Brewer, *Sinews of Power*, pp. 128–9; Mathias and O'Brien, 'Taxation in Britain and France', pp. 636–9.
25. W.R. Ward, *The English Land Tax in the Eighteenth Century* (Oxford, 1963); G.J. Wilson, 'The Land Tax Problem', *Economic History Review* 35 (1982); J.V. Beckett, 'Land Tax or Excise: The Levying of Taxation in Seventeenth and Eighteenth-Century England', *English Historical Review* 100 (1985).
26. Brewer, *Sinews of Power*, pp. 101–2, 130; P.K. O'Brien, 'The Political Economy of British Taxation, 1660–1815', *Economic History Review* 41 (1988): 23–6.
27. Brewer, *Sinews of Power*, pp. 69–87, 101–14; O'Brien, 'Political Economy', pp. 26–8; T.C. Barker, *The Glassmakers: Pilkington: The Rise of an International Company, 1826–1976* (London, 1977), pp. 34–5, 39, 41–3; entry on Smiths of Glenlivet in *Oxford Dictionary of National Biography*.
28. Velde and Weir, 'Financial Market and Government Debt Policy', pp. 15–19, 36; D. Stasavage, *Public Debt and the Birth of the Democratic State: France and Great Britain, 1688–1789* (Cambridge, 2003), pp. 96–7; Brewer, *Sinews of Power*, pp. 114–26. On the operation of the loan market in Britain, see Dickson, *Financial Revolution*.
29. See Velde and Weir, 'Financial Market and Government Debt Policy', pp. 9–10, 37; Macdonald, *Free Nation Deep in Debt*, p. 252.
30. Stasavage, *Public Debt*, pp. 92, 95; R. Bonney, 'The Eighteenth Century II. The Struggle for Great Power Status and the End of the Old Fiscal Regime', in Bonney (ed.), *Economic Systems and State Finance*, p. 347; Doyle, *Oxford History of the French Revolution*, pp. 78–85.
31. Velde and Weir, 'Financial Market and Government Debt Policy', pp. 18–19; Macdonald, *Free Nation Deep in Debt*, p. 250; see also P. Hoffman, G. Postel-Vinay and J.-L. Rosenthal, *Priceless Markets: The Political Economy of Credit in Paris, 1660–1879* (Chicago, 2000), pp. 173–6.
32. Stasavage, *Public Debt*, pp. 89–90; Doyle, *Venality*, pp. 14, 42–3, 95–6, 99, 122–6; D. Bien, 'Offices, Corps and a System of State Credit: The Uses of Privileges under the Ancien Regime', in K.M. Baker (ed.), *The French Revolution and the Creation of Modern Political Culture* (Oxford, 1987); H. Root, 'Tying the King's Hands: Credible Commitment and Royal Fiscal Policy during the Old Regime', *Rationality and Society* 1 (1989): 247–9; M. Potter, 'Good Offices: Intermediation by Corporate Bodies in Early Modern French Public Finance', *Journal of Economic History* 60 (2000): 603.

33. Potter, 'Good Offices', pp. 599–626; M. Potter and J.-L. Rosenthal, 'Politics and Public Finance in France: The Estates of Burgundy, 1660–1790', *Journal of Interdisciplinary History* 27 (1997): 577–612; Stasavage, *Public Debt*, p. 90.
34. Dickson, *Financial Revolution*; Macdonald, *Free Nation Deep in Debt*, p. 242.
35. Velde and Weir, 'Financial Market and Government Debt Policy', p. 4; Macdonald, *Free Nation Deep in Debt*, p. 243.
36. The differences are outlined in Macdonald, *Free Nation Deep in Debt*, pp. 242–8, 251; on annuities, see Velde and Weir, 'Financial Market and Government Debt Policy', pp. 3–4, 28–36; D.R. Weir, 'Tontines, Public Finance, and Revolution in France and England, 1688–1789', *Journal of Economic History* 49 (1989).
37. Macdonald, *Free Nation Deep in Debt*, p. 245.
38. Velde and Weir, 'Financial Market and Government Debt Policy', pp. 3, 36.
39. The estimate of Macdonald, *Free Nation Deep in Debt*, p. 227.
40. H. Bolingbroke, *Some Reflections on the Present State of the Nation* (1749), in *The Works of Henry St John Bolingbroke*, iv (1809), p. 388; on republican virtue, see J.G.A. Pocock, *Virtue, Commece and History: Essays on Political Thought and History, Chiefly in the Eighteenth Century* (Cambridge, 1985).
41. The thinking of political economists on the debt is outlined in T. Dome, *The Political Economy of Public Finance in Britain, 1767–1873* (London, 2004); M. Daunton, *Trusting Leviathan: The Politics of Taxation in Britain, 1799–1914* (Cambridge, 2001), pp. 39–40.
42. Stasavage, *Public Debt*, pp. 24, 39, 99, 129, 154, 156, 172.
43. E. Burke, *Reflections on the Revolution in France* (1790; Everyman edition, 1910), p. 106.
44. J. Hoppit, 'Attitudes to Credit in Britain, 1680–1790', *Historical Journal* 33 (1990): 316–17; Brewer, *Sinews of Power*, pp. 142–3, 161.
45. On credit, see C. Muldrew, *The Economy of Obligation: The Culture of Credit and Social Relations in Early Modern England* (Basingstoke, 1998) and P. Hudson, *The Genesis of Industrial Capital: A Study of the West Riding Wool Textile Industry, c1750–1850* (Cambridge, 1986), Part III; on the changing composition of bond-holders, Dickson, *Financial Revolution*; on the use of mortgages, Macdonald, *Free Nation Deep in Debt*, p. 230.
46. Macdonald, *Free Nation Deep in Debt*, p. 339; J.F. Wright, 'British Government Borrowing in Wartime, 1750–1815', *Economic History Review* 52 (1999): 356.
47. For the debate on crowding out, see J.G. Williamson, 'Why was British Growth so Slow during the Industrial Revolution?', *Journal of Economic History* 44 (1984) and C.E. Heim and P. Mirowski, 'Interest Rates and Crowding Out during Britain's Industrial Revolution', *Journal of Economic History* 57 (1987); Wright, 'British Government Borrowing', p. 360.
48. A. Hope-Jones, *Income Tax in the Napoleonic Wars* (Cambridge, 1939), pp. 2, 28–9, 68–9.
49. Bonney, 'Struggle for Great Power Status', pp. 380–2 citing O'Brien, 'Political Economy', pp. 13, 22; P. O'Brien, 'Public Finance in the Wars with France, 1793–1815', in H.T. Dickinson (ed.), *Britain and the French Revolution, 1789–1815* (Basingstoke, 1989), pp. 177, 182–3; Mathias and O'Brien, 'Taxation in Britain and France', pp. 610–1 and tables 7 and 8; F. Crouzet, *L'economie britannique et le blocus continental, 1806–1813* (2nd edn, Paris, 1987), p. lxii; F. Crouzet, 'The Impact of the French Wars on the British

Economy', in Dickinson (ed.), *Britain and the French Revolution*, p. 208; E.A. Wrigley, 'Society and Economy in the Eighteenth Century', in L. Stone (ed.), *An Imperial State at War: Britain from 1689 to 1815* (London, 1994), pp. 74–5.

50. Bonney, 'Struggle for Great Power Status', p. 386; L. Bergeron, *France Under Napoleon* (Princeton, 1981), pp. 41–2, 44–51.

51. Daunton, *Trusting Leviathan*, p. 54; Doyle, *Oxford History of the French Revolution*, pp. 131; Aftalion, *French Revolution*, 86–95; Bonney, 'Struggle for Great Power Status', pp. 347–8; R. Bonney, 'The State and its Revenues in Ancien Regime France', *Historical Research* 65 (1992): 175–6.

52. Bonney, 'Struggle for Great Power Status', pp. 349–52; S.E. Haris, *The Assignats* (Cambridge, MA, 1930); Velde and Weir, 'Financial Market and Government Debt Policy', pp. 17–18; Aftalion, *French Revolution*, ch. 4 and pp. 184–7; S. Woolf, *Napoleon's Integration of Europe* (London, 1991), p. 17.

53. M.D. Bordo and E.N. White, 'A Tale of Two Currencies: British and French Finance during the Napoleonic War', *Journal of Economic History* 51 (1991): 314–15; Bergeron, *France Under Napoleon*, pp. 37–51; Bonney, 'Struggle for Great Power Status', pp. 353–7 citing Aftalion, *French Revolution*, p. 178; T.C.W. Blanning, *The Origins of the French Revolutionary Wars* (London, 1986), p. 196; S. Schama, 'The Exigencies of War and the Politics of Taxation in the Netherlands', in J. Winter (ed.), *War and Economic Development* (Cambridge, 1975), pp. 111–12, 117–18; S. Schama, *Patriots and Liberators: Revolution in the Netherlands, 1780–1813* (London, 1977), pp. 207, 238, 293–5, 305, 385, 446; Woolf, *Napoleon's Integration of Europe*, p. 172.

54. Bergeron, *France Under Napoleon*, p. 40; A. Grab, 'The Politics of Finance in Napoleonic Italy', paper delivered to conference in Cambridge, 2005; Woolf, *Napoleon's Integration of Europe*, pp. 172–3; Aftalion, *French Revolution*, pp. 177–8; Bonney, 'Struggle for Great Power Status', p. 355.

55. For details, Bonney, 'Struggle for Great Power Status', pp. 358–60; on Prina's reforms and demise, Grab, 'Politics of Finance in Napoleonic Italy'.

3
The War of Words: French and British Propaganda in the Napoleonic Era

Simon Burrows

In April 1816 the British foreign minister Castlereagh justified continued government funding of French-language propaganda newspapers to Parliament in strikingly contemporary language. They were, he said, for 'Conveying instruction to the Continent when no other means could be found.'[1] This brief statement reveals much about international propaganda warfare in the Napoleonic period. First, Castlereagh implies that British use of these newspapers was a reaction to a novel set of circumstances which created unprecedented difficulties 'conveying instruction' to mainland Europe. Second, this situation arose because normal channels of communication had broken down. Ten months after Waterloo, when Castlereagh addressed Parliament, they were still not back to normal. Third, he implied that the British propaganda effort was about information ['instruction'] rather than polemic. This explains why newspapers were the preferred propaganda vehicle. Fourth, he revealed that the British government response to this situation was to farm out responsibility for conducting its propaganda war to the motley collection of French émigré journalists who produced these newspapers. Finally – since the British government only subscribed for about 600 of these newspapers – Castlereagh intended to instruct a very narrow political élite spread across several continental states. This was a very different readership to the 'bourgeois' audience that, according to most recent historians, was by the late eighteenth century the primary constituent of a political 'public' whose 'opinion', across much of Europe, was increasingly influential.[2]

This chapter seeks to explore the British propaganda strategy and explain how it arose as a result of Napoleonic policy and political-military hegemony. This is largely uncharted territory.[3] For paradoxically, although Napoleon Bonaparte has always been acknowledged as a master propagandist, international propaganda warfare – even more than espionage – is the forgotten branch of the Napoleonic conflict.[4] In consequence, the chapter maps the broad contours of a large field, in order to illustrate the fundamental importance of propaganda warfare in the Anglo-French struggle.

I

Since Britain's propaganda campaign was reactive – i.e. a response to Napoleonic policy – it is necessary to begin by considering the French propaganda campaign. Remarkably, Napoleonic France had no ministry of propaganda. Nor did Napoleon develop new propaganda techniques or technologies. Instead, he rationalized and systemized existing practices, drawing heavily on *ancien régime* precedents, while supervising propaganda and press campaigns himself. This represented a limit on resources, but also made for a far more focused and consistent policy than under the *ancien régime*, where several ministers and a plethora of censors holding conflicting jurisdictions exercised sway over the printed word.[5] Moreover, Napoleon consistently made propaganda and press control a political priority and, from the very beginning of his career, devoted a considerable amount of time and energy to it.

Indeed, Napoleon's political ascension was as much a product of successful image manipulation as military success. Through his self-aggrandizing military bulletins and the army newspapers he established in Italy and in Egypt (thereby founding the first ever printed newspaper in both Africa and the Islamic world), which were widely copied in the French domestic press, he managed to remain a hero despite being checked in the Near East.[6] Once in office he continued to make assiduous use of both the press and *bulletins de la grande armée*, and frequently wrote key articles for the official *Moniteur* newspaper himself.[7]

Even the most cursory dip into Napoleon's correspondence reveals that he used almost every trick of the modern propagandist's trade and assiduously instructed ministers, vassals and viceroys to place disinformation stories in newspapers to mislead or intimidate the enemy, and incite popular anger or enthusiasm. His letters contain endless suggestions concerning the fabrication of propaganda prints, pamphlets, academic and school books, newspaper stories, pageants, religious ceremonies, art and architecture.[8] A typical order, sent to his police minister, Joseph Fouché, on 21 April 1807, ordered him to use the provincial press in Brittany, the Vendée, Piedmont and Belgium (some of the most militantly Catholic areas of the empire) to whip up feeling against the Anglican Church on account of its persecution of Irish Catholics. The story would then be taken up nationally by the *Journal de l'Empire*, and the minister of religions [cultes], Portalis, would encourage the bishops to offer intercessions that the persecution might cease.[9] On another occasion, in October 1809, he wrote to the war minister, General Clarke, telling him to reprimand his brother Joseph, King of Spain, and make him understand

> that nothing is more contrary to military usage than to reveal the strength of his army, whether in orders and proclamations, or in his official newspapers; that, when forced to speak of his own forces, he ought to exaggerate them and make them appear formidable by doubling or trebling their number; and when he speaks of the enemy, he should reduce his strength by an half or a third ... that the King disregarded this principle when he said that he had only 40,000 men and when he announced that the enemy had 120,000 ... that this was to proclaim his weakness throughout Spain, [and] in a word to deprive himself of the moral advantage and give it to his enemies.[10]

Equally, Fouché and his agents watched the foreign press to gauge allied intentions and actions. Fouché's daily police bulletin to Napoleon of 28 May 1805 offers the following report concerning a British-sponsored propaganda organ: 'The *Courier de Londres* is much more reserved. We conclude from this that someone [the author] is afraid or peace is imminent.'[11] Indeed, monitoring the foreign press was part of Napoleon's daily routine. During the Consulate, as Hélène Maspero-Clerc has noted, his secretary Bourrienne describes how Napoleon would have the British papers read to him while at his *toilette*,[12] and by 1810 he was receiving a daily digest of stories from the British press along with his daily police reports.[13]

Like his British adversaries, Napoleon saw newspapers as the main means of international propaganda. This is unsurprising, for by the late eighteenth century, the newspaper had everywhere replaced the pamphlet as the 'primary medium' for the communication of political messages. It might be added that a third propaganda vehicle, the caricature, although well-capable of crossing linguistic boundaries, does not appear to have done so in any great numbers until late in the Napoleonic Wars.

Moreover, outside France, continental anti-Napoleonic caricatures were few in number prior to 1808.[14] This slow progress was probably due to the linguistic and visual complexity of many British caricature images, and the danger of producing caricatures anywhere within the French sphere of influence.[15]

Newspapers had several key advantages over pamphlets. First, they offered a regular contact with their readers, and thus provided an opportunity to develop continuous relationships with them, based on trust and recognized authority. Pamphlets, in contrast, appeared only once, and each individual pamphlet lacked an established audience. But newspapers also had disadvantages as propaganda organs. Since they had to advertise a regular place of publication, gather subscription and advertising revenue, and be distributed by post, they were poor vehicles for carrying clandestine and deeply subversive messages into hostile territory. Notwithstanding futile efforts by British-sponsored smugglers to deposit trunks full of newspapers on the French coast in *chouan* areas, or fantastic proposals to drop newspapers over France from unmanned balloons bearing Bourbon symbols using timing devices, in general international newspaper propaganda in this period targeted neutral or wavering states.[16]

Newspapers were also expensive to direct or control, both because they were relatively costly commodities and because, although steam technology was not used to produce newspapers until 1814, the late eighteenth-century European reading public was extensive.[17] Although individual titles usually sold only a few hundred to a few thousand copies, combined daily or weekly sales were massive. Subscriptions to Parisian newspapers probably peaked at 300,000 copies daily in the early revolution, while British stamp duty records show that by 1801 London newspapers (daily and otherwise) sold about 20,000 copies per day and provincial weeklies a further 180,000 per week. Moreover, the following two decades saw a massive growth in British newspaper sales, despite punitive stamp duties.[18] In Germany, whose patchwork of small states formed the main propaganda battlefield until 1806, the market was more extensive still, and in the early 1800s a single title, the *Hamburgische Unpartheyische Correspondent* achieved print-runs in excess of 40,000.[19] Faced with such figures, any government that wished to influence opinion across Europe could not hope to do so by time-honoured traditions of bribery and corruption.[20] More subtle and effective means were required.

II

The Napoleonic solution to this problem was to control news flows rather than newspapers. The model for this Napoleonic media policy, as so much else, was the policy of late *ancien régime* governments. Before the revolution, the Bourbons had controlled domestic news reporting by licensing newspapers, limiting their numbers, and employing pre-publication censors for each title. Their official paper, the *Gazette de France*, held a monopoly over political news, and other papers had to pay to copy its coverage. In the provinces, one commercially-orientated paper was permitted in each major town.[21] Gradually, the Napoleonic government resurrected this system. On 17 January 1800 a proclamation closed all but 13 Parisian newspapers. Sixty papers, including all titles with Jacobin sympathies, were forced to close. Although the government stopped short of introducing direct censorship, it made clear that any paper that upset the government would be closed, and thus imposed a desperate self-censorship on editors. It was tacitly understood that it was dangerous to publish political news unless taken from the *Moniteur*, the regime's official newspaper. This was made explicit to the departmental press by a decree of 1810, and in 1811 the same measure was extended to the kingdom of Westphalia.[22] By this time too, further suspensions and forced mergers had reduced the Parisian daily press to just four titles. A decree of 1807 limiting provincial newspapers to one per *département*, produced under the Prefect's watchful eye, made control of local papers easier still.[23] In addition, as detailed below, whole classes of news were subject to blanket bans.

One effect of these measures, as Napoleon doubtless hoped, was to depoliticize the revolutionary public and reduce the audience for newspapers. Pierre-Louis Roederer's figures from the *Bureau des ouvrages périodiques* in the spring of 1803 indicate that the daily press had a total of 35,580 subscribers inside France. There were a further 10,919 subscribers to non-quotidiens, mostly specialist or literary periodicals.[24] Thus the French market for all categories of newspaper and periodical late in the Consulate totalled just 46,500 subscriptions, little more than in 1781[25] and perhaps just one tenth the scale of sales in the early 1790s.[26] Although much of the slump occurred under the Directory, it is clear that the Napoleonic reduction in titles, together with reader rejection of a highly controlled press, pushed newspaper readership in France to record lows for the post-revolutionary period. This helped keep the costs of press control low.

In parts of Europe – especially Germany – where the newspaper reading public was much more extensive, it was not feasible to exercise control by relying on French-subsidized newspapers. Hence control methods used successfully in France or elsewhere were extended to French-occupied and satellite territories. A press censor was established in Amsterdam early in the Napoleonic period, and in Switzerland the press was effectively shackled following the Act of Mediation (1802).[27] However, the German press was only subjugated following Napoleon's victories of 1806–07, whereafter serious resistance became unthinkable. In June 1806, the summary execution of the bookseller-publisher J.P. Palm, who was seized from neutral Nuremburg and shot after he refused to name the author of *Deutschland in siener tiefen Erniedrigung*, sent out a clear message.

Thereafter few publishers within range of the French sphere of influence dared to defy Bonaparte. Moreover, following the twin victories of Jena and Auerstädt (14 October 1806), many of Germany's most prestigious French-language gazettes were suppressed, including the *Courier du Bas-Rhin*, the *Gazette de Frankfort*, the *Gazette de Bayreuth*, together with many German-language papers including the *Mainzer Zeitung*, *Aachener Merkur*, *Kölnische Zeitung* and several Hamburg titles.[28] By 1812, the *Hamburgische Unpartheyische Correspondent*, which had been reduced to a bilingual French propaganda organ, had lost over 85 per cent of its subscribers, much to Napoleon's chagrin.[29] The only significant German paper to escape the direct control of the French government or its satellites was the *Allgemeine Zeitung*. However, even it was effectively bent to Napoleon's will and forced to draw its political content from the *Moniteur*.[30]

Napoleon also resurrected and refined Bourbon methods in his attempts to control the press beyond his frontiers and turn the European public sphere into French-dominated space. This model was not inappropriate, for after 1770 the Bourbon government exercised an unprecedented level of control over French coverage in the foreign newspaper press. Between late January and March 1771 it placed so much diplomatic pressure on the government of the Netherlands that the influential Dutch international gazettes were obliged to stop hostile coverage of the Maupeou crisis.[31] This was not a marginal victory over marginal papers. The Maupeou crisis of 1771–74 was the Bourbon monarchy's biggest domestic political crisis since the Frondes of the mid seventeenth century, while subscriptions to Dutch French-language gazettes accounted for perhaps one quarter of newspapers sold in France.[32] They were considered a quality press, being less overtly censored than their French rivals, and circulated widely across Europe.[33] As France was the biggest single market for these papers, the threat of exclusion from Bourbon territory was usually enough to bring them to heel.[34]

Increasingly, too, the Bourbons controlled news from Paris at source. In 1781, the freelance correspondents who supplied the international press were rounded up and briefly imprisoned in the Bastille. On their release, a select few were licensed to continue their trade under government supervision. Thus, even apparently independent news bulletins in the international press were in reality produced under government aegis.[35] Nevertheless, like other *ancien régime* governments, the Bourbons found the international press could not be controlled entirely, not least because it served their purposes that these sources seem at least partially independent and worthy of credit. Moreover, the means of control tended to be crude. Threats of banning an individual title from France were often effective, but if actually enacted, the French would lose all suasion over that paper.[36]

Like the Bourbons, Napoleon sought to silence or convert hostile journalists beyond his sphere of influence, particularly émigrés, using a mixture of intimidation, financial inducements, argument and diplomatic complaints.[37] Indeed, in retrospect the decree of 17 January 1800 can be seen as a first stage in a campaign to control news media across Europe. If this campaign was not the result of a preconceived plan, it certainly involved systematic attempts to control the press, starting with French domestic titles before spreading outwards, and at times drove rather than followed foreign policy. Hence, after persuading the Hamburg Senate to suppress the émigré-edited *Censeur* and arrest its authors as early as July 1800,[38] and converting two other leading émigré editors, Louis Baudus of the *Spectateur du nord* and Montlosier of the *Courier de Londres*, to the new regime in 1801,[39] Napoleon attempted during the Peace of Amiens (1802–03) to suborn British newspaper editors and proprietors. However, although he sent agents, including Joseph Fiévée, to buy their support, British newspapermen saw little commercial gain in supporting the French dictator, and hence Napoleon singularly failed to silence British journalistic criticism. Nevertheless, Napoleon's two most vociferous critics in the London press were the veteran émigré journalists Jean-Gabriel Peltier, the author of *Paris pendant l'année* (1797–1802) and *L'Ambigu* (1802–18), and Jacques Regnier, a *pur* royalist who took over as editor of the *Courier de Londres* when Montlosier returned to France in 1802.

These papers were on the receiving end of a series of diplomatic complaints in which Napoleon insisted that the British ministry take tough action. Although the Addington ministry was keen to mollify Bonaparte, it repeatedly reiterated that it would not be lawful to expel

Peltier, and that the only possible remedy was an *ex officio* legal action for criminal libel. Thus, on 21 February 1803 Peltier was brought before the Court of King's Bench and found guilty. Nevertheless, Napoleon felt that the British refusal to punish Peltier by executive fiat was provocative hypocrisy, especially as pro-French writers were expelled under the provisions of the Alien Act in both 1793 and 1803. The dispute rapidly soured relations between Britain and France, as both sides became convinced that the other acted through malevolence and hence – I have argued elsewhere – hastened the descent into conflict.[40] As for Peltier, he escaped sentencing, due to the outbreak of war.

III

The objective of French press policy at home and abroad was to prevent certain types of news becoming known, especially those damaging to the army, France's allies, or social harmony. Many subjects, including troop movements, religious affairs, and Napoleon's actions or speeches had to be mentioned in *Moniteur* before they could be covered elsewhere. In 1808 there were temporary interdicts on events in Rome and Spain, while in 1813 the French press failed to report the Austrian declaration of war on France. In 1804 the seizure and judicial murder of the duc d'Enghien was covered in a tiny paragraph in the *Moniteur*, without colour or context.[41] Yet this event was perhaps the most sensational single news story of a momentous decade, and turned Alexander I against Bonaparte. Mention of the exiled Bourbon royal family was also banned, and mention of the word 'Poland' forbidden. Military defeats were either passed over in silence, or, if that proved impossible, 'buried' under good news. Thus the defeat at Trafalgar, which the French press initially reported as a victory, was eclipsed by blanket coverage of Ulm and Austerlitz once the stream of casualties returning to France meant it could no longer be concealed.[42] Bans on coverage had a dual purpose. They were intended to portray Napoleon as the only public actor in Europe and to keep French citizens and subject peoples in ignorance. But more importantly, they were intended to establish a French monopoly over the distribution of information, keeping enemies and wavering allies alike in the dark about French intentions, dispositions and weaknesses.

Were these aims fulfilled? It is, of course, notoriously difficult to measure the impact of contemporary 'propaganda' systems, let alone historical ones. Nevertheless, there is little doubt that the primary news media of any historical period has enormous power to set the political agenda of individuals and states. However, they rarely dictate what people think directly, since readers appropriate texts for their own purposes, assimilating them into existing experience and belief systems. Indeed, much evidence suggests French and European readers saw through Napoleon's propagandist statements as readily as British satirists, such as George Woodward in 'John Bull exchanging news with the continent', which juxtaposes French and British reports of Trafalgar, or George Cruickshank in 'Boney Hatching a Bulletin or snug winter quarters', which ridicules Napoleon's 27th military bulletin from the *grande armée* in Russia (27 October 1812).[43] Instead, primary media use 'agenda-setting information' to provide a menu of issues for people to think about, discuss with others, and base their actions upon. By continuous suggestion, moreover, primary news media have the power to shape perceptions of reality and redefine it through the construction of powerful myths.

The testimony and actions of some of Napoleon's arch-enemies certainly suggest that he was remarkably successful at this. The émigré journalist Peltier, for one, noted in 1809 that Napoleon's control of the media had a vital impact on political decisions:

> This man, master of all the presses of the Continent save those of Austria, has the greatest means to intercept all news which might reveal his true position to his enemies; and when he tells a diplomatic lie, or proclaims a victory that he has not won, the effect he desires has long been achieved by the time his imposture is discovered.[44]

Peltier might seem a little too self-interested to trust in isolation, but occasionally it is possible to catch glimpses of Napoleon's successes with his media policy. For example, the ban on mentioning the Bourbons apparently bore fruit. French prisoners of war in Russia in 1806–07 were reportedly stunned to be visited by the pretender Louis XVIII in Courland, having not known of his existence.[45] Likewise, explosive news of Napoleon's excommunication on 10 June 1809 was kept a closely-guarded secret for several months. It only seeped into Spanish America in early 1810 via Peltier's *Ambigu* of 30 October 1809, which contained a translated version of the bull of excommunication in a Spanish-language supplement which was rapidly reprinted in Mexico City.[46]

Hence, as alternative sources of information broke down in the Napoleonic period, the British government found itself in an increasingly difficult position. Postal services between combatants were interrupted. Merchant activity and correspondence were inhibited, especially after the instigation of the British blockade and Napoleon's continental system.

Diplomatic reports, themselves often partly reliant on press sources, were constrained by censorship, blockade and war. Even foreign travellers, traditionally a useful information source, found their movements inhibited by the new 'rules' of revolutionary warfare, especially after Napoleon arrested all Britons unfortunate enough to be in Paris at the opening of hostilities in 1803.

IV

Starved of reliable sources, the British government was forced to obtain its information from self-serving spy-masters like Fauche-Borel and the comte d'Antraigues and – as noted in Castlereagh's testimony at the start of this chapter – to use French-language newspapers to transmit it.[47] Thus it hired émigré newspapers to fight a targeted propaganda war, including the *Courier de Londres*, Peltier's *L'Ambigu* and a further paper produced by Regnier, the *Courier d'Angleterre* (1805–15). Initially, not all their hirelings published their papers in London, for they also employed a succession of émigré journals produced in Germany by François-Etienne Paoli de Chagny and others between 1803 and 1805.[48] However, even before the Jena campaign, French counter-measures were restricting the circulation of British-sponsored papers, and in 1804–05 Bonaparte obtained the suppression of Paoli de Chagny's *Mercure universel* at Regensburg and pressured the Hamburg Senate until it agreed to discover and punish the printer of his *Annales politiques du dix-neuvième siècle*. Likewise he achieved bans on Regnier's *Courier de Londres* in the Batavian republic, Hamburg and Saxony.[49]

After the Napoleonic victory in Germany in 1806–07, the British propaganda campaign shifted to Sweden and Russia, where the *Courier d'Angleterre* was distributed *gratis* to leading courtiers and politicians.[50] In 1808–09, it was extended to the Iberian Peninsula, where the *Courier de Londres* was translated into Portuguese and the *Courier d'Angleterre* sent free of charge to Spanish editors. Its accounts of British military successes were translated into Spanish and published as separate pamphlets.[51] The aim of this strategy – which was much more limited in scope than Napoleon's press propaganda campaigns – was to reach élites close to government, and hence influence policy, by providing agenda-setting information which supported pro-British executive decisions in the *lingua-franca* of the era: such information was often translated from official documents in the government's *London Gazette*.

Nevertheless, reliance on émigré auxiliaries could be problematic. In April 1805, following British government pressure, Regnier was sacked

from the editorship of the *Courier de Londres*, apparently to remove an
obstacle to peace negotiations.[52] His successor, a Scottish career journalist
named Robert Heron, in a letter to Lord Petty, the future third Marquess
of Lansdowne, recently deposited in the British Library, reveals both the
motives for his own appointment at the request of the Foreign Office,
and that relying on émigré publicists was a two-edged sword:

> My business has been chiefly to keep it [the paper] free from those
> foolish indecencies of invective by which the French Emigrants had,
> at one time, embarrassed Government with almost every Foreign
> Court – to prevent its being made a vehicle of clumsy and irritating
> falsehoods, and to make it a fairer and fuller representation of the
> details of English life and policy, than might, otherwise, be circulated
> on the continent, in the French language.[53]

Yet in 1806, the British government nevertheless re-hired Regnier and
his new journal, the *Courier d'Angleterre*.[54] Reliance on such auxiliaries
seems proof of the British government's difficulties when faced by
Napoleon's near monopoly over Europe's traditional public information
system. Although the government devoted more money to subsidizing
these papers than had been spent 'corrupting' the entire British domestic
press in the 1780s and 1790s, the émigré journals were for the most
part financially self-sufficient. Hence their support for British policy was
contingent not absolute. Moreover, the government was reluctant to
interfere too overtly in the day to day running of the émigré papers
because it hoped that its influence would remain undetected. Thus the
editors of British propaganda papers were able to expound disagreeable
doctrines in polemical articles. These included incitements to assassinate
Napoleon that led to outraged questions in Parliament.[55] It seems fair to
suggest, therefore, that the British propaganda policy was to some extent
a result of desperation and lack of alternative means – just as Castlereagh
asserted – and that this provides further evidence of the Napoleonic
empire's success in establishing an ideological and informational *cordon
sanitaire* around much of Europe, even beyond the frontiers of France
and her satellite states.

V

Thus, although propaganda budgets in the Napoleonic period were low,
the stakes in the struggle were high. The key international propaganda
battle was not – in contrast to the 1790s – an ideological one, but rather

a struggle to disseminate agenda-setting data. A 'war of information' had superseded a 'war of ideas'. In the Napoleonic era timely flows of high quality information – just as much the lifeblood of executive decision-making as finances are the sinews of power – was at a premium. Using newspapers as their primary battleground, the French aspired to control the public sphere across Europe and sought to drive the public from the public sphere in order to portray Bonaparte as the only public actor in Europe. Napoleon's strategy was facilitated by the cumulative dysfunction of traditional communications networks caused by war, press controls, blockade, the interruption of civilian travel, the disruption of postal services and the stagnation of trade, which made the transfer of news much more problematic than in previous wars.

At the same time, French hegemony made it much easier for Napoleon than his predecessors to bully and cajole continental governments into bowing to his whims, and when that did not work, he could resort with apparent impunity to direct action in neutral territories, as when he seized Palm or d'Enghien. The British responded by attempting to maintain information flows to members of the European élite who could influence policy. Although this was less visible than other aspects of the war, it was nonetheless vital if the British were to prevent Napoleon establishing a monopoly over the dissemination of news information inside France and much of Europe. For both protagonists, in different ways, information warfare was an integral part of the war effort.

Notes

1. Hansard, *Journals of the House of Commons*, XXXIV, 101 (debate of 30 April 1816).
2. The classic treatment of the rise of the public, which has shaped almost all subsequent work, is Jürgen Habermas, *The Structural Transformation of the Public Sphere*, trans. Thomas Burger (Cambridge, MA, 1989). For recent critiques, see Hannah Barker and Simon Burrows (eds), *Press, Politics and the Public Sphere in Europe and North America, 1760–1820* (Cambridge, 2002), James van Horn Melton, *The Rise of the Public in Enlightenment Europe* (Cambridge, 2002).
3. The only general study of Napoleonic propaganda, Robert B. Holtman, *Napoleonic Propaganda* (Baton Rouge, 1950), is over 50 years old, a remarkable book researched and written during and just after the Second World War without access to French archives. Since then relatively little has been added to our knowledge of propaganda warfare in the period. A recent bibliographical essay in Philip G. Dwyer (ed.), *Napoleon in Europe* (Harlow, 2001), pp. 264–88, cited just one subsequent study – my essay 'The Struggle for European Opinion in the Napoleonic Wars: British Francophone Propaganda, 1803–14', *French History* 11 (1997): 29–53. However, since Dwyer's book went to press, one could

add Simon Burrows, *French Exile Journalism and European Politics* (Woodbridge, 2000) and Wayne Hanley, *The Genesis of Napoleonic Propaganda, 1796–1799* (New York, 2005). In addition, the full text of Napoleon's propagandistic *bulletins de la grande armée* have recently been combined into a single volume in English translation for the first time: see J. David Markham (ed.), *Imperial Glory: The Bulletins of Napoleon's Grande Armée* (London, 2003). While the British domestic propaganda campaign unleashed during the invasion scare of 1803–05 – which was of unprecedented scale and social reach – has attracted historical attention, the international dimension of Britain's propaganda campaigns remains largely unexplored.

4. On espionage see especially Elizabeth Sparrow, *Secret Service: British Agents in France, 1792–1815* (Woodbridge, 1999); Olivier Blanc, *Les Espions de la Révolution et de l'Empire* (Paris, 1995). Studies of leading spies, notably d'Antraigues (see note 47 below), are also useful as, for the revolutionary period, are a series of essays and papers by Michael Durey, especially 'The British Secret Service and the Escape of Sir Sidney Smith from Paris in 1798', *History* 84 (1999): 437–57, and 'Lord Grenville and the "Smoking Gun": The Plot to Assassinate the French Directory in 1798–1799 Reconsidered', *Historical Journal* 45 (2002): 547–68. More topical for the purpose of the current collection of essays, although it deals with the mid 1790s, is Jane Knight, 'Nelson's "Old Lady": Merchant News as a Source of Intelligence: June to October 1796', *Journal of Maritime Research* (May 2005).

5. Holtman, *Napoleonic Propaganda*, especially pp. 37–43, 244–6.

6. On Napoleon's use of propaganda in Italy and Egypt see Hanley, *Genesis of Napoleonic Propaganda*.

7. For the bulletins of the *grande armée* from 1805 see Markham (ed.), *Imperial Glory*; on his journalistic contribution, A. Périvier, *Napoléon journaliste* (Paris, 1918).

8. The interested enthusiast will find that all these themes recur in the translated selection of correspondence in J.M. Thompson (ed.), *Napoleon's Letters* (London, 1998, first published 1934 as *Napoleon Self-Revealed*), which also contains the letters to Fouché and Clarke of 21 April 1807 and 10 October 1809 cited later in this paragraph (letters 146 and 195). I have cited the original published sources below and provided my own translations, since Thompson's translations are rather loose.

9. See Léon Lecestre (ed.), *Lettres inédites de Napoléon Ier*, 2 vols (Paris, 1897), I, 93–4, letter no. 150, Napoléon to Fouché, 21 April 1807. For Napoleon's instructions to Portalis on the same subject, see *Correspondance de Napoléon Ier publiée par ordre de l'Empereur Napoléon III*, 32 vols (Paris, 1858–69), XV, 156–7, no. 12436, Napoleon to Portalis, 21 April 1807.

10. *Correspondance de Napoléon Ier*, XIX, 666–7 no. 15933, Napoleon to Clarke, 10 October 1809.

11. E. d'Hauterive, *La Police secrète du premier empire*, 5 vols (Paris, 1908–68), I, para #1402.

12. Hélène Maspero-Clerc, *Un Journaliste contre-révolutionnaire: Jean-Gabriel Peltier, 1760–1825* (Paris, 1973), p. 148.

13. Copies survive in the Archives nationales, AF[IV] series. They are incorporated into daily police bulletins in AF[IV] 1508–34 and survive separately in AF[IV] 1564–89.

14. There is at present no systematic international survey of anti-Napoleonic caricatures, so the observations made here are necessarily impressionistic. There are also some caveats. For example, British prints may well have been exported to the Netherlands from early in the Napoleonic period, and the Curzon collection's 500 Continental cartoons from the period – which will shortly be available on-line – contains about a dozen Italian caricatures of Napoleon from the late 1790s. Nevertheless, the Curzon collection, as well as the smaller selection of prints published in Catherine Clerc, *La Caricature contre Napoléon* (Paris, 1985), generally supports the impression that the output of Continental caricaturists (excepting the French) only really took off after 1808. I wish to thank Dr Mark Philp of Oriel College, Oxford and Dr Alexandra Franklin of the Bodleian Library for supplying information on the Curzon collection database and the export of British prints.

15. For treatments of Napoleon in caricature see: Alexander Meyrick Broadley, *Napoleon in Caricature, 1795–1821* (London, 1911), John Ashton, *English Caricature and Satire on Napoleon I* (London, 1888); Clerc, *La Caricature contre Napoléon*. See also Pascal Dupuy, 'La Caricature anglaise face à la France en révolution (1789–1802)', *Dix-huitième siècle* 32 (2000): 307–20.

16. For the futility of using smugglers and alternative proposal for using balloons, see London, National Archives, FO27/91, George Davis to Lord Bathurst, 14 October 1812.

17. For literacy rates, see R.A. Houston, *Literacy in Early Modern Europe: Culture and Education, 1500–1800* (London and New York, 1988). On newspaper audience figures in various European countries see Barker and Burrows, *Press, Politics and the Public Sphere*.

18. The French figure is from Jeremy D. Popkin, *Revolutionary News: The Press in France, 1789–1799* (Durham, NC, 1990), p. 82. The British figure is drawn from stamp office records showing that 7,000,000 newspaper stamps were sold to London newspapers and 9,400,000 to the provincial press in 1801: see Hannah Barker, 'England' in Barker and Burrows (eds), *Press, Politics and the Public Sphere*, pp. 93–112 at p. 103.

19. Paris, Archives nationales, AF[IV] 1521, 'minute of police bulletin, 8 April 1812'.

20. In fact, the degree of corruption in the eighteenth-century European press seems to have been exaggerated. In the British case, the classic Whig narrative of a corrupt eighteenth-century press being transformed into a model of respectability and rectitude in the nineteenth century has been convincingly debunked by Hannah Barker, *Newspapers, Politics, and Public Opinion in Late Eighteenth-century England* (Oxford, 1998). The most scholarly version of the Whig narrative is Arthur Aspinall, *Politics and the Press, c. 1780–1850* (London, 1949).

21. The best treatment of the structure of the French pre-revolutionary press, and especially the local advertising papers, the *Affiches*, is Jack Censer, *The French Press in the Age of Enlightenment* (London and New York, 1994).

22. Holtman, *Napoleonic Propaganda*, pp. 46, 53.

23. Ibid., pp. 44–5.

24. Paris, Archives nationales, 29AP/91 (Roederer papers) fo. 52. Roederer's figures also include a third category, works sold through subscription. However, since

none of these were periodicals in the regular sense of the word, I have not included them in these figures.

25. Gilles Feyel, 'La Diffusion des gazettes étrangères en France et la révolution postale des années 1750', in Henri Duranton, Claude Labrosse and Pierre Rétat (eds), *Les Gazettes européennes de langue française (XVIIe–XVIIIe siècles)* (Saint-Etienne, 1992), pp. 81–99; Censer, *French Press*, pp. 10–11. In 1781, postal records show that there were 14,000 subscriptions to foreign-produced international gazettes in France and 30,000 for French titles.

26. Popkin, *Revolutionary News*, p. 82.

27. Holtman, *Napoleonic Propaganda*, pp. 51–2.

28. Ibid., pp. 46–7, 57. Holtman's reference to the *Gazette du Bas-Rhin* clearly should read *Courier du Bas-Rhin*.

29. Paris, Archives nationales, F^{18} 12 no. 43 and AF^{IV} 1521, 'minute of police bulletin, 8 April 1812'. In January 1811 the paper had 17,425 subscribers, but in January 1812 only 5,850. This compares with 40,000 subscribers a decade earlier.

30. Daniel Moran, 'Cotta and Napoleon: The French Pursuit of the *Allgemeine Zeitung*', *Central European History* 14 (1981): 91–109.

31. Jack Censer, 'Maupeou et la presse politique', in Duranton, Labrosse and Rétat (eds), *Gazettes européennes*, pp. 290–8.

32. Feyel, 'Diffusion des gazettes étrangères', pp. 96–8. As has been stated above (note 25), in 1781 about 14,000 out of 44,000 French newspapers subscriptions (i.e. almost one-third) were to foreign-produced international gazettes. By then, German gazettes, notably the *Courier du Bas-Rhin* (founded 1767) and the London-produced *Courier de l'Europe* (founded 1776) had established themselves alongside the Dutch gazettes as important players in the French market. In the early 1770s the main players, save for the *Courrier d'Avignon* (which was produced in a Papal enclave), were all Dutch journals, notably the *Gazette d'Amsterdam* and *Gazette de Leyde*, but also the *Gazette de La Haye* and *Gazette d'Utrecht*. Assuming roughly constant ratios, it thus seems fair to suggest that the Dutch held one quarter of the market at this time.

33. This point is made cogently in Jeremy D. Popkin, *News and Politics in the Age of Revolution: Jean Luzac's Gazette de Leyde* (Ithaca, NY, 1989).

34. See especially Pierre Rétat, 'Les Gazetiers de Hollande et les puissances politiques: une difficile collaboration', *Dix-huitième siècle* 25 (1993): 319–35; Jean Vercruysse, 'La Reception politique des gazettes de Hollande, une lecture diplomatique', in Hans Bots (ed.), *La Diffusion et lecture des journaux de langue française sous l'ancien régime* (Amsterdam, 1988), pp. 39–47.

35. Simon Burrows, 'The Cosmopolitan Press', in Barker and Burrows (eds), *Press, Politics and the Public Sphere*, pp. 23–47, p. 33; Popkin, *News and Politics*, pp. 72–3; Jeremy D. Popkin, 'The *Gazette de Leyde* and French Politics under Louis XVI', in Jack Censer and Jeremy D. Popkin (eds), *Press and Politics in Pre-Revolutionary France* (Berkeley, 1987), pp. 75–132, pp. 82–3.

36. Burrows, 'Cosmopolitan Press', pp. 31–2; Popkin, *News and Politics*.

37. Burrows, *French Exile Journalism*, pp. 106–42; Simon Burrows, 'Struggle for European Opinion'.

38. Bibliothèque historique de la ville de Paris, MS 723, 'Journaux bibliographie', fo. 61 (1); London, National Archives, FO27/56, Comtesse de la Chapelle to Grenville, 9 August 1800.

39. Paul Hazard, 'Le *Spectateur du Nord'*, *Revue d'histoire littéraire de France* (1906): 26–50, 45–50; Hélène Maspero-Clerc, 'Montlosier, journaliste de l'émigration', *Bulletin d'histoire économique et sociale de la révolution française*, année 1975 (1977): 81–103, pp. 95–7; Burrows, *French Exile Journalism*, pp. 50, 106, 188–91.

40. See Simon Burrows, 'Culture and Misperception: The Law and the Press in the Outbreak of War in 1803', *International History Review* 18 (1996): 793–818; Burrows, *French Exile Journalism*, pp. 107–28. For other treatments of the press issue see Maspero-Clerc, *Un Journaliste contre-révolutionnaire*, pp. 139–79, and Hélène Maspero-Clerc, 'Un Journaliste émigré jugé à Londres pour diffamation du Premier Consul', *Revue d'histoire moderne et contemporaine* 18 (1971): 261–81; Périvier, *Napoléon journaliste*, pp. 200–25; T. Ebbinghaus, *England, Napoléon und die Presse* (Munich-Berlin, 1914), pp. 144 ff. It should be noted that the most comprehensive treatment of the Peace of Amiens to date, John D. Grainger, *The Amiens Truce: Britain and Bonaparte, 1801–1803* (Woodbridge, 2004), argues that the press was not a significant factor in the deterioration of Anglo-French relations, contending that the French only used it as a bargaining chip to distract British attention. However, Grainger has not consulted the main source on which my claims and those of other press historians rest: the diplomatic correspondence in the French foreign ministry archives in Paris. The timing of complaints might equally be explained by Peltier's long periods of silence in 1802.

41. Holtman, *Napoleonic Propaganda*, pp. 52–3; Burrows, *French Exile Journalism*, pp. 206–7; Périvier, *Napoléon journaliste*, p. 110.

42. British and allied publicists seized on the mendacious French reports of Trafalgar and republished them: see for example the *Gibraltar Chronicle*, 1 February 1806. A copy of this edition was exhibited in the National Maritime Museum's 'Nelson and Napoléon' exhibition, but is not listed in the official catalogue because it was a late acquisition. I thank Margarette Lincoln of the National Maritime Museum for supplying me with supplementary data about this newspaper edition.

43. Copies of these prints can be consulted in Margarette Lincoln (ed.), *Nelson and Napoléon* (London, 2005), p. 248 (cat. No. 283) and M. Dorothy George, *English Political Caricature, 1793–1832: A Study of Opinion and Propaganda* (London, 1959), plate 53, respectively.

44. *L'Ambigu*, 217 (10 April 1809) p. 63.

45. *L'Ambigu*, 193 (10 August 1808), p. 226.

46. Burrows, *French Exile Journalism*, p. 138; *Traduccion del numéro 237 del Ambigu, en que se incertan las lettres Apostolicas … en 10 de Junio de 1809* (Mexico City, 1810).

47. For d'Antraigues' services see especially Jacques Godechot, *Le Comte d'Antraigues* (Paris, 1986) and Colin Duckworth, *The d'Antraigues Phenomenon: The Making and Breaking of a Revolutionary Royalist Espionage Agent* (Newcastle-upon-Tyne, 1986). These are the best and most recent among several studies of d'Antraigues. Fauche-Borel outlines his supposed services in Louis Fauche-Borel, *Mémoires*, 4 vols (Paris, 1829).

48. According to French secret police lists of émigré agents, other German-based journalists in British pay included the barons d'Angely (*père* and *fils*) who edited the *Abeille* at Altona and Sabatier de Castres: see Paris, Archives

du Ministère des affaires étrangères, Mémoires et documents, France, 620, 'Statistique, 1810' and Paris, Archives nationales, AN, AF^{IV*} 1710 'Statistique des Bourbons et des consorts'. Paoli de Chagny's journals were entitled *Le Mercure universel*; *Le Pour et le contre*; and *Annales politiques du dix-neuvième siècle*. Paoli de Chagny details his services to the British in two letters to the Foreign Office, dated London, 24 March 1805 and Hamburg, 6 July 1816: see London, National Archives, FO27/71 and FO27/144. See also Burrows, 'Struggle for European Opinion'.

49. D'Hauterive, *La Police secrète*, vol. 1 paragraphs 441, 1061; vol. 2 paragraphs 533 and 605; *Courier de Londres*, LVI.22 (14 September 1804) and LVII.25 (26 March 1805); Paris, Archives du Ministère des affaires étrangères, Mémoires et documents, France 1774, fo. 94, Napoleon to Talleyrand, 1 November 1803. See also Burrows, 'Struggle for European Opinion', p. 44.

50. For the fullest treatment of the circulation of émigré propaganda in the north of Europe see Simon Burrows, 'British Propaganda for Russia in the Napoleonic Wars: The *Courier d'Angleterre*', *New Zealand Slavonic Journal* (1993): 85–100. See also Burrows, 'Struggle for European Opinion', pp. 45–8, and Burrows, *French Exile Journalism*, pp. 134–8.

51. Burrows, *French Exile Journalism*, p. 138; Burrows, 'Struggle for European Opinion', pp. 48–9. Copies of Spanish and Portuguese materials survive in the Bodleian Library.

52. Burrows, 'Struggle for European Opinion', p. 41; Burrows, *French Exile Journalism*, p. 130.

53. London, British Library, Bowood papers, B115 fos 82–4, Heron to Petty, 15 Feb. 1806, at fos 83–4. I would like to thank Dr Matthew Shaw of the British Library for informing me of the accession of this document and communicating its content.

54. The first purchases of the *Courier d'Angleterre* in November 1806 are recorded in civil service receipts in London, British Library, Add. MS. 51464 fos 70, 73.

55. Burrows, *French Exile Journalism*, pp. 90–4. According to the *Courier de Londres* LXIX.52 (28 June 1811), Lord Howick complained in Parliament about an incitation to the assassination of Napoleon, copied from Lewis Goldsmith's *Anti-Gallican Monitor*, which appeared in the *Courier d'Angleterre* no. 642. The precise date and content of this number, which does not survive, are unknown. In addition, Regnier translated the infamous interregnum justification of tyranicide *Killing noe murder* (1657) into French and published it in the *Courier de Londres* (6–17 January 1804) and in pamphlet form.

4
The Fleets at Trafalgar: The Margin of Superiority

Roger Knight

One of the most pleasant and useful developments in the English-speaking naval historical world over the last 20 years has been increasing contact with French, Spanish and Dutch historians. Their work and judgements have begun to permeate the history written on this side of the Channel and in North America, and one of the main strands of this chapter is to review the agreement – or otherwise – between the historians of the different countries involved in the Battle of Trafalgar.

Success in this battle depended upon the relative strengths of the industrial resources of the different countries in bringing such concentrations of force together at the right time, while warfare itself was labour intensive. Nelson commanded 27 ships, approximately 17,000 men and 2,148 guns. The Combined Fleet under Villeneuve numbered some 30,000 seamen and soldiers and 2,632 guns. Seventeen ships were French and 16 were Spanish. The sheer numbers were impressive. Without counting the men and armaments of the frigates of both sides, 60 ships of the line and slightly under 50,000 men took part in the battle. Where were the margins of superiority, of both quantity and quality, in the ships and men across these opposing fleets? Was Sir Julian Corbett correct when he wrote in 1910 that at Trafalgar 'Ship for ship' the British fleet had a clear advantage.[1]

I

The first area of broad agreement is that the French Navy was no longer at the peak of condition or performance that it reached in the middle of the American Revolutionary War, and that the Spanish Navy had similarly declined. The task of keeping a navy at sea and effective was one of the most formidable tasks facing an eighteenth-century nation. Daniel Baugh, in a recent essay, gives a graduated definition of the tasks and costs of an eighteenth-century navy:

> Building warships, even very good warships, was rather easy. Consistently repairing and replacing them over the years was harder. Manning them with competent seamen, feeding those men and preserving their health was harder still. And, finally, keeping squadrons at sea, especially for extended cruises and on distant deployments, was hardest (and most expensive) of all.[2]

Both the French and Spanish navies had continued building through the years of peace after 1783, but for different reasons both were starved of funds from 1790 and began to fail at these tasks through the 1790s. French historians agree that France had lost the naval shipbuilding race, long before the turmoil of the French Revolution hit both the navy and the dockyards. Most would now accept Baugh's judgement that the French Navy in 1790 began a period of prolonged decline.[3] No Spanish ship of the line was launched after 1796 due to 'the pitiful state of Charles IV's treasury', whereas three or four had been the average in previous years.[4] All the same, according to Jan Glete's calculations, in his great survey of the sailing navies, if France and Spain combined in 1793 as they had done between 1779 and 1783, the Bourbon powers would have at least 34 per cent more warships than Britain.[5]

The condition of those French and Spanish warships was, however, another matter. Tonnage figures alone mask the advantage that England had gained by infrastructure improvements financed by William Pitt's government after 1783. Parliament, smarting after the defeats of the American war and the loss of the colonies, had granted money for steadily launching new ships of the line through the 1780s. Perhaps more significantly, money was also granted for investment in dockyards, dry docks, yard buildings, victualling facilities and fortifications of overseas yards. A critical factor at the time of Trafalgar was the difference in the number of graving docks necessary for the regular maintenance required by late eighteenth-century warships: the French had one for every ten ships of the line, while the British and Spanish had one for every 7.5, and with more investment in the late 1780s, the British increased this advantage.[6] By the middle of the 1790s, the British had developed a formidable system of dry docks leading off a wet dock in Portsmouth, begun in 1789 (substantially those you can see today, with the *Victory* in one of them), and a further dry dock at Plymouth begun in 1784. Professor Rodger has outlined these improvements in *The Command of the Ocean* and these developments will now be more fully understood.[7] Further, the southern coast of England is blessed with twice daily tides of substantial height, and, once a fortnight, the high range of spring tides enabled ships of the line to dock or re-float, an advantage shared by the French only in their northern bases at Brest and Rochefort. It is probably true to say that French and Spanish historians do not fully appreciate the effort and commitment made by the politicians and naval administrators in London before the war began in 1793.

The operational importance of these frontline facilities can be illustrated by a small example from Trafalgar itself. Cuthbert Collingwood's 100-gun *Royal Sovereign* was first to reach the line of the Combined Fleet, ahead of Nelson's *Victory*. Many have noted that this was the only time that Collingwood beat Nelson to anything, but few have realized that the real reason for his speed was that the copper sheathing on the normally slow-sailing *Royal Sovereign* had just been renewed, and thus she was clear of weed and barnacles – a substantial advantage in the light winds on 21 October. The ship had returned after three years' service in the Mediterranean and been docked in Plymouth in mid August, sailed on 10 September, and joined Nelson's fleet off Cadiz eight days before the battle.[8] Turning around large ships in so few days was difficult to match.

The other resource advantage enjoyed by Britain from its domination of the entrance to the Baltic is, however, well appreciated by our French and Spanish colleagues. Shortages of hemp, pine timber for masts, good quality Swedish iron and canvas dogged both France and Spain and attempts to stockpile Baltic naval stores in peacetime were doomed to failure, for hemp, in particular, deteriorates if kept in store for any length of time. Agustin Roderiguez notes the difficulties of supplying Baltic naval stores to the Spanish fleets, as inferior Spanish products were substituted with resultant breakages and accidents in difficult conditions.[9] In France the British blockade off Brest from June 1803 caused the dockyard to stop shipbuilding because of a shortage of timber and naval stores and by February 1805 coastal traffic supplying the dockyard had almost ceased.[10]

II

All the evidence points to a very significant British advantage in the performance of every aspect of seamanship: keeping the seas in all weathers and all seasons, in the shiphandling of individual ships and the manoeuverability of squadrons and fleets. British skills showed a marked improvement from 1793. Compare, for instance, the Mediterranean fleet under Hood and Hotham in the mid 1790s with the fleet under Nelson between 1803 and early 1805. In the earlier period ships were continually in trouble in the unpredictable weather, particularly in winter, when winds are no less fierce than in the great oceans of the world. Collisions were frequent, the 74-gun *Berwick* rolled her masts away, the 64-gun *Ardent* disappeared, presumably from an explosion. Captain Nelson in the *Agamemnon* (64) was taken aback several times, and suffered hull damage when he did so. Individual ships and sometimes the whole fleet spent inordinate times in Leghorn refitting.

By contrast, a decade or so later, by 1803 Nelson had evolved his system of loose blockade, keeping below the horizon off Toulon, and for 20 months the fleet kept at sea without, as Nelson accurately claimed, the loss of a spar. When the north-west gales blew the fleet lay under bare poles, drifting to leeward – but safe, with no lee shore for several hundred miles. Regular convoys arrived from England with naval stores and equipment and provisions; more efficient arrangements were made for obtaining fresh provisions from local sources, and there was little sickness. The fleet was either at the rendezvous off Toulon or engaged in purposeful cruising for 75 per cent of the time. When Villeneuve made his first breakout from Toulon in January 1805, one of these gales battered his fleet so severely that it had to return immediately to Toulon. Nelson's fleet rode the storm out unscathed. 'What a contrast to the Spanish and French fleets', Contre-amiral Remi Monarque has written recently, 'which were usually prevented from setting out to sea, prisoners in their ports due to the strict blockade, and so cruelly lacking training. With little or no preparation they had to face bad weather and encounter an enemy both seasoned and well trained through long months at sea.'[11]

Britain also had a numerical advantage in its seamen. Both France and Spain suffered from a lack of seamen, whereas while the British were under pressure, they managed enough for a continually increasing fleet. Estimates of the number borne in the British Navy average 110,000 in 1805 and they continued to increase every year until they stood at about 140,000 in 1813.[12] Spanish numbers declined during these years, straining the marine register of 65,000 men in 1793 and remained static through to the early 1800s: Carla Rahn Phillips estimates that Spain would have needed 111,000 to man the ships which Charles IV and his ministers planned to build.[13] Morale declined as delays in pay to the seamen and shipyards became longer. Nelson saw the weaknesses in the quality of Spanish seamen almost before the war started after he had been allowed to visit Cadiz dockyard in June 1793: He wrote to his wife: 'In vain may the Dons make fine ships, they cannot however make men.'[14]

III

It is over the crucial question of gunnery that there seems to be most differences in interpretation. Roderiguez remarks that the idea that British fire was faster than their enemies is a British 'patriotic legend' and that it 'has become part of folklore that the British crews were capable of shooting three times faster than their enemies'. Even if British gun crews were better trained, the enormous physical effort involved in firing heavy guns would limit the rate of firing, and that guns would need time to cool so that they would not ignite gunpowder needed for the next firing. Thus, he argues, it was not technically possible to have achieved a markedly greater rate of fire. Roderiguez attributes the difference between the effectiveness of the British and Combined fleets to the tactics adopted by the British, who waited until they were very close to the enemy ship before opening fire, thus conserving not only their shot, but the energy of their crew.[15]

Of this last point there can be no doubt, and the British close quarters tactics were dictated by their preference for the use of the carronade, withholding fire until opposing ships were very close. These short guns, effective only at close range, were the reasons for the desire of British commanders-in-chief such as Howe, and followed pre-eminently by Nelson, to get close to the enemy. From his time in the *Agamemnon* Nelson had always carried two 68lb carronades on board his ships.[16] How fast the crew was able to fire them was critical. There is some evidence provided by the inventory of the gunner of the *Captain*, Nelson's ship at the Battle of Cape St Vincent, which survives (because it has Nelson's signature) in the Houghton Library at Harvard. Close action in this battle lasted just under three hours, and in that time the ship expended 146 barrels of gunpowder, 2,773 round, grape and double-headed shot, and one ton, seven hundred weight of 'junk', made of unpicked hemp rope, which formed the wads rammed home behind each shot. Over a thousand shot had been fired by the *Captain*'s long 32 pounders, a rate of one broadside every four and a half minutes. Her two carronades, so short that they could be easily loaded and fired, fired 117 shot, one every two and a half minutes, although this does not allow for double-shotting these lethal weapons which was certainly done at the beginning of the action to reduce muzzle velocity, which caused wider, more jagged shot holes.[17]

To fire at this rate required seamen to be confident that their guns would not burst, with the consequent dreadful carnage on the gundeck, and here the British had a distinct advantage. Ordnance reforms had begun in the 1780s. The entire gun-stock of the navy and army was tested, weak ones condemned and replaced under the direction of Thomas Blomefield, Inspector of Artillery. This very long and expensive process had, by the late 1790s, started to improve the performance of British guns. Blomefield also pushed up the standards of guns made for the navy by instituting the '30 round proof', requiring the firing of a gun made by a contractor 30 times before it was accepted by the Ordnance. By this means, he forced contractors to improve their guns, achieved especially by reducing the sulphur content of iron, thus making it less brittle. Blomefield also introduced a newly designed long gun in 1787. French and Spanish gun foundries could not match British technology. Napoleon himself reckoned that his navy was ten years behind the British; Nicholas Rodger estimates that the French were 20 years behind in the manufacture of carronades.[18] The British, too, produced gunpowder with more explosive force, manufactured from saltpetre from India, denied to the French. Further, the British used gun locks, which had been in general issue since 1793, and which the French were only just beginning to adopt. This had the advantage of allowing the captain of the gun crew to fire looking down the barrel of the gun by pulling a long lanyard attached to the gunlock. In the pitching and rolling of a line of battleship – and the calm conditions at Trafalgar, with a long Atlantic swell made accuracy at long range difficult – these were critical advantages. After the battle a report to the French Minister of Marine from the army officer in command of the troops on board Villeneuve's fleet noted that 'the swell took our ships abeam, made them roll heavily and rendered our aim uncertain'.[19]

The *Victory*'s shot expenditure for the battle, recorded by the Gunner, survives in the Royal Naval Museum at Portsmouth: in four hours and 20 minutes of firing, the ship expended a total of 3,041 shot. Her 32 pounders fired 997 shot, the 24 pounders 872, the 12 pounders 800 (they were on the upper deck where heavy casualties occurred). As the *Victory* was engaged on both sides this implies that an average of seven shots an hour per gun was achieved, although it is difficult to be accurate with this figure, as most of the firing took place in the first two hours and it is not known how much these guns were double shotted. Seven and half tons of powder were expended, three tons of junk in wads, 3,000 musket balls, 1,000 pistol shot.[20] No direct comparative figures exist for French or Spanish rates of fire, but it seems reasonable to agree with Professor Rodger when he concludes his analysis of Trafalgar: 'The French and

Spanish ships were more numerous and more heavily manned; they were fought in most cases with desperate gallantry and in many cases with some skill. So complete a defeat in spite of so many advantages can only be explained by the crushing superiority of British gunnery tactics.'[21] And one of the quartermasters on board the *Victory* wrote to his wife after the battle: 'After the [French] prisoners came on board they sayed that the Devil loded the guns for it was impossible for men to load and fire as quick as we did.'[22]

IV

There is further difference of opinion between French and Spanish historians, on the one hand, and the British on the other, as to the numbers of ships available to the combatant nations. Roderiguez's view is that: 'Trafalgar was only the confirmation of a crushing superiority that had already existed for many years', and goes as far as saying that 'the British could have afforded to lose at Trafalgar' and still have won the naval war.[23] But in the years immediately before the battle, the British did their best to throw away their hard-won advantages. Firstly, the fleet was ageing. Only 33 battleships were launched between 1793 and 1805, a rate of 2.5 a year. In the 1780s ten a year had either been built or had been given a major repair, and this was the minimum that was calculated to be needed to keep up with the deterioration of a fleet of oak-built battleships.[24] Although the dockyards were kept at full stretch on maintenance and repair work, the age and condition of the fleet steadily deteriorated.

The greatest inroad into the British advantage in ships of the line was caused by the baleful administration of Lord St Vincent, the First Lord of the Admiralty from February 1801 to May 1804 in Henry Addington's administration. St Vincent's attempts to cut the navy down to size and reduce costs during the Peace of Amiens, a process carried out in an atmosphere of political vindictiveness, with the Navy Board and the shipbuilding and timber contractors as the First Lord's main target, was nearly to prove Britain's undoing. The dockyards were demoralized to the point of paralysis, timber and naval stores were short, merchants and private shipbuilders unwilling to contract with the navy. St Vincent himself refused to use the contractors, although they were integral to the British naval effort.[25] Just how bad the situation had become can be judged by the plight of the British Mediterranean fleet under Rear Admiral Sir Richard Bickerton during the Peace of Amiens, when he was based at Malta. Food became scarce by June 1802 and by December he was reporting scurvy; in January 1803 he described his situation to the Admiralty as 'almost destitute'. He had to cope with crew sickness on a large scale, a situation made worse by the Admiralty order to close the naval hospital at Malta. In March 1803 Bickerton reported that 408 men were sick and that 53 of them had died, and the situation was only relieved by the long-delayed arrival of transports and victuallers in Malta in April 1803. Ships were not relieved and their condition had deteriorated sadly. Bickerton's own flagship, the *Kent*, lost all her masts in a storm in December 1801 because her bowsprit and foremast were rotten.[26] And this was peacetime. It is not too much of an exaggeration to say that the condition of the British fleet denoted nothing less than a ship repair crisis.

After three years of bad tempered attempts at naval reform, which achieved almost nothing, Henry Addington's administration fell from power. William Pitt then appointed Henry Dundas, just raised to the peerage as Lord Melville, to be First Lord of the Admiralty on 15 May 1804. Melville was only to last a year in office, a period which has largely been overlooked because it was overshadowed by political scandal, which led to the First Lord's impeachment in April 1804, and to his resignation on 2 May 1805: but Melville's contribution to the preparation of the Fleet before Trafalgar was critical.

British naval commitments were extensive and world-wide, with the greater number of ships, and those in better condition, given to Admiral Cornwallis in the Channel. In September 1804 he had 44 ships of the line under his command, with 16 off Brest itself, seven off Rochefort, and another seven off Ferrol. Admiral Keith in the North Sea had more, but there were also other stations at Jamaica, the Leeward Islands, North America, the Cape of Good Hope and the East Indies to cover.[27] After he had been appointed Melville locked himself away in his house at Wimbledon with all the information he could get out of the Admiralty and navy offices. Doubtless he had the advice of his relative, Sir Charles Middleton, who had been Comptroller of the Navy Board for many years, and was a member of the Board of Admiralty in the 1790s. But Melville's logical mind and fresh thinking went into 'a very laborious Investigation into the State of the Ships now in commission', as he called it, and he reworked the distribution of the fleet through the world and made radical changes.[28] He produced a number of important memoranda for his Cabinet colleagues through the second half of 1804. On 14 June he wrote:

So many Rumours have of late gone abroad respecting the insufficiency of our Naval Force … I have thought it my earliest duty to investigate

... not with a view of insinuating Blame ... but for the purpose of applying every Remedy within the Resources of the country ... for the important object of putting permanently the British Navy upon such a footing as to preserve the Dominion of the Seas.[29]

Melville graded by condition the ships needed for each station, and he came up with new figures. He concluded that Britain desperately needed more ships at sea. His decisions in the next few months were just as radical and determined as the reforms that St Vincent had been trying to force through, though the two men were ideologically opposed. He shifted control away from the Navy Board and brought in private sector ideas and resources to meet the crisis. Within days of taking office he ordered contracts for building a large number of gun ships and gun brigs, while some were purchased already built.[30] He ordered three 64-gun ships and six frigates lying 'in Ordinary' in the Medway to be sailed to the Thames merchant shipyards to be repaired, as well as some smaller ships, making a dozen in all.[31] This order broke a long tradition that all major warship repairs were undertaken in the royal yards, and thus directly overseen by the Navy Board. In this decision he was guided by Charles Middleton, who was Comptroller of the Navy Board at the end of the American war when merchant yards had been used briefly, 'in cases of absolute necessity, and confined to frigates only'.[32]

At the same time the Navy Board lost its control of quality and price that it had defended since the Seven Years War.[33] It was now forced to make contracts in which price was not stipulated and where quality control could not be exercised. For instance, the contract for the repair of 64-gun ships *Belliqueux* and *Stately* with John Wells was to be fulfilled at the going rate: 'according to the Rate and prices charged by the Shipbuilders in the River Thames for performing similar works to the Ships belonging to the East India Company and the Merchants', while 'thickstuff or plank, withinside or withoutside, should be charged wrought, that it shall be done at the same prices as are charged for works of the like kind to Merchant ships'.[34]

Melville then drove through a reform which the Navy Board and the dockyards liked even less that the merchant yards encroaching upon their repairing role. He ordered them to change their system of repair to a method known as 'doubling'. This was first proposed by Gabriel Snodgrass, the Surveyor to the East India Company, with which Lord Melville was closely associated. Snodgrass, who started his career in the Royal Dockyards, had long been a critic of ships designed by the Surveyors in the Navy Office and built by the Royal Dockyards, holding that they were not nearly strong enough. He even went as far as to say that between 1775 and 1784 66 ships had foundered because of green timbers and bad workmanship. He advocated the use of more iron to strengthen ships, a material used in East India ships and, for that matter, in the French Navy (see Plate 1).[35] What he proposed now was radically different from the Navy Board practice of dismantling rotten timbers and replacing them with new:

> No ship should ever have what is called a thorough repair, or *any timbers* shifted; instead of this, their bottoms and upper works should be doubled with three inch oak plank from keel to gunwale, and strengthened with iron knees, standards, and even with iron riders, if necessary; all of which might be done at a small expence and ships so repaired would be stronger and safer, and be able to keep the seas longer, in the worst weather, than any new ships in his Majesty's Navy … All ships of the Navy are every way deficient of iron to strengthen and connect the sides and beams together, they should be built with diagonal braces …with the knees, standards, breast-hooks and crutches of iron, it being obviously impossible, by any means, to make a ship equally strong with wooden knees etc.[36]

The brittleness of the iron of the time was much distrusted by the shipwrights in the Royal Dockyards and Snodgrass's ideas for 'doubling with riders' had become thoroughly politicized, nor was the new method welcomed by St Vincent's administration. Thomas Troubridge, at that time on the Board of Admiralty, had written to Nelson in May 1803: 'I have long reprobated Riders. Every Taylor in the Country knows they destroy a Ship. We have for many months call'd on the Surveyors of the Navy to report their opinion on them, & after consulting all the Carpenters in Ordinary, they do not <u>feel competent to give an Opinion. So much for our Surveyors.</u>'[37] St Vincent and Troubridge, however, were hardly likely to get an opinion out of the civil administration of the navy when relations were so bad within it.

Melville then galvanized the Navy Board and the dockyards into action to implement the new ideas. The ships in ordinary were surveyed to find those in better condition and most able to get to sea. In February 1805 he despatched Sir Andrew Snape Hamond, the Controller of the Navy Board and Sir William Rule, the Surveyor of the Navy, down to Portsmouth dockyard, and they travelled on to Plymouth in early March. At both yards they laid down a precise programme of repair for the officers to follow, stipulating which drydock was to be used for each ship, and

Table 4.1 Ships doubled and strengthened before Trafalgar 1805 (in order of sailing from refitting port)[38]

	Repaired at	Docked	Cost	Date sailed	Station
Belliqueux (64)	Perry, B'Wall	20 Oct 1804	£23,720	13-Apr	East Indies
Prince George (90)	Portsmouth	30 Jan 1805	£11,764	30-Apr	Channel
Stately (1784)	Perry, Thames	3 Nov 1804	£22,422	01-May	North Sea
Thunderer (74)	Plymouth	16 Mar 1805	not given	03-Jun	Med
Majestic (74)	Chatham	12 May 1805	not given	15-Jun	North Sea
Zealous (74)	Portsmouth	11 June 1804	mid repair	21-Jun	Med
Caesar (80)	Plymouth	Aug 1802	£37,300	25-Jun	Channel
Dictator (64)	Cox & Co, Thames	20 Oct 1804	£26,061	24-Jul	North Sea
Captain (74)	Plymouth	26 Jun 1805	£27,505	05-Aug	Channel
Edgar (74)	Chatham	16 Mar 1805	£19,605	08-Aug	North Sea
Audacious (74)	Plymouth	16 Apr 1805	£27,429	18-Aug	Channel
Bellona (74)	Portsmouth	13 Apr 1805	£27,613	20-Aug	Channel
Powerful (74)	Perry, Thames	16 Mar 1805	£30,065	24-Aug	Channel
Africa (64)	Pitcher, Northfleet	30 Oct 1804	£32,208	Aug	Med
Nassau (64)	Perry, Thames	19 Mar 1805	£22,012	08-Oct	Thames
After battle					
Pompee (80)	Plymouth	30 May 1805	£41,229	02-Dec	Plymouth
London (90)	Plymouth	30 Apr 1805	£35,990	17-Dec	Plymouth
Canada (74)	Portsmouth	27 May 1805	£33,035	18-Dec	Portsmouth
Formidable (90)	Plymouth	30 May 1805	not given	25 Jan 1806	Plymouth
Resolution (74)	Chatham	29 May 1805	not given	9 Mar 1806	?
Ganges (74)	Portsmouth	25 Jul 1805	not given	24 May 1806	Channel
Gibraltar (80)	Portsmouth	6 Jul 1805	£30,643	15 Mar 1806	Portsmouth

specifying the spring tide they were to be docked and undocked.[39] They were able to do this because the Snodgrass method enabled them to forecast accurately the length of time for each repair. The complex task of making the iron straps and standards was undertaken in London, supervised by the Master Smith of Woolwich Yard, and then taken down to Plymouth by transport.[40] At Portsmouth 11 ships of the line were to spend between two weeks and a month in dock, and nine at Plymouth. By the summer of 1805 they were to be repaired and in commission. The Navy Board's order to the Portsmouth officers ended with an unusual formality: 'And in respect to strengthening such ships as may require it you will be governed by the orders you have recently received from the Navy Board in Town, in pursuance to directions to that effect from the Right Honourable the Lords Commissioners of the Admiralty.'[41] Though the yards did not manage to adhere too accurately to the programme, they managed to keep broadly in line with it.

Melville left office after the impeachment proceedings by Parliament in May 1805, just five months before the battle, when Charles Middleton, now Lord Barham, took over as First Lord. By that time, those rapidly-repaired ships found their places, in the main, as guardships or in the Channel, enabling others to take their place in Nelson's fleet and on distant stations. Of those ships, only the *Africa* (64) took part in the battle; but the significance of the number of ships on station represented by the steadily ascending graphs (see Figures 4.1 and 4.2), hardly affected by the casualties at Trafalgar, was not lost on contemporaries. The blockades were maintained and British grip on sea control was not loosened.

Thus Melville succeeded in generating an urgency which the dockyards had not demonstrated through the malaise of St Vincent's time as First Lord. An indication of how tough the bureaucratic battle had been comes from a letter written to him in early 1806 by John Barrow, the Second Secretary of the Admiralty:

As the measure of bringing forward ships from a state of ordinary by doubling and strengthening them with diagonal braces, according to the plan of Mr. Snodgrass, is wholly your own, and was adopted in spite of a determined prejudice against it every one of His Majesty's Dockyards, it may not be unsatisfactory to your Lordship to know the success of an Experiment which was undertaken in every department by something like compulsion and carried into effect with the utmost reluctance.

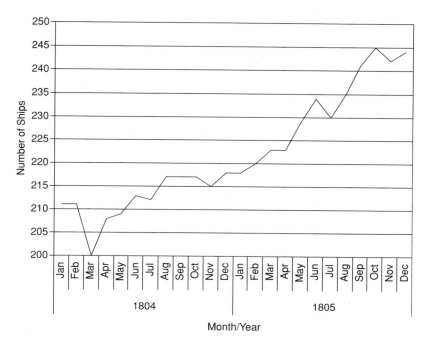

Figure 4.1   Ships on station, January 1804 to December 1805

Source: (UK) NA: PRO, ADM 8/87-90.

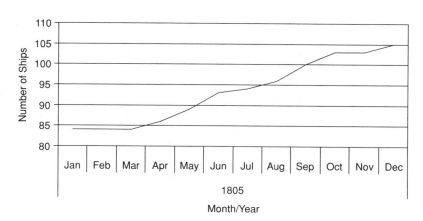

Figure 4.2   Ships of the line on station, January to December 1805[42]

Source: (UK) NA: PRO, ADM 8/87-90.

Barrow had no doubt of the importance of the measures:

> It might be thought perhaps going to far to say that the battle of Trafalgar would not have taken place if the new mode of repairing ships had not been adopted ... instead of 34 sailing of the Line, the Mediterranean Fleet would not possibly have exceeded 24 sail of the line at the time the action happened ... by the ordinary mode of repairing ships. Not one third of the number could have been brought forward in the same time as by the plan of Snodgrass.[43]

In November 1805 Sir John Sinclair, the noted naval and political commentator, wrote to Melville: 'What pleasure you must feel from our late naval successes? For though not present at the Head of the Admiralty, we would not have had such fleets at sea had it not been for your exertions.'[44]

V

Early analyses of the battle Trafalgar centred on Nelson and his command. Theodore Containine, the major general in command of the soldiers in Villeneuve's fleet reported to the Minister of Marine: 'Without doubt the greatest misfortune was that the enemy fleet was commanded by a man, uniting genius to daring, [who] knew how to profit by the rare opportunity of such a situation.'[45] Since there were 33 French and Spanish ships, to 27 British, it was perhaps an understandable reaction to account for the result of the battle to 'genius' and 'daring', but at the distance of 200 years it is perhaps easier to see the qualitative superiority of the British ships over the those of the Combined Fleet. In Remi Monarque's words: it was 'the culmination of a long process which brought the British Navy to that superior state of combat readiness which was so overwhelming at Trafalgar. ... the superiority ... was not just a fluke but the result of policies and attitudes prevalent at the Admiralty of the time, as well as the genius of Nelson'.[46] One Spanish historian, Jose Alcala-Zamora, concludes that: 'it did not really need either Cape St. Vincent or Trafalgar to explain Spanish naval decline'.[47] Not surprisingly, differences of interpretation of the overwhelming nature of the British victory remain between the historians of different countries today, but all are making assessment based on the capability of each of the fleets, and their views are perhaps now converging.

In terms of numbers of ships on active service, it was, however, a closer run thing. The relative neglect of the systematic replacement of old and worn out ships during the 1790s and St Vincent's disastrous administration nearly sacrificed the advantage gained from the investment of ten years before: the wisdom of the Pitt administration's expenditure between 1783 and 1793 is quite apparent. In 1804 the forgotten man of British naval administration, Lord Melville (Plate 2), by swift and radical measures, effectively gave the British another fleet of some 20 battleships. Though it was only a temporary advantage, its impact was similar to the effect of that other risky and costly ship-repair decision taken 25 years earlier during the American Revolutionary War. The decision to sheath the bottoms of the entire British fleet with copper was taken in exactly the same circumstances, when the British Navy had its back to the wall.[48] Melville's measures only just pushed the British Navy past the safe limit of numbers by the time of the Battle of Trafalgar. But the knowledge of the qualitative superiority enjoyed by each British ship over those of France and Spain provided Nelson with the confidence to adopt the tactics that he did to aim for comprehensive victory.

Notes

1. Sir Julian Corbett, *The Campaign of Trafalgar* (London, 1910) p. 53.
2. Daniel A. Baugh, 'Naval Power: What Gave the British Navy Superiority?' in Leandro Prados de la Ecosura, *Exceptionalism and Industrialisation: Britain and its European Rivals, 1688–1815* (Cambridge, 2004), p. 235.
3. Baugh, 'British Naval Superiority', p. 236; Martine Acerra and Jean Meyer, *Marines et Revolution* (Rennes, 1988), pp. 71, 74; William S. Cormack, *Revolution and Political Conflict in the French Navy, 1789–1794* (Cambridge, 1995), pp. 291–301; Jonathan Dull, 'Why Did the French Revolutionary Navy Fail?', *The Consortium on Revolutionary Europe: Proceedings for 1989* (Athens, GA, 1990), pp. 121–37.
4. Agustin R. Roderiguez Gonzalez, 'The Spanish at Trafalgar: Ships, Cannons, Men and a Problematic Alliance', *Journal of Maritime Research*, <http://www.jmr.nmm.ac.uk> April 2005.
5. Jan Glete, *Navies and Nations: Warships, Navies and State Building in Europe and America 1500–1860* (Stockholm, 1993), I, pp. 272, 276, 313.
6. N.A.M. Rodger, 'Form and Function in European Navies, 1660–1815', in Leo Akveld et al. (eds), *In het kielzog. Maritiemhistorische studies aangeboden aan Jaap R. Bruijn hij zijn vertrek als hoogleraar zeegeschiedenis aan de Universiteit Leiden* (Amsterdam, 2003), p. 97. Rodger addressed the ship design issue in this article and finds the British fleet well-built and 'fit for purpose', and the French and Spanish less so.
7. N.A.M. Rodger, *The Command of the Ocean: A Naval History of Britain 1649–1815* (London, 2004), chapter 24; also Paul Webb, 'The Rebuilding and Repairing of the Fleet 1798–1793', *Bulletin of the Institute of Historical Research* 50 (1977): 194–209; Jonathan G. Coad, *The Royal Dockyards 1690–1850: Architecture and Engineering Works of the Sailing Navy* (Aldershot, Hants, 1989), p. 97.

8. (UK)NA: ADM 180/6, Progress and Dimensions Books.
9. Acerra and Meyer, *Marines et Revolution*, pp. 54–64; Roderiguez, 'Spanish at Trafalgar'.
10. Rodger, *Command of the Ocean*, p. 530.
11. Remi Monarque, 'On Board HMS *Alexander* (1796–9)', *Mariner's Mirror* 89 (2003): 212.
12. Rodger, *Command of the Ocean*, appendix VI.
13. Carla Rahn Phillips, 'Recruiting Sailors in Eighteenth-Century Spain, *Mariner's Mirror* (2001): 439.
14. G.B.P. Naish, *Nelson's Letters to His Wife* (London, 1958), p. 83.
15. Roderiguez, 'Spanish at Trafalgar'.
16. e.g. Roger Knight, *The Pursuit of Victory: The Life and Achievement of Horatio Nelson* (London, 2005), pp. 196, 617.
17. Rodger, *Command of the Ocean*, pp. 420–1; Knight, *The Pursuit of Victory*, pp. 139–40, 226.
18. Rodger, *Command of the Ocean*, pp. 310, 423.
19. C.L. Eastwick (ed.), *The Naval Campaign of 1805: Trafalgar by Edouard Desbrieres* (Oxford, 1933), II, 145, 20 November 1805.
20. Royal Naval Museum, 1998/41/1, Gunner's Notebook, *Victory*, 1804–5.
21. Rodger, *Command of the* Ocean, p. 542.
22. Royal Naval Museum, MS1963/1, 5 November 1805, Benjamin Stevenson to his wife.
23. Roderiguez, 'Spanish at Trafalgar'.
24. Webb, 'Rebuilding and Repairing', p. 209.
25. Rodger, *Command of the Ocean*, pp. 476–80; see Roger Morris, *Naval Power and British Culture, 1760–1850: Public Trust and Government Ideology* (Aldershot, 2004), chapter 8, for a valuable analysis of the background to this traumatic period.
26. Knight, *The Pursuit of Victory*, pp. 442–3.
27. Glete, *Navies and Nations*, II, p. 378; Rodger, *Command of the Ocean*, p. 531.
28. G. Cornwallis-West, *The Life and Letters of Admiral Cornwallis* (London, 1927), p. 448, Melville to Cornwallis [1804].
29. William L. Clements Library, University of Michigan, Melville Collection, 14 June 1804.
30. (UK)NA: PRO, ADM 3/150, Board of Admiralty Rough Minutes, 2 June 1804.
31. NMM, CHA/E/80, Navy Board to the Chatham dockyard officers, 4–22 September 1804.
32. J.K. Laughton (ed.), *Letters and Papers of Charles, Lord Barham*,III, p. 68, Middleton to Melville, 17 March 1805; British Library, Add. Mss. 41079, Dundas Papers, fos. 127–8.
33. R.J.B. Knight, 'The Building and Maintenance of the British Fleet during the Anglo-French Wars, 1688–1815', in Martine Acerra et al. (eds), *Les Marines de Guerre Europeennes XVII–XVIII siecles* (Paris, 1985), pp. 37–43.
34. NMM, SPB/27, contract between the Navy Board and John Wells for the repair of the *Belliqueux* and *Stately*.
35. Gabriel Snodgrass, *Letter to the Rt. Hon. Henry Dundas…on the mode of improving the Navy of Great Britain* (London, 1797).

36. *Naval Chronicle*, V, 1801, pp. 130–1, letter of 9 November 1796. Snodgrass's ideas were first aired publicly in his evidence of 12 May 1791 to the Parliamentary Commission 'appointed to enquire into the State and Condition of the Woods, Forests and Land Revenues of the Crown'.

37. NMM, CRK/13, Phillipps-Croker collection, Troubridge to Nelson, 19 May [1803].

38. This list is compiled from Portsmouth and Plymouth dockyard records and (UK)NA: PRO, ADM 180/6, Abstract of Progresses, with information from Rif Winfield, *British Warships in the Age of Sail 1793–1817: Design, Construction, Careers and Fates* (Chatham, 2005). The list does not correspond with that given by J.K. Laughton, *Barham Papers*, III, p. 273. The document which Laughton reproduced is NMM, MID/13/4, but Laughton inserts the list of ships with no indication of his source. For instance, the *Thunderer*, originally on the list to be doubled, was found when docked not to require it, while the *Zealous* had had a year-long repair. Other ships of the line were being docked for a short time and refitted (rather than repaired) during this period: e.g. *Majestic, Formidable, Orion, Temeraire*.

39. NMM, POR/A/47, Navy Board to the Portsmouth dockyard officers, 26 February 1805 (UK)NA: PRO, ADM 174/41, Navy Board to the Plymouth dockyard officers, 7 March 1805.

40. (UK)NA: PRO, ADM 174/41, Navy Board to the Plymouth dockyard officers, 22 March 1805; also NMM, POR/A/47, 19 February 1805.

41. NMM, POR/A/47, 26 February 1805.

42. (UK)NA: PRO, ADM 8/87–90, Admiralty List Books, 1804–5.

43. William L. Clements Library, Melville collection, 2 February 1806, John Barrow to Melville.

44. William L.Clements Library, Melville collection, Sinclair to Melville, 20 November 1805.

45. Eastwick, *Trafalgar*, II, p. 147.

46. Remi Monarque, 'HMS *Alexander* (1796–9)', pp. 207, 212.

47. Roderiguez, 'The Spanish at Trafalgar', fn. 5.

48. R.J.B. Knight, 'The Introduction of Copper Sheathing into the Royal Navy, 1779–1786', *Mariner's Mirror* 59 (1973): 301.

5

The Significance of Trafalgar: Sea Power and Land Power in the Anglo-French Wars

N.A.M. Rodger

It seems to be worth beginning a discussion of the significance of the Battle of Trafalgar by considering the meaning of battle and victory at sea, and of a number of related terms, such as 'strategy', 'tactics', 'offensive' and 'defensive', which help us, or ought to help us, to think clearly about the meaning of victory at sea. For several reasons, however, such terms have in the past generated, and not infrequently still generate, as much confusion as clarity. This is partly because there is an acute – and, as I shall suggest, a double – problem of anachronism in using them, and partly because they are all in origin military terms borrowed from land campaigning, which have often been applied to naval warfare without establishing exactly how they might be applicable or inapplicable.

The problem of anachronism necessarily confronts the historian, who must apply the mind of the modern world to understand the past, when people thought differently. This is particularly the case when we are using words, and therefore ideas, which did not exist at the time in question. When we speak of 'strategy', we must be continually aware that the word was unknown in eighteenth-century Britain. It is first recorded in 1810,[1] when its meaning was close to its Greek original: it referred to the art of the general, not the admiral, and mainly in what we would call the tactical rather than the strategic dimension. Fleets and armies existed in the eighteenth century, of course, and men had of necessity ideas about how to use them, but the slowness of communications, the weakness of intelligence and the absence of any central military or naval staffs made it both less important and more difficult for them to engage in detailed military or naval planning. As a result they tended not to distinguish very clearly the strictly military or professional aspects of what they would have called 'policy' about the employment of naval and military forces. Other useful terms like 'tactics', offensive' and 'defensive' were already in use, but again much more often about armies than navies.[2]

I

We owe most of our thinking about naval strategy and tactics to a group of historians and naval thinkers who wrote about the end of the nineteenth century. These men, above all Sir Julian Corbett whose *Some Principles of Maritime Strategy*[3] remains the foundation of all serious study of the subject, and whose *The Campaign of Trafalgar*[4] is arguably still the indispensable book on the battle, were not simply historians engaged in a dispassionate search for the truth about the past. They were also campaigners closely engaged with the Royal Navy of their own day, who used history as an intellectual tool to shape its policy and reform its thinking. Some, like Sir John Laughton, were engaged in a Positivist search for the laws of naval war which would guide their Service and their pupils to certain victory. Others, like Corbett himself who first imported the ideas of Clausewitz into naval strategy, embraced a more fluid and sophisticated reading of the past. For all of them, however, the past was at the service of the present.[5] Their history was a history for their own time, and their own purposes. Corbett's maritime strategy was distilled from his lectures to senior officers attending the War Course at the Royal Naval College Greenwich; this was the intellectual formation of the admirals of the First World War. Though its material is drawn entirely from the seventeenth and eighteenth centuries, we cannot separate it from the generation who nearly lost the Great War because of their inability to think logically about the convoy problem.

At the root of their difficulty, I would argue, lay a simple but disastrous confusion between two senses of the word 'offensive'. On the one hand it indicates a mode of making war by advancing to attack the enemy. In this sense the offensive is essential to victory in an aggressive or conquering war, though not necessarily in a defensive or limited one. It is not always needed, and it almost always calls for a superiority of force or position which may not be available. During the American War of Independence, for example, the American rebels themselves had little need of the offensive. Having early gained political control over the core of 'their' territory, they needed only to defend their position.

Though their offensive campaigns (notably the 1776 invasion of Canada) were defeated, their defensive successes gained their essential political objectives. Across the Atlantic, however, their ally Spain went to war to recover lost territories – Gibraltar, Minorca, Florida and Jamaica – and planned a direct attack on Britain. For this the strategic offensive was indispensable, and in its most difficult form, for all of these targets except Gibraltar required long-range amphibious operations. Two of them, those against Florida and Minorca, succeeded, and Spain was accordingly the only European belligerent in this war which made real territorial gains. One kind of war, one type of war-aim required the offensive, but in another successful defence was all that was needed. Both allies could claim victory, or at least partial victory, though their different situations called for different strategic approaches.

In another sense the word 'offensive' refers to an attitude of mind, that aggressive determination to fight and win which has marked great military leaders in every age, and which is all the more essential to the commander whom circumstances oblige to stand on the defensive or to retreat. Certainly an offensive strategy generally requires an offensive attitude – a timid or complacent aggressor is unlikely to overcome determined resistance unless the balance of forces is very much in his favour – but it is often in resistance and retreat, in facing fearful odds, that the real qualities of leadership are most evident. At Quiberon Bay in 1759 Hawke had a rough equality of forces and a real superiority in quality, but he could only deploy them because he was willing to run grave navigational risks to bring the enemy to action. This was surely an example of the offensive mentality, and in a tactically offensive situation – but in strategic terms the French were mounting the invasion, and Hawke was on the defensive. In the Mediterranean in 1941 Cunningham's determination to rescue British troops from Crete in spite of heavy losses showed exactly the same unflinching resolve in the face of disaster, though his strategic posture – evacuating a defeated army – was as far from the offensive as it could well have been. In time the tide of war turned and the Mediterranean Fleet was able to go onto the offensive. Cunningham's aggressive determination, his offensive spirit, remained as strong as before, only now circumstances allowed him to adopt an offensive strategy.

Muddling the two meanings of 'offensive' led British admirals of the early twentieth century into acute difficulties. 'In the foregoing remarks', the Admiralty magisterially assured the 1902 conference of colonial prime ministers, the word *defence* does not appear. It is omitted advisedly, because the primary object of the British Navy is not to defend anything, but to attack the fleets of the enemy, and by defeating them, to afford protection to British Dominions, supplies and commerce ... The traditional role of the Royal Navy is not to act on the defensive, but to prepare to attack the force which threatens – in other words to assume the offensive.[6]

In this remark truth is mingled with error and confusion. In reality the prime role of the Navy had always been to defend Britain against invasion, and to defend the trade on which her livelihood depended. 'Afford protection' is here a synonym for 'defend'. Opportunities for victory had always been welcomed (for reasons to which we shall return), but for long periods they had been unavailable. Having missed two opportunities of victory in the early months of the Seven Years War, the Royal Navy spent nearly four exhausting years of cruising and blockade, trying to force decisive battle on a reluctant enemy, until at last in 1759 both Boscawen at Lagos and Hawke at Quiberon Bay found (or made) their opportunities. Even when victory was obtained, it seldom solved all the problems of defence. Applied in 1915 and 1916 to the novel threat of submarine attack on merchant shipping, this muddled thinking led to the adoption of methods (essentially high-speed steaming to nowhere in particular) which felt satisfyingly aggressive, but which in reality minimized the chance of meeting the enemy. Allowing merchant ships to sail individually dispersed them in such a way as to maximize the enemy's chance of finding them. Though that fact was mathematically demonstrable and these officers were advanced mathematicians, they did not analyse their decisions mathematically or logically.

Even when they were forced to adopt convoy they do not seem to have understood how and why it worked – and confusion on this critical point continued to attend Admiralty thinking on the subject throughout most of the twentieth century.[7] In fact convoy is tactically defensive, but strategically offensive. It forces the enemy to attack at that point at which the defence is concentrated; to fight, therefore, at the maximum disadvantage, or to abandon his strategic purpose. It may be possible for the enemy to concentrate superior forces against a convoy and overwhelm the escort, as for example in 1707 when the combined squadrons of Duguay-Trouin and Forbin took or sank most of the escorts and one tenth of the merchantmen of a British troop convoy. Even in these cases, however, convoy was the right choice because it permitted the defenders to fight at the least available disadvantage, and yielded the best result possible at odds of more than two to one – a costly French victory from which nine-tenths of the convoy escaped. By contrast all schemes of patrol lines or defensive barriers necessarily involve the maximum dispersal of the defence, and offer the attacker the most perfect opportunity of concentrating against an isolated portion of the defence, or of avoiding the defence and achieving his end without fighting at all. On land man-made fortifications or geographical positions such as mountains or rivers may make up for the weakness inherent in a defensive line – but not at sea.

All this is more relevant to Trafalgar than at first it seems, because the intellectual world which produced this confusion was the same which produced the seminal studies of Trafalgar and its significance on which we still depend. The fullest treatment we possess of Lord Barham, the First Lord of the Admiralty in office in 1805, is still the three volumes of his papers which Sir John Laughton edited for the Navy Records Society between 1906 and 1910.[8] In these volumes we see relatively little of Sir Charles Middleton, the great but controversial Controller of the Navy and political intriguer who contributed so much to the reform of naval administration in the 1770s and 1780s. Instead we meet the statesman-strategist who guided the Trafalgar campaign and coined the phrase 'First Sea Lord', and behind him we cannot avoid seeing, as we are meant to see, another shore-based naval administrator and political operator who very much wished to be remembered as the statesman-strategist who had guided the Navy to overwhelming victory, the man who revived the term 'First Sea Lord' for himself: Sir John Fisher. It is impossible in the early twenty-first century to examine the significance of Trafalgar without passing through the intellectual categories and assumptions of the early twentieth, so that we face a double layer of anachronism.

Unfortunately there is no alternative to employing some modern concepts if we are to cut through the eighteenth century's own muddled thinking. Just over 300 years ago, for example, the allied main fleet fought the French off Malaga. If we explain this battle in modern strategic terms, we must say that it arose from the recent allied capture of Gibraltar. The French fleet sailed from Toulon to recapture the place, and on the day of battle it was between the allies and their new possession. The battle itself was bloody but indecisive, but on the next morning the French were still between the allies and Gibraltar. The allies, moreover, after a long bombardment before the battle, were almost out of ammunition, though the French do not seem to have known this. What should have been clear to them was that their objective was still within their grasp if they renewed the action. Instead the French council of war concluded that 'what we did yesterday will suffice for the reputation of the navy and the king's arms'.[9] Knowing that Gibraltar has remained in British hands ever since, we can hardly deny that this was a battle with strategic consequences, but well-informed contemporaries did not understand it in these terms at all.

The ancient concepts of honour and reputation which they did use were of course borrowed from the world of land warfare, and so was (and is) much of the language of naval strategy. This makes it important to be clear about the similarities and differences between the two. Most wars on land are fought for the control of territory, because it is the ultimate location of wealth and political power. Many battles are therefore fought for positions which give access to territory. Very often armies fight for key communication points such as bridges, passes or road junctions. For this reason such points were in the eighteenth century often fortified. Fortresses which guarded the crossings of a major river on an obvious invasion route, such as Namur and Maastricht on the Maas or Nijmegen and Arnhem on the Rhine, were repeatedly fought over down the centuries. The strategic motives which led William III to besiege Namur in 1695 and British airborne troops to attack Arnhem in 1944 were identical: capture of the bridges would force the river line and allow advance into the country beyond. For the defenders, heavy capital investment in fortifications made it possible for a small garrison to hold up a large field army; in the eighteenth century it was usually stated that a major fortress ought to be able to sustain a siege of about six weeks. This left the defending army at liberty to campaign elsewhere, or to catch the besiegers at a grave disadvantage. Whether armies fought for a fortress or in open country, it was clearly position for which they fought, and as a rule of thumb it was safe to say that the side which was left in possession of the field of battle was clearly the winner.

Applied to naval battles, however, most of this was meaningless. After indecisive naval battles such as Ushant in 1778, there was sometimes a controversy as to which side had conceded defeat by 'abandoning the field of battle'. In reality neither side knew their position accurately enough to tell, and the question was in any case wholly unimportant. At sea there are few or no positions, other than those directly associated with land warfare in the case of landing operations, coastal sieges and the like. There was a naval analogy with siege warfare, but it was at the tactical level of individual ships. The conduct of an artillery fight between individual ships (whether alone or in a squadron) was guided by assumptions similar to those of siege warfare, which governed how long it was reasonable to expect the weaker party to resist, and provided procedures for honourable surrender when the proper moment arrived. At the strategic level, however, there was no equivalent to the capture of a fortress or the occupation of territory. The sea itself is not inhabited and cannot be occupied. Though naval fortresses existed, they were essentially fortified fleet bases whose value derived from the fleet which was based on them. The Spaniards based a powerful squadron on their West Indian fortress of Havana, which as a result exercised a strategic leverage out of all proportion to the size and activity of the squadron. The French, by contrast, never stationed a squadron at Louisbourg.[10] The place had some deterrent value in the defence of Canada, because it was always possible that ships might have been based there (for which reason the British went to the trouble of capturing it in 1758 before their main campaign), but it is nonsense to suggest that it blocked the entrance to the St Lawrence. The Cabot Strait is 70 miles across, and a fortress unprovided with a fleet controlled nothing beyond the range of its guns.

Fleets at sea do not fight for position, and those who think automatically in terms of land warfare will be hard-pressed to explain why they fight at all. This is indeed precisely the problem of many commentators on Trafalgar. So long as it could be believed that Trafalgar had defeated the French invasion of Britain, the victory could be celebrated in terms comprehensible to everyone. Once it became clear that Napoleon's invasion schemes had already collapsed, for unrelated reasons, the meaning of Trafalgar seemed to have collapsed too. Napoleon at Ulm and Austerlitz had visibly and obviously conquered territory, wealth and population, while Nelson at Trafalgar had not. The most that could be claimed was that Trafalgar had eliminated the possibility of the Grand Army returning from Austerlitz to Boulogne to resume its invasion project.

This was the problem which Corbett, almost alone among his contemporaries, identified and confronted. Right at the end of his life, as he worked on the official history of the Navy in the Great War, he was asking himself 'what material advantage did Trafalgar give that Jutland did not give?'[11] In other words, in what respect was a decisive victory really necessary? This was not a question which the admirals wanted asked, still less answered, and when the third volume of Corbett's official history, covering the Battle of Jutland, appeared in 1923 the Board of Admiralty attached an official note warning that 'Their Lordships find that some of the principles advocated in the book, especially the tendency to minimise the importance of seeking battle and forcing it to a conclusion, are directly in conflict with their views.'[12] Had they known as much naval history as Corbett they would have known that the eighteenth-century Navy, however ardently it desired to fight and win fleet actions, was for long years denied the opportunity by reluctant enemies. Alternative methods, in particular blockade and convoy, made it possible for Britain to build up supremacy at sea without crushing victories. Even when decisive victories were obtained, they did not usually remove the necessity for continued blockade and convoy – as Trafalgar very clearly showed. The war lasted almost ten years more, during which period Napoleon sank large sums in rebuilding a battle fleet, but it was never again risked at sea, and therefore the British never had the chance of another fleet action. Yet their control of the sea was progressively strengthened, not weakened, by the steady pressure applied by blockade, convoy and patrol. Naval battles, it seems, were both precious and unnecessary.

II

The key to this paradox, it may be suggested, lies in the ways in which naval warfare differs fundamentally from campaigning on land. The object of war at sea is to gain the use of the sea – for trade, for the movement of armies, for fishing – and to deny it to the enemy. Ships and squadrons can control the sea only so far as their own guns can carry, and the vast area of the sea has always been essentially uncontrolled, available to any belligerent. However great the disparity of forces at sea may grow, a belligerent with a seacoast and some minimum resources of ships and seamen can always use it, if he is prepared to run the risk. 'Command of the sea', unlike command of the land, is relative rather than absolute. The term may usefully be applied to that power which has built up so dominant a position that the enemy can only use the sea in strictly limited ways, or with completely disproportionate risk. Almost invariably in British naval history, that position was achieved, if it was achieved, by long years of grinding struggle punctuated by only occasional battles. It was so during the Napoleonic War, in spite of Trafalgar, and it was to be so again in the great wars of the twentieth century. The characteristic mode of naval warfare has always been attrition of the constituent elements of seapower, namely capital, technology and skilled manpower. Battles were valuable because they represented a speeding-up of the clock of attrition; a major victory might degrade the enemy's resources as much in an afternoon as a year or more of regular warfare. To that should be added the intangible but real losses of morale, reputation and financial credit. British officers and men were quite right to yearn for battle as a major step towards victory and peace, but the mechanism by which victory in battle contributed to victory in war was quite different from that which operated on land.

Trafalgar was essential for Britain in part because Lord St Vincent's destructive efforts to 'reform' British naval administration had inflicted all but fatal damage on the Navy's seagoing strength. By 1805 the British were markedly inferior in numbers of ships, and the prospect was of further rapid decline. A great victory alone could abruptly reverse the process of attrition. Trafalgar provided it – but it did not stop French squadrons putting to sea, or eliminate the threat to British seagoing trade. In the immediate aftermath of that crushing defeat, the French Navy had four major squadrons at sea in the North Atlantic alone, two of which sailed after the battle. In the event two of the four squadrons were eliminated (Dumanoir's refugees from Trafalgar by Strachan in the Bay of Biscay, Leissègue's by Duckworth in the West Indies), while the other two French admirals (Allemand and Willaumez) cruised for months without being intercepted, but were unable to locate any vulnerable targets. British strength, and British victory, had not eliminated the French capacity to make war at sea, but they had considerably limited it. In the Indian Ocean, where France had a base, Mauritius, which was remote from attack but well situated to threaten British trade, French frigates remained active and dangerous until the island was finally captured in 1810.

Blockade and convoy remained necessary throughout the war, and continued progressively to build up Britain's material superiority without the aid of further fleet victories. Though St Vincent had made a great victory urgently necessary, naval history shows many examples of ultimate victory obtained without any great fleet battles. In the War of the Spanish Succession there was only one unequivocal allied naval victory of any consequence, at Vigo in 1703. The war continued for another ten years, and led in the end to the elimination of the French battle fleet, and largely of the French Navy, but with no more fleet actions. There was continuous and often heavy fighting, mainly between convoy escorts and attacking squadrons, but the main fleets did not meet again. In the Second World War, the prolonged campaign which is misleadingly known as the 'Battle of the Atlantic' was in fact made up of numerous smaller operations and engagements with no fleet battle at all, but its result was in the end as decisive and clear-cut as the most ardent advocate of fleet action could have desired. At no stage during this war did the British have any absolute command of the sea. German submarines could and did put to sea right up to the last days of the war, and so did German surface ships in coastal waters, within reach of friendly air cover. It was in using the contested sea, in passing their expeditions and convoys to and fro that the allies ground down German and Italian naval resources and established a growing superiority which in the end became incontestably dominant. The British would certainly have welcomed fleet battle, but for most of the war it was neither necessary nor possible.

Exactly the same comment can be applied to the bulk of the Napoleonic War, which had only just started when Trafalgar was fought. Though in the special circumstances of 1805 a fleet victory was urgently needed, Trafalgar in a sense re-established the ordinary workings of British seapower as it gradually built up a dominant position, all the while assuring the overseas trade on which Britain's livelihood and war effort depended, and denying the same to the enemy. Dominant seapower forced Napoleon to depend on indirect modes of warfare, namely the denial of trade, and this in turn made worse a characteristic problem of military victory. Armies campaign on land, usually over the fields and among the homes of the civilian population. Even the best-behaved army will have many easy ways to make itself hated, let alone Napoleon's armies which depended on looting and extortion to live. Add to this an economic policy which explicitly aimed to ruin trade and beggar merchants throughout the French empire in order to hurt the enemy, and it is easy to see how Napoleon's military victories were also his political defeats, so many reasons for the people of Europe to unite against him. Naval battles, by contrast, were fought between professionals in a neutral environment which did not affect non-combatants or their property. A victory like Trafalgar did not have to arouse hatred and resentment; in fact the chivalrous exchanges between British and Spanish enemies after the battle laid the foundations of alliance three years later, when the cruelties and exactions of French armies drove the Spaniards to rebel against their domineering ally. In political as well as military terms, the meaning of victory at sea was very different from that on land.[13]

III

Trafalgar had two strategic consequences. In the short term it made up for the damage St Vincent had done to the Navy and restored numerical superiority. In the longer term, it restored what we might call the normal mechanism of British seapower, which secured home defence, protected trade and opened strategic possibilities all over the world outside Europe. At the same time it did exactly the opposite to the Napoleonic empire: exposing it to coastal attack, denying it the wealth and economic growth generated by trade, and eliminating Napoleon's hopes of breaking out of the strategic limitations of Europe. Confined within Europe, his military and political system inflicted growing damage on itself, and in the end provoked the resistance which destroyed him. To understand these factors, however, calls for sophisticated analysis and a long historical perspective. It requires a good knowledge of matters such as naval administration and wartime trade which were unknown to the public then, and unfashionable among historians until recently. It does not offer the immediate gratification and self-evident significance of a great victory on land. It is not difficult to see how Trafalgar was in some ways a disappointment to the British public of the day, and why the admirals of later generations were so eager to misinterpret it. The simple doctrine that big battles win wars automatically and immediately was attractive and accessible. It promised swift victory. The complex reality of seapower demanded thought and study. It threatened a long and costly route to victory. The British admirals of the early twentieth century, and not a few commentators since, have tended to shy away from the true meaning of Trafalgar towards the simple answers.

Notes

1. By the *Oxford English Dictionary*.
2. N.A.M. Rodger, 'Die Entwicklung der Vorstellung von Seekriegsstrategie in Grossbritannien im 18 und 19 Jahrhundert', in Seemacht und Seestrategie im 19. und 20. Jahrhundert ed. Jörg Duppler (Vorträge zur Militärgeschichte Band 18, Hamburg, 1999), pp. 83–103; revised and translated as 'The Idea of Naval Strategy in Britain in the 18th and 19th Centuries', in Geoffrey Till (ed.), *The Development of British Naval Thinking: Essays in Memory of Bryan Ranft* (London, 2006). I have also discussed aspects of this theme in 'The West Indies in Eighteenth-Century British Naval Strategy', in Paul Butel and Bernard Lavallé (eds), *L'éspace Caraïbe: théâtre et enjeu des luttes impériales, XVIe–XIXe siècles* (Bordeaux, 1996), pp. 38–60; and 'Sea-power and Empire, 1688–1793', in P.J. Marshall (ed.), *The Oxford History of the British Empire*, Vol. II, *The Eighteenth Century* (Oxford, 1998), pp. 169–83.
3. London, 1911.
4. London, 2nd edn 1919, 2 vols.
5. D.M. Schurman, *The Education of a Navy: The Development of British Naval Strategic Thought, 1867–1914* (London, 1965). Andrew Lambert (ed.), *Letters and Papers of Professor Sir John Knox Laughton, 1830–1915* (Navy Records Society Vol. 143, 2002).
6. Nicholas Tracy (ed.), *The Collective Naval Defence of the Empire, 1900–1940* (Navy Records Society Vol. 136, 1997), p. 7.
7. Early drafts of BR1806, *The Fundamentals of British Maritime Doctrine* (London, 1995) in the revision of which the present author had a small share, showed this very clearly.
8. Sir J.K. Laughton (ed.), *Letters and Papers of Charles, Lord Barham, Admiral of the Red Squadron, 1758–1813* (Navy Records Society Vols 32, 38 & 39, 1906–10). John E. Talbott, *The Pen and Ink Sailor: Charles Middleton and the King's Navy, 1778–1813* (London, 1998) is a short life concentrating on his administrative achievements.

9. 'Ce que nous fîmes hier suffit pour la réputation des armes du roi et de la Marine ...': J.P. Ausseur, 'Le mentor du Comte de Toulouse', *Neptunia* 91 (1968): 2–8, at p. 6.
10. J.R. McNeill, *Atlantic Empires of France and Spain: Louisbourg and Havana, 1700–1763* (Chapel Hill, NC, 1985).
11. Quoted from Corbett's Creighton Lecture by John B. Hattendorf, 'Sea Power as Control: Britain's Defensive Naval Strategy in the Mediterranean, 1793–1815', in *Français et Anglais en Méditerranée de la Révolution française à l'indépendence de la Grèce (1789–1830)* (Service Historique de la Marine, Vincennes, 1992), pp. 203–20, at p. 205.
12. Sir Julian Corbett and Henry Newbolt, *History of the Great War: Naval Operations* (London, 1920–31, 5 vols in 10). Corbett died the same year, leaving Newbolt to complete the work.
13. N.A.M. Rodger, 'La naturaleza de la victoria naval', in Agustín Guimerá, Alberto Ramos and Gonzalo Butrón (eds), *Trafalgar y el mundo atlántico* (Madrid, 2004), pp. 113–25; also in English as 'The Nature of Victory at Sea', *Journal for Maritime Research* (July 2005).

Part Two:
The Battle in History

6
Politics and Memory: Nelson and Trafalgar in Popular Song[1]

Mark Philp

John Harkness, a Preston printer in business between 1840 and 1866, published a ballad sheet, probably in the mid 1840s, containing two songs. *The Comforts of Man* retails the story of a young man who, thinking he ought to have the comforts of a wife, asks young Betty, his sweetheart, to marry him. She consents, but the marriage turns sour as our hero is subjected to repeated spousal abuse. His final verse rues 'the day that ere I was married' and concludes 'what a plague is the comforts of man'. The other song is entitled *Grand Conversation on Nelson Arose*. It lists Nelson's achievements, at the Nile, Copenhagen and Trafalgar, and it recounts his fearlessness and the loyalty of his officers and men. The later verses suggest that the song was written soon after the completion of Nelson's column (1843) and Trafalgar Square. The most striking feature of the song, however, is that the title and the implied tune are borrowed from a slightly earlier and better known song that achieved wide circulation and that has lodged itself in the oral tradition: *The Grand Conversation of Napoleon*. As in life, so in death: Nelson and Napoleon remain locked in an engagement in which their posthumous reputations contest for ascendancy. Moreover, they do so in the popular song, one of the most important but largely neglected channels for information and public memory in the eighteenth and nineteenth centuries. I want to go some way to correcting this neglect by examining the range of songs we have about Nelson and by setting them in the context of the intense ideological mobilization that took place in England in the mid 1790s and again at the height of the invasion threat in 1803–05. The chapter is primarily concerned to indicate the sheer volume and range of Nelson songs, to go some way towards an analysis of the provenance of the songs, and to consider the role they played in the memorializing of Nelson. I return in conclusion to reflect on the contrast between Nelson and his implicit antagonist, Napoleon.

I

Although *Rule Britannia* is still widely sung and it is possible to find the words and music for *Hearts of Oak*, *Roast Beef of England* or *Britons Strike Home*, and although there is some general awareness that these songs would have been sung in ships, at dinners, and at public entertainments, during the military campaigns against first Revolutionary and subsequently Napoleonic France, there is substantially less acknowledgement that Nelson himself was directly celebrated and commemorated in song, and that such songs formed an important part of a much wider campaign to rouse British resistance to Bonaparte and to encourage public support for the navy and the military. There are a number of reasons for the neglect of this aspect of Nelson's reputation: many songs were ephemeral, their provenance and subsequent histories are not easy to track, and it is not easy to grasp their significance without having a sense of the other songs being written, sung and circulated in the period and a sense of the political context in which such songs figured. To address the neglect we must address these obstacles.

In the winter of 1792–93 the Association for the Preservation of Liberty and Property Against Republicans and Levellers was set up to encourage all loyal persons to correspond with the Association, to inform on local subversives, and to send in copies of material to be published to sway the minds of the lower orders against the surge in popular radicalism spreading through the country. One of the Association's female correspondents shrewdly drew attention to the importance of popular song in the political struggle:

> I have had many opportunities of observing the influence of the new seditious doctrines upon the lower class of people, that class that the wicked and designing intend to use as their Engine, they are incapable of reading or understanding any good or serious address to set them right; but through the medium of popular ballads surely much instruction might be convey'd and much patriotic spirit awakened.[2]

The suggestion was taken up with enthusiasm, with the Association and its sympathizers initiating the prosecution of ballad sellers caught selling works with more insidious and subversive messages and positively encouraging the writing, printing and circulation of songs and ballads supporting King and constitution, and attacking the ideas of the reformers and some of their principal supporters – especially Tom Paine.

From the beginning of 1793 until the end of the decade, the ideological and political confrontation between the government and reformers ratcheted up in intensity, with the government launching a series of prosecutions of leaders of the reform movement in 1794 and with some reformers becoming prepared to countenance more radical opposition to what they saw as Pitt's tyranny. The insurrection and subsequent landing of a French invasion force in Ireland, and growing demands for peace, coupled with rioting over food shortages and recruitment practices, only strengthened the government's intransigence. In parallel, as contestation over the public's loyalties intensified, the government, loyalists and local magistrates increasingly silenced popular songs and singers that were critical of the government or supportive of France and published street ballads become more consistently loyalist in character. There are one or two ballads sympathetic to the Spithead and Nore mutinies in 1797, and some ballad writers with reformist leanings do remain at work throughout the period – such as John Freeth in Birmingham, Robert Burns or Robert Anderson – but there is very little published in popular broadsides in England that is openly critical of Pitt or of the handling of the war, or which is expressive of the widespread unrest that marked the country in 1798–99 and 1800–01. In contrast, in Ireland the circulation of popular songs with political content (both radical and loyalist) was widespread until the insurrection of 1798, and songs from that insurrection circulated widely throughout the country thereafter, even if many were expressly proscribed in an attempt to extinguish them.[3] Indeed, as the Irish case shows, even if repression could largely eradicate printed songs sympathetic to reform, this does not mean that such songs did not exist – ballad and song collectors early in the nineteenth century found many songs traceable to the period preserved within the oral tradition that made their way into print forms only when government repression relaxed and political opposition again began to flourish, tentatively in England after 1805, and more vigorously after 1815.

That loyalist sentiment becomes the only acceptable script for popular politics does not mean that this sentiment is entirely manufactured. Sympathy for reform did not necessarily entail an unwillingness to defend one's country or hostility to those who did. And some with sympathies for reform certainly contributed to celebrations and commemorations of British victories and British heroes. John Thelwall, the leading radical and the third major defendant in the treason trials of 1794, ventured into print after Trafalgar with a poem on Nelson's death; and John Freeth, for all his Whig and reformist sympathies, wrote several songs celebrating British victories, including 'From the mouth of the Nile, flush'd with glory behold' (All shall yield to the mulberry tree) *On Admiral Nelson's Victory, Britannia Triumphant* to celebrate the Nile.[4] So one dimension of this relative silence for reformers may well be that their hostility to Pitt and to the political system was leavened by their suspicion of the French and their sense of the importance of national self-defence – wanting an end to the war was not the same as not being concerned about losing it. Nonetheless, although loyalists and the government had every interest in ensuring that people saw support for national defence as entailing support for the administration and for the constitution, we have considerable evidence at the end of the 1790s of widespread unrest over the continuation of the war, recruitment, the price of bread, and the unresponsiveness of government to demands for political reform. What is striking is how far this unrest is absent from the broadsides and popular songs of the late 1790s and early 1800s, despite the fact that these normally provided one of the key conduits for public commentary on events and for the expression of concerns and grievances.

In contrast, loyalist songs flourished, especially around the invasion threats of 1797–98 and 1803–05. Loyalist and government-sponsored presses pumped out songs and broadsides to meet every occasion.[5] This investment in popular song is certainly not new, election songs were common throughout the eighteenth century, and there is evidence of massive spending on the part of the Treasury to secure the election of certain candidates in London in the elections in the late 1780s and early 1790s and thereafter.[6] But, in such cases, there were usually two or more sides to the controversy, each having their say. What is distinctive about the time of the Revolutionary and especially the opening of the Napoleonic War is the degree of dominance that loyalist forces secured over this dimension of popular culture and the consequent lack of contestation.

The intense politicization of songs and singing in this period has implications for the broader understanding of the significance of popular culture in this period. Many scholars examining the published material of the period 1793–1815 have been tempted to speculate about the creation of a sense of national unity and national spirit in response to the threat of French invasion, suggesting for example that the massive enlistment in the Volunteers in 1803–05 (when some half a million men joined volunteer regiments) is a function of their ideological commitments against the French. There are, in fact, more prosaic explanations, not least the immunity from impressment and militia duty that it gave those who volunteered.[7] Such accounts also understate the complexity of popular attitudes to politics, their leaders, and the enemy. Popular songs and ballads offer one window on this suggestion of a national unity in the face of French invasion, although it is a complex one. There are many songs but we need care in how we read them because many were the products of members of a social and political élite concerned to generate, reinforce and express a sense of unity in their audiences and to achieve dominance over potentially contending voices.

I emphasize 'printed' material but this was not the only vehicle for the transmission of popular song. The literature in general draws a distinction between popular ballads, sustained and transmitted through the oral tradition, popular broadsides which were published, usually singly or in pairs in a strip sheet, popular songs that originated in music hall performances and then might also be sold in broadside form, or were collected together in cheap collections of songs, and more élite forms of song that were performed in public by recognized singers of the day and published with music and orchestration for several instruments. Moreover, these categories are not hard and fast, perhaps especially in this period. In part because of the intensity of loyalist pressures, and partly associated with an interest among the middle and upper classes with more popular traditions of song, material moves across such boundaries, with music hall songs being transmitted into oral culture and being collected a century of more later in the oral tradition, and popular songs being appropriated (both music and words) by composers at the end of the eighteenth and beginning of the nineteenth century who drew on 'folk' elements for their compositions – a transmission repeated at the end of the nineteenth century with Vaughan Williams' appropriation of folk songs and ballads to form the basis for his own work.

This background is important for appreciating some of the aspects of the songs that emerged about Nelson. A considerable number were written expressly for loyalist purposes, to celebrate his victories, but also to demonstrate and to rouse others to show their attachment to their country and their hostility to Britain's enemy, the French (and after 1803 to Bonaparte in particular). This is not true of all the songs, but the dramatically heightened ideological stakes of the period without doubt influenced what was written, what was circulated, and what survived the immediate crisis.

II

The survival of popular songs relies heavily on printed material – in the form of strip sheets of ballads sold in the street by pedlars (who would advertise their wares by singing them), cheap garlands of collected songs that also sold to a popular but slightly wealthier audience, songs that appear in journals, newspapers and periodicals of various kinds, and songs published with music for performance in public and at home. However, we also have sources drawing on the oral tradition from the beginning of the nineteenth century, so it is also possible to identify ballads and sometimes to date them to a particular period. As to who wrote the songs, here the information varies considerably. At one end we know of local ballad writers, such as John Freeth in Birmingham, Robert Burns in Scotland and Robert Anderson in Carlisle, and we have publications and manuscript material from them that allows us to identify their loyalties and to date some of their material.[8] But none of them offer a great deal in relation to Nelson in particular. For example, Freeth, a publican with reformist leanings, wrote songs to existing tunes to entertain his customers and periodically published collections of his material; despite his generally reformist outlook he wrote several songs celebrating British victories.[9] Clearly, sympathy for reform did not entail antagonism to Britain's navy or a lack of concern with her military defence.

At the other end of the scale, we know the composers and the lyricists for a number of songs written for Covent Garden, the Theatre Royal, and other large-scale, public occasions, and we know in detail the musical entertainment output of Charles and Thomas Dibdin: the former a prolific writer and performer of songs and entertainments in which the sturdy British tar in particular was celebrated; the latter, his son who also turned to composition and wrote several pieces on Nelson.[10] But otherwise a great deal remains anonymous – and that material ranges from traditional street and naval ballads, which were a major conduit for reporting battles and British victories, to a considerable bulk of material clearly written by educated members of the public and designed for performance in loyalist and volunteer organizations and at local events. This last group of material is significantly more insistent in ideological tone and message, lauding Britannia, her King and constitution, and celebrating stout British tars in general, while generally lacking much of the specificity that many of the more apparently popular ballads exhibit.

We need now to indicate the scale of this material. Quantification is difficult, because apparently different songs sometimes turn out on closer inspection to share the same core, because it is impossible to cover every possible source of material (and I make no claims to having done so), and because of the diverse locations in which such material is to be found. But, accepting these caveats, I have thus far identified around 90 songs from the period that feature Nelson in some way. I am certain more exist, but this is already a very substantial group, dwarfing, for example those in praise of Howe or others of Nelson's contemporaries. The only major contender getting equivalent (and possibly more) attention is Napoleon, but the great bulk of that is critical, at least until the end of the war! In marked contrast to that material I have been unable to identify anything that would count as a critical or hostile song (even in relation to his less successful endeavours) in all the Nelson material. I have also failed to find a single scurrilous ballad about him – an even greater source of surprise since he was not exactly spared on this front by Gillray and other caricaturists.[11]

The scale of the outpouring of songs on Nelson is certainly linked to the demand for popular songs as a means to interpret, commemorate and, in a sense, complete the events of the day in a period of major national anxiety and crisis. The absence of any later revisionism or emerging counter-interpretation reflects the extent to which the material and messages penetrated deep in the public culture, fixing certain elements of a national historical memory and folklore. His victories, at the Nile, Copenhagen and Trafalgar, restored British confidence in a Navy (and its leadership) that had been racked by the Spithead and Nore mutinies of 1797. For the political élite, and for ordinary members of the public who feared the collapse of British naval resistance to France, Nelson's successes (following Duncan's at Camperdown) struck a major chord and it is not difficult to read considerable relief in the accompanying lyrics. When the political climate again became more contested after 1805, with the emergence of new political opposition, events had moved on and Trafalgar and its hero were securely past – and in many respects remained a monument to military heroism with which the rest of the war found it hard to compete (John Moore's death in the Peninsular Campaign of 1809 might have contended for heroic status but the controversies over the war – the corruption in its equipping and the incompetence in its leadership – meant that there was (in contrast to Nelson) little sense of unanimity in his commemoration).[12] A further indication of Nelson's standing is that some of the songs continue to be printed and sold until the late nineteenth century. There was clearly a market for material in his own lifetime, although some was clearly 'supply-led', with loyalist organizations paying for the cheap or free publication and circulation of songs, but there is no doubt the songs also responded to popular demand and that his reputation remained marketable for a number of years.

III

Of the 90 or so songs, there are a number of productions clearly designed for élite circles, such as the piece by William Shield and T. Goodwin of the Theatre Royal in Covent Garden, 'When the Victory weigh'd anchor' (printed) *Lord Nelson's Victory*.[13] Two similar contributions from Mr Braham are 'In death's dark house the hero lies' (printed) *The Victory and Death of Lord Viscount Nelson* and 'Cease vain France, ill-manner'd railer' (The Storm) *The Death of Nelson*, Upton and Shroeder contributed 'Genius of Britain, why that down cast eye' (printed) *The Hero of the Sea, or Nelson Immortal*, and Charles Frederick Horne produced 'A Navy, Colonies and Trade, the Tyrant cried' (printed) *Trafalgar an Heroic Song*. These songs are, for the most part, too intricate and verbally convoluted to move easily into the street ballad or oral tradition. The one exception is Braham and Arnold's *Death of Nelson* – 'O'er Nelson's Tomb, with silent grief oppress'd, Britannia mourns her hero, now at rest: but those bright laurels ne'er shall fade with years; Whose leaves, whose leaves are watered by a Nation's tears' – which is reprinted on ballad sheets throughout the nineteenth century. Although I have quoted the recitative, the actual verses are considerably more robust, and singable, beginning: 'Twas in Trafalgar's bay/We saw the Frenchmen lay/Each heart was bounding then;/We scorned the foreign yoke/Our ships were British Oak,/Hearts of oak were our men', and in some cases the song was reprinted without the recitative. There are also several songs by Charles Dibdin including: 'I say my heart', *Nelson and the Navy*; 'Be the great twenty-first of October recorded', *The Death of Nelson*; and 'Ah, Hark the signals round the coast', *The Arrival of Nelson's Corpse*. Dibdin was an energetic composer and performer who took his one-man shows of songs around the country to considerable public acclaim, and whose work consistently appropriated and subsequently re-emerged in popular songs. His son, Thomas, though less renowned, also added to the Nelson canon.

Not all the more élite songs were concerned with Nelson's death – although this certainly was a major focus. There are also earlier pieces: Charles Dibdin celebrated a succession of naval heroes in 1799 with 'Why I'm singing ...' *Naval Victories*; William Shield produced a piece on Copenhagen 'For glory, when with fav'ring gale' *The Danish Expedition*; Dussek wrote an instrumental celebrating Copenhagen; Haydn composed his *Battle of the Nile*; and a celebration of the Nile, 'Never yet in ancient story did more gallant deeds appear' (printed) *Welcome Nelson Home Again* was 'set to music by a lady of fashion'.[14] And, of course, there are similar pieces celebrating victories by Howe (1794), Duncan (Camperdown,

1797), and others. The Nelson songs, although considerable in number, are probably outweighed numerically (although not by much) by a host of generic anti-Napoleonic songs, and songs in praise of volunteering and of bold British tars, both of which are largely for the more élite audiences. Indeed, one feature of many of the loyalist songs of the period is their more general character – they do not focus on detail or narrative, they sketch broad positions of support for King and constitution, and they attack their enemies. There is also a good deal of repetition, with songs being adapted by a phrase here or a word there to suit one Volunteer Regiment rather than another.

An indication of the transmission between the popular ballad and the music hall is Charles Dibdin's work. A number of his songs, such as *A Salt Eel for Mynheer* (on Duncan and Camperdown – but appearing also as *A Salt Eel for Monsieur* celebrating the Nile), and *Nelson and the Navy*, are published as street ballads until well after the end of the war, as well as in collections of popular songs, something which is evident in relatively few other cases. This is partly because they are lively songs, written in clear and idiomatic English, which themselves drew on popular material and tunes. Dibdin's son Thomas also followed suit with a song, written for the music hall with a theatrical setting and sung by Mr Fawcett with 'unbounded applause in the interlude of the musical entertainment, *Nelson's Glory*, at the Theatre Royal, Covent Garden': 'Of our Island we've sung til the welkin has rung', *The Great Nation, A song* that essentially compares the aspirations to be a great nation on the part of France with the British: 'John Bull like a fool, says he wont go to school/From home, for a French education.' (A more fanciful song, not by one of the Dibdins but betraying a similarly musical entertainment origin, is 'The watry god, great Neptune lay' *The Watry God* (written by Wagnell), which has Neptune expostulating over the number of naval heroes that Britain has – so many that the ruler of an island producing such men must himself be a god!) Many of Charles Dibdin's songs, some of Thomas Dibdin's, and several of those of others, formed parts of whole programmes of musical entertainment. This may also have been the case with a song by Mr J. Stawpert of Newcastle, linked to the Theatre Royal, about *John Diggins*, in which Diggins is bullied by his father into coming to town (to 'Buy myself a blue jacket, and put off the clown, and fight for my country and king'), where he hears a poor beggar boy singing:

> He sung how that Nelson had lately been shot
> O – I verily thought I'd have died on the spot,
> For father told I that lead, e'en boiling hot,
> Wou'd ne'er take the life of this man

> At length the boy prov'd e'er he ended his song,
> That nature and valor however so strong
> Must still bow to fate, so poor father was wrong,
> And Nelson's gone, – dead – after all

With the conclusion that he vows to write to Collingwood, straight for a place ... 'So I may chance to revenge Nelson's wrongs.'

Charles Dibdin also contributed 'Now listen my honeys a while if you please' *The first of sweet August* (also published in broadside) and his son Thomas wrote a whole musical entertainment called *The Mouth of the Nile or the Glorious 1st of August*, loosely arranged around the Nile (although the final section is pretty much the only explicit reference), including two untitled songs that feature Nelson in one way or another 'When the world first began' and 'In the midst of the sea, like a tough man of war.' Charles Dibdin's 'I say, my heart, why, here's the "works"' *Nelson and the Navy* also commemorates the victory – and gives most prominence to Nelson, whereas 'Our anchors weighed to sea we stood' *Warren Triumphant* gives greater prominence to Warren (for the dispersal of the French Invasion Fleet near Ireland) and Nelson gets only a minor mention.

There are a number of songs that refer to Nelson only in passing, for example, alongside a range of other naval and/or military leaders: 'Come now heroes of this war' *Heroes of this War* hymns Howe, Jervis, Duncan, Mitchell and Abercrombie – 'Says gallant Nelson at the Nile, Egad I'll have the day – And so he had a glorious spoil – But two could run away.'[15] 'What matter your ditties, your jokes and narrations' *The Tars who've Lathered the World*, also links Nelson and Duncan as finishing off a job started by Howe and Jervis. Similarly, *Dumplings for Bonaparte* has a chorus that praises the admirals in succession. Nelson's 'turn' is as follows:

> But let us sing of the great Buonaparte,
> Of that wonderful hero I'll something impart,
> They say that bold Nelson has stopt him awhile,
> And has dish'd his great fleet at the mouth of the Nile,
> Huzza for brave Nelson, for brave Nelson huzza, and
> *Like them lets be ready and steady, boys, steady.*
> On the first of August, let us never forget,
> Twas that proud day they engag'd at sunset,
> And of their supper Nelson gave them enough,
> But the dumpling from Norfolk they found rather tough,
> *Huzza for brave Nelson etc.*

Charles Dibdin's *Naval Victories* does much the same, ending:

> But as if British tars, to their country so hearty,
> Was determined still honour on honour to pile,
> Ninety-eight, first of August, did up Bonaparte,
> By the wonders that Nelson performed at the Nile.
> But Lord how I talk, ain't the nation bestowing
> A pillar to tell about tars and their lives?
> And 'tis gloriously done, for to them 'tis all owing,
> That we've laws and religion, and children and wives.[16]

A slightly different form of inclusion is exemplified in the adaptation of more traditional songs and themes to link them with Nelson. For example, *A new song called the Victory*, is for all its title, essentially a simple ballad story – 'I am a youthful lady, my troubles they are great'. Her lover, of whom she dreams each night, is too poor to satisfy her parents, he is then press-ganged into the navy and comes to serve on the *Victory*, and – in the final verse – we get the first mention of Nelson, along with the denouement:

> Here's a health unto the *Victory* and crew of noble fame,
> And glory to the noble lord, bold Nelson was his name,
> In the battle of Trafalgar the *Victory* cleared the way,
> And my love was slain with Nelson upon that very day.

Another version was collected that does not get beyond the verses on the press-gang suggesting that this is an earlier ballad adapted for the occasion. Nonetheless, it clearly becomes a part of the oral tradition being collected in the 1840s, and it is still around in 1951 in Nova Scotia.[17] 'As early one morning in the groves I was walking' *The Damsel in Tears*, is a similarly traditional song about the loss of a lover alongside Nelson at Trafalgar. A more maudlin connection between the two is established in the sentimental, 'Stay lady stay for mercy's sake' *The Orphan Boy*, in which a boy sings to a stranger of his father's death at Trafalgar followed quickly by his mother's of a broken heart, but even this is more persuasive than the pastiche in 'It was early one morning', *The Widow's Lamentation* – where the narrator comes across a widow and child and offers her (rather unconvincing) comfort that her husband died with Nelson. There are also songs in which the narrative is more directly about a sailor (unmediated by the lover) who dies alongside Nelson, such as 'Tom Splice was a tar in whose bosom was blended' *Nelson and Victory*.

There are also a range of other songs, such as 'Oh my comrades ...' *The Sailor's New Leg*, that have a much more tenuous connection with Nelson. This is a quasi-comic song (of a type much exploited by Charles Dibdin[18]) about a sailor having his leg blown off by a cannon ball during Trafalgar (although it really could have been set anywhere); its opportunism being evident by the lack of any mention of Nelson's death. A still more extreme version of a traditional song which is fitted to the occasion is *Crippled Jack of Trafalgar* in which neither Nelson nor Trafalgar are mentioned in the body of the song – but which is clearly designed for the ballad pedlar to sell his wares as highly topical.

Perhaps the largest single category of songs relating to Nelson (often with a popular pedigree and lasting well into the nineteenth century) are the battle-narrative ballads – essentially similar to those celebrating Howe's 1 June victory, or Duncan's victory over the Dutch at Camperdown in October 1797, or many other naval battles throughout the centuries.[19] In Nelson's case the boundaries of the category are somewhat blurred, since while there are several songs commemorating each battle, there are also a number of others that smack of élite attempts to pastiche more traditional songs but which generally lack the detail and incident that mark the more narrative ballad.

IV

The first group of songs to feature Nelson are those celebrating his victory at Aboukir Bay, or the Battle of the Nile. The core of these songs (of which there are some 13) are traditional battle narratives that give a basic account of the events of the battle with a degree of objectivity in the commentary.

'Come all you valiant heroes and listen unto me' *Defeat of the French Fleet/A new song of the total defeat of the French Fleet*, details the chase across the Mediterranean and onset of the battle.[20] It is not sanitized, as many songs are, but refers to the many who were slain – 'While the blood it poured from the decks and stained the watery main' – and it refers to Nelson and some hundred others being wounded. It also emphasizes, as do most of the songs, the number of French ships captured or destroyed and the very few that escaped. 'Come all you British sailors bold, and listen to my song' *The Battle of the Nile*, of which Firth gives only an incomplete version, is one of the most detailed of the battle narratives relating to Nelson.[21] It gives an account of being unable to find the French fleet until they caught up with the *Reguli*, which gives news from Malta and sends them on to Alexandria. When they catch the fleet the ships are named in order, and the battle described, with the destruction of the *L'Orient* as a centrepiece:

Now the glory and the pride of France the *L'Orient* was called,
And in the centre of their line she got severely mauled;
Gave her a dreadful drubbing, boys, took fire and up she blew,
With fourteen hundred souls on board which bid this world adieu.

'Now ye sons of Britannia, attend to my strains' *Capture of the French Fleet* provides a basic narrative, and says 'some hundreds were wounded and many were slain, still Britons are masters and lords of the main' – but it ends with a direct bid for charity: 'May a blessing attend those that give some relief,/To the widows and children that now are in grief,/For the loss of their husbands are now in distress,/And left with their children to moan fatherless.' This is certainly not unusual and is likely linked to the use of the songs as a way of raising money through street performance. In the case of 'Twas on the ninth day of August, in the year ninety eight' *The Battle of the Nile* the battle narration is provided (implicitly) from the perspective of the *Majestic*, whose Captain, Westcott, was killed early in the action and replaced by Mr Cuthbert.[22]

Full fifty seamen we had slain, which grieved our hearts full sore;
Two hundred more were wounded, lay bleeding in their gore.
But early the next morning most glorious for us to see
Our British ships of war, brave boys, were crowned in victory

The dating to the 9th might suggest a degree of authenticity, as does the still later dating in 'Twas on the twenty-second we fought in Aboukir Bay' *The Battle of Aboukir Bay*, collected by Greig and Duncan which centres around 'little Jim' a powder monkey who sings the chorus 'Soon we'll be in London town, sing my lads yo ho!' only to be picked off by a musket bullet in the last verse, leaving not a dry eye on board.[23]

In 'It was in the forenoon of the first day of August' *Mouth of the Nile* the explosion of *L'Orient* is celebrated but the narrative is muddled. However, there is a detail absent in other songs:

As the night came on, we formed a plan
To set fire to one hundred and twenty guns;
We selected with skill, and unto them did thrill,
We secur'd our shipping, and laugh'd at the scene.

Freeth's song, 'From the mouth of the Nile, flush'd with glory behold' (All shall yield to the mulberry tree) *On Admiral Nelson's Victory, Britannia Triumphant* is a reworking of a song written to celebrate the naval victory of Russell and adds little in terms of detail. Much the same can be said for 'Never yet in Ancient story did more gallant deeds appear' *Welcome Nelson Home Again* which is a more élite song: it is brief, lacking in battle details and concludes with a verse on 'Eager crowds around him pressing' welcoming back the hero of the Nile. In a similar vein, 'Fame let thy trumpet sound' *The Voice of Fame* mentions the battle off Egypt's coast and Brueys being sent to the shades but is a typical loyalist song, sung to *God Save the King*.

'Arise! Arise! Britannia's sons arise!' *The Battle of the Nile* is, in many respects, a typical loyalist effusion – over-convoluted in style, and lacking detail, objectivity and distance – 'For the genius of Albion, victory proclaiming/Flies throughout the world, our rights and deeds maintaining … Mars guards for us what freedom did by character gain'. Surprisingly, it is also available as a street ballad, and while, in some versions, the chorus is sometimes simplified, the ballad is basically unchanged. Nonetheless, it cannot be described as a narrative song, and its aim seems wholly laudatory. However, its tune is re-used on a number of occasions (in one case in the Peninsular War, where the brave sons of Spain are enjoined to 'Drive hence, the Tyrant's minions back to France') and there is no doubt that it enters into popular and folk memory, although it is interesting that on more than one occasion it is paired on broadsheets with 'Ye gods above protect the Widow', *Death of Parker*, the major ballad on the execution of Parker, the leader of the mutineers at the Nore in 1797.

'Arise, muse, arise, assist me to sing' *Britannia's Triumph or Nelson Honoured* is similar but does have slightly more detail – 'At the setting of the sun, the battle it begun./Broadside for broadside for fourteen hours long;/We sent them cruising in the air/Which made the Frenchmen all to stare, /They struck their flags their fate to share,/With bold Nelson' – but it does not expressly mention the Nile and it is, most likely, a loyalist song written directly after to celebrate the victory. The same applies to 'With strains melodious make the heavens ring/Ode – sovereign lyre – this noble action sing' *The Conqueror: On the glorious Victory obtained by Lord Nelson*, whose verses remain as convoluted as the opening lines and where the location is mentioned entirely *en passant* – 'Majestic Nile beheld the bloody fight/And rear'd his sovereign head to view the knight.' It is not a great success as a song!

Charles Dibdin's 'I say me heart why here's your works' *Nelson and the Navy/aka Nelson and Warren* is a piece directed to celebrate the English successes in Egypt more generally – 'between the English and the Turks they'll lose both their army and their Navy'. His 'Now listen my honies awhile if you please' *The First of Sweet August* (Dibdin), is another typically eulogizing song celebrating the British victory but lacking any detail of the battle. These are classic Dibdin territory, cheery and lively songs, short on detail and the realities of the encounter, but plugged into the need to reflect national pride in the achievements: 'Bold Nelson went out with determined view,/to keep up our National glory,/So of thirteen large ships he left mounseer Two,/Just to tell the Directory the story.' Finally, the ubiquitous sailor's girl, Nancy, features in a widely published ballad 'Near a clear chrystal stream, where sweet flowers do grow' *Nancy's complaint for the loss of her sailor, who was killed by the French on the first of August*, in which she mourns for his loss. Although it shares many of the tropes of a traditional lament it does seem to have been written for the occasion, with Nelson being mentioned in three of the five verses.

The Nile ballads are, on the basis of internal evidence, written up quickly after the event. As we have seen, the dates given for the battle vary and the details of the battle remain local to each song and while most of the songs mix description with a certain amount of eulogizing, this is not exceptional in comparison with other battles and other heroes. The several more élite songs tend to lack the detail and they also focus on Nelson far more (while the battle narratives often tell the story from the perspective of a particular ship), and they add in considerably more reference to the defence of England and her liberties. Those that have been collected in the oral tradition tend to be those with more detail and 'locality'; those that we find published and reprinted in the nineteenth century tend to be Dibdin's and the more élite 'Arise! Arise! Britannia's sons arise …'*Battle of the Nile*. Being confident about the later publishing history of popular songs is extremely difficult, but few others seem to be reprinted, probably because later events will have rendered these songs less relevant, both for immediate purposes when new victories were being added, and for subsequent generations, for whom Trafalgar partially eclipses the Nile.

V

'Of Nelson and the north, sing the day' *Copenhagen/Battle of the Baltic* is a 27-verse account of the battle, which mentions Nelson only in the opening line and focuses largely on the action and on the celebrations that will greet the news.[24] It has the hallmarks of a more élite song, possibly written by one of the officers, in the complexity of some of its phrasing, which is only marginally less present in the other version we have – 'Of Nelson and the North sing the glorious day's renown' *The Battle of the Baltic*. For example,

But the might of England flush'd	Three cheers of all the fleet,
To anticipate the scene	Sung Huzza!
And her van the fleeter rush'd	Then from centre, rear, and van
O'er the deadly space between	Every captain, every man,
	With a lion's heart began
'Hearts of oak' our captains cried,	To the fray
When each gun	Oh, dark grew soon the heavens –
From its adamantine lips	For each gun
Spread a death-shade round the ships,	From its adamantine lips
Like the hurricane eclipse	Spread a death-shade round the ships
Of the sun	Like the hurricane eclipse
	Of the sun

'You undaunted sons of Britannia lend an ear' *Action off Copenhagen/The Siege of Copenhagen*, although briefer, manages more detail and is less complex. It also accords a greater role to Nelson, not so much in the battle as in the wrapping up (which was, of course, seen by many as an integral part to the battle and to the claiming of a victory).[25]

'The Russians, Swedes, and Danes combine/In colleague France to join' *Nelson's Thunder or the Danish Submission* treats the Danish Prince as ambitious for British territory after the capture of Hamburg but being seen off by Nelson's tactical skills, but there is little detail of the battle. 'Nelson the great he is the man' *Nelson and Victory* provides a narrative but, like *Nelson's Thunder*, this really revolves around Nelson, who features in several verses for his courage in taking on the Danes, his joining in the attack, and, finally, his clemency in rescuing drowning Danes 'Nelson the Great he form's a plan/to snatch from death each hostile Dane; The boat was mann'd without delay/To save each Danish seaman.' 'Draw near, ye gallant seamen, while I the truth unfold' *A New Song on Lord Nelson's Victory at Copenhagen* is similarly laudatory, but linking Nelson with his tars in the final stanzas:

Now drink a health to gallant Nelson the wonder of the world,
Who, in defence of his country his thunder loud has hurl'd;
And to his bold and valiant tars who plough the raging sea,
And who never were afraid to face the daring enemy

Finally, Shield's 'For glory, when with fav'ring gale' *The Danish Expedition*, is a typically rousing élite song, lacking in detail and with resounding patriotic conclusions to each verse. It does, however, pay due respect to Parker as the Commander of the fleet, acknowledging that it was Parker who sent Nelson to the Danes to negotiate, thereby conveying a sense of protocol and authority that is not entirely in keeping with the events of the battle!

Copenhagen is relatively under-sung, in comparison with the Nile. However, there are several good quality battle narratives, although the line between these and the more loyalist effusions that was relatively clear in the case of the Nile is less easily drawn here. In this case the brief invasion scare in England in 1801 following the battle, the general war-weariness, and perhaps the apparent distance of the Danish concerns from the more pressing demands of the French, may have led to less attention being paid to the victory.

The only song I have been able to identify that tackles one of Nelson's less successful sallies concerns the attack on Boulogne in August 1801, 'On the second of August, eighteen hundred and one' *Second of August*, but this seems to be both well-informed (except about the date) and well-disposed to the commander of the operation:

> On the second of August, eighteen hundred and one.
> As we sail'd with Lord Nelson to the port of Boulogne
> For to cut out their shipping, which was all in vain:
> But to our misfortune they were all moor'd and chain'd
> Our boats being well mann'd at eleven at night
> For to cut out their shipping, excepting they fight:
> But the grapes from their batteries so smartly did play
> Nine hundred brave seamen killed and wounded there lay
> ...
> Our noble commander with heart full of grief
> Used every effort to afford us relief
> No ship could assist us, as well you might know;
> In this wounded condition we were toss'd to and fro
> And you who relieve us, the Lord will you bless
> For assisting poor seamen in the time of distress.
> May the Lord put an end to all cruel wars,
> And peace and contentment be to all British tars

As Roy Palmer, who includes a full (marginally different) version of the song in his *Boxing the Compass*[26] acknowledges, the song is partly an appeal for financial aid for seamen, which may account in part for its restrained tone towards Nelson's enthusiasm for the task and the failures of intelligence that wrecked the attack.

VI

There are at least eight traditional battle narratives of Trafalgar, although several of them also have different versions. 'Arise, Arise brave Britons, Perform your loudest lays' *Nelson's Glorious Victory at Trafalgar* is essentially the same as 'Come all you jolly sailor's bold, in chorus join with me' *A New Song Called Nelson's Victory*; 'The twenty-first day of October' *Brave Nelson* (but with significant variation);[27] and 'We got ready for the battle,/To face the daring foe' *Nelson's Victory at Trafalgar*.[28] The versions emphasize the smaller number of British ships, Nelson's death, and the number of ships taken (although the numbers given vary between these songs).

'Come all you gallant heroes and listen unto me' *N[elson's] Glorious Victory*, emphasizes the chasing of the French fleet from 19 October, the formation of two columns of attack, and the engagement lasting four hours and ten minutes when Nelson was slain on the point of victory. 'Come all you gallant seamen that unite a meeting' *A new song composed on the Death of Lord Nelson* is a classic narrative that also includes reference to his past glories. It features a verse of the 'then up steps the doctor' variety, but the focus is essentially on Nelson asking how the battle had gone, and on commemorating his memory.[29] 'It was daylight the next morning'/[Alt] 'Great deeds of former heroes' *Nelson's Fame and England's Glory* focus on the detail of the battle – the first engagement with a French 84-gunner, manned by 900 French boys, the sinking of the *Trinidad*, and the numbers taken (although these vary between the versions). Interestingly, neither version mentions Nelson's death.[30]

'You true sons of Britain, give ear to my ditty', *A New Song Called Lord Nelson*, is a curious song that interweaves a battle narrative in classical form with a whole range of biblical reference:

> As we sailed from Moab to the plains of Jericho
> Where Joshua was praised and trumpets did sound
> Seven times there we sounded, surprised their city
> Our foes we destroyed and their walls tumbled down.
> Seven broad sides that immortal Lord Nelson
> Pour'd in on those Frenchified traitors with might,
> They all struck their colours, were forced to surrender,
> Unto him as he was a true Israelite

In many other respects it is a straightforward battle narrative with many similar details to others. 'Come list you lads where ere you be' (Arethusa) *Nelson's Victory and Death* is distinctive in mentioning 'While he was contending with his foes/Was oft implored to change his clothes/No, No, said he, I'll stand in those/As Admiral of my squadron./As they, his captains, he addressed/A ball smote him fatal on the breast.' 'I'll sing of famed Trafalgar if you'll listen to me' *Trafalgar* misses that detail but includes: 'We marked the man that did the deed, that aimed the fatal ball/And picked him from the rigging, riddled through with English lead.' 'Ye sons of Britain in chorus join and sing' *Nelson's Death and Victory* is essentially a narrative ballad, but ends with the hope that the battle will bring peace and a restoration of trade![31]

In addition to these eight and their variations, there are a number of others that appear to be written directly for loyalist purposes. The contrast is tentative and the lines somewhat blurred, but unlike the former group of battle narratives these songs seem not to be trying to convey anything distinctive about Nelson or about the experiences of the battle. They also lack objectivity and distance – tending to insist on a moral and an assertion of patriotism. For example, there are several songs in which the narrative is essentially swamped or excluded by the glorification: 'Britons! You heard Trafalgar's Story/You triumph in your country's glory;/Mourn o'er the relics, pale and gory,/Of brave immortal Nelson' *Nelson and Collingwood*, is one such instance – and the opening has some of the better lines! But while such songs seem clearly linked to loyalist propaganda, there are several others that combine narrative and effusion more subtly: 'Britannia musing o'er the deeds' *Britannia's Revenge for the Death of Her Hero*, while it has elements of narrative is essentially a call to avenge Nelson's death, as is 'When Neptune first at love's command' *When Neptune &c.* 'Ye sons of old Albion for valor renown'd' *The Departed Hero* gives a potted summary of Nelson's various victories, combined with an effusive commemoration, as does 'Since the birth day of Britain a period long fled' *Chapter of Victories*.

'When Nelson saw off Trafalgar' (Rule Britannia) *England Expects each man will do his duty* is certainly effusive – 'Weep, sons of Britain the godlike Nelson's dead/With victory crowned, he nobly bled' – but it lacks any real detail. 'When Nelson first at Britain's call,/To rule the ocean undertook' *Britannia Mourn the Hero Slain* has essentially similar problems, whereas 'From the direful scene returning, where grim carnage stalk'd around' *The Fight off Trafalgar* provides an odd combination of an over-convoluted beginning followed by increasing narrative style, with first person narrator. Similarly, *Death and Victory* starts in typically loyalist style, 'When the navy of Gaul, our inveterate foe, called the valour of England their rage to oppose/Brave Nelson who never in battle would yield/For Britain and George nobly enter'd the field/To be true to the true land of freedom he swore;/As the blue that adorn'd the proud standard he bore.' But this is followed by a verse on his death in battle, and the final verse has a sentimental, but not unballad-like twist, with the flagstaff being planted beside his grave 'Where as gratitude's tear wou'd the spot oft bedew/Thus moisten'd – at length to a laurel it grew.'

The songs that focus directly on mourning Nelson's death, rather than seeing it as integral to the action in Trafalgar, are almost entirely of the more élite form. That there should be so few popular songs expressly on his death and commemoration of his deeds is not, I think, surprising, since the natural context for popular songs would be the narrative of Trafalgar, rather than a more abstract concern with a contribution to his country. Dibdin provides two such songs: 'Come messmates rejoice' and 'Ah Hark, the signals round the coast.' There are also two sung by Incledon, the renowned Covent Garden tenor: 'Cease vain France' (The Storm) *The Death of Nelson* and 'Fate uncontroll'd by human prayer' *Nelson's Tomb*. And the equally well known John Braham sang 'In death's dark house' (printed) *The Victory and Death of Lord Viscount Nelson* – 'received with unbounded applause at the Theatre Royal, Drury Lane, in the melodramatic piece commemorative of that remarkable event' (written by R. Cumberland). Two similar pieces are: 'In the temple of fame, where the ghosts of the brave, ascend from the mouldering tombs' (printed) *Britannia's Hero: or Nelson eclipsing the Heroes of Yore*; and 'Let Britons Nelson's valour sing' (Arethusa) *A small tribute to the memory of the late gallant Lord Nelson* (written by J. Pratt and containing the thought that as Nelson was dying Victory caught him in her arms, and to the sounds of success in battle, he soared to heaven).

Perhaps the most striking group of songs are those that effectively enjoin us to move on, thereby both celebrating Nelson as a hero, and preparing us to recognize others who will do the same for their country. There is some indication of a wish to draw a line under the war during the peace of Amiens, when the first verse of *The Newcastle Bellman* begins – 'Talk no more of brave Nelson, or gallant Sir Sydney,/Tis granted they're tars of a true British kidney/And people are curious, such heroes to see/But neither are half so much follow'd as me (*viz* the Town Cryer).' But in the case of the post-Trafalgar songs the motive is not war-weariness so much as a need for closure to the mourning of Nelson, and for reassurance that his loss will not expose the country to the French: 'Though with tears we lament our great Nelson's demise,/Let the nation rejoice that more

Nelsons arise' *Admiral Strahan's Victory* (chorus: Hearts of Oak).[32] And, 'In a battle you know we Britons are strong' (Chapter of Kings) *Trafalgar's Battle*, the sole purpose of the song seems to be to introduce and underline the importance of Collingwood. Indeed, many of the Trafalgar songs were keen to reference other naval leaders (see the last verse of 'Arise, Arise, Brave Britons' *Nelson's Glorious Victory at Trafalgar*, which hymns Collingwood and Hardy; and 'Britons, you've heard Trafalgar's story' *Nelson and Collingwood* – 'Mourn for Nelson in his grave; Rejoice and cheer the living brave/With modest, gallant Collingwood'). 'Come all you gallant seamen' *A new song composed on the Death...* similarly concludes: 'Here's God bless all seamen that speak for his good/May the heavens go with you, and ten thousand blessings/Still rest on the fleet and brave Collingwood.'[33] While 'Old England's long expected heavy news from our fleet ...' *Nelson's Death*, does not go so far, Collingwood is also central,[34] and in 'We got ready for battle' *Nelson's Victory at Trafalgar*, Hardy and Collingwood again feature in the final verse.[35] In contrast, 'Where now my dear Boney is your grand combined fleet' *Lord Nelson's Victory* brings on Strahan to sweep up the remainder of Napoleon's fleet. (See also Dibdin's manuscript 'When Nelson fell, the voice of fame' *When Nelson Fell.*) While there are variations here it is clear that many of these songs are about shoring up national confidence in the wake of Nelson's death and providing a positive form of closure.

More unusual is 'Britons all attend, while I sing of your friend' *Gallant Lord Nelson*, to the tune of God Save the King, which is essentially a song about Nelson's funeral, the last three verses essentially detailing the attendance of captains, lieutenants, admirals and sailors:

> Lords Dukes and Judges there
> So grand the sight
> Did appear,
> And great was the throng,
> Princes, earls and Squires too,
> Lord-Mayor and Sheriffs also,
> The body followed its true
> Of Admiral Nelson.

The picture is of a unified nation paying homage to Nelson. If it is unusual to have a penny ballad written for your funeral, it is doubly so to be able to match this with two whose occasion is the creation of the national memorial to your last battle. 'Old England/Britain's long expected ...' *Nelson's Death/Nelson's Monument* announces the intention to build a monument to his victories – 'A monument for Nelson, and a sword for Collingwood.'

'As some heroes bold, I will unfold' *Grand Conversation on Nelson* in part celebrates the building of Trafalgar Square and Nelson's column in the 1840s. This later ballad, however, has features that distinguish it from almost all the other material on Nelson, even if it is not a particularly successful song. Nelson is depicted as committed to liberty, yet in the following verse Nelson, Hardy and Collingwood are credited with causing 'some thousands to be slain, while fighting on the raging main', and this is followed by the middle verse that has considerably more objectivity and ambiguity in it than most of the other songs connected to Nelson:

Many a gallant youth, I'll tell the truth, in action have been wounded
Some left their friends and lovers in despair upon their native shore,
Others never returned again, but died upon the raging main,
Causing many a mother to cry, my son, and widows to deplore.
When war was raging, it is said, men for their labour were well paid
Commerce and trade were flourishing, but now it ebbs and flows
And poverty it does increase, tho' Britons say they live in peace,
This grand conversation on Nelson arose.

It is not difficult to find fault with the song as a song, but it is markedly different from the songs of 1797–1806 – indeed different from anything else about Nelson in the nineteenth century: it is complex, ambiguous, open to interpretation, partly critical, and it comments on contemporary affairs and, at least by implication, government. In fact, those qualities are pretty standard fare for many street songs and penny ballads in the eighteenth and nineteenth centuries, but they are qualities that are effectively silenced in relation to Nelson by a combination of repression, prosecution and propagandizing, especially when the government was fiercely embattled by internal dissent and threats of invasion in 1796–99 and when it was most threatened by Napoleon between 1803 and 1805. Not that songs about Nelson were singled out for such censorship – but Nelson's ascendancy coincided with the key period of loyalist dominance and government resistance to radicalism, and by the time the political context again became more contested and pluralist Nelson's exploits are a matter of past record and new issues exist to task the ballad writers.

VII

Songs were also performances, and most of these songs were written for public performance, and in some cases for public participation. For loyalists the performance was part of the process of bringing together and uniting in sentiment an audience. Earlier in the 1790s there are instances of rival clubs meeting in the same taverns and singing songs that borrow each other's tunes but put them to new purposes – so that many performances were multi-layered processes of ideological contestation and confrontation. For loyalists those early lessons had certainly been learnt by 1803–05: both the value of the medium for arousing public participation and commitment, and the importance of silencing the opposition. To encourage participation many loyalist songs were written to existing tunes, with existing choruses, thereby facilitating identification with the cause espoused (using especially *God Save the King*; *Rule Britannia*; and *Hearts of Oak*). That so many of these songs (especially those relying on established tunes) proved ephemeral would not have been thought significant by their writers and those who circulated them: their fundamental purpose was to contribute to and help to manage the historical moment, rather than to provide a lasting tribute. Nonetheless, some songs did endure, and it is in their endurance that they help play a deeper part in the creation of a popular cultural memory.

The outpouring of material on Nelson was, I have suggested, partly a function of the loyalist dominance of the presses, linked to a sense of relief associated with naval success in the wake of Spithead and the Nore, and an élite sense of the importance of commemoration and celebration of the achievements for maintaining the support of the wider British public – an issue that the 1790s had brought to the centre of the political stage. It was also informed by more traditional practices of celebrating battles in narrative songs. The absence of any counter-Nelson songs, associated, for example with his less successful endeavours (for example, Santa Cruz), or any songs containing a whiff of scandal or scurrility, is, I am suggesting, partly a function of the extent to which popular culture had, by the mid 1790s, become tightly policed, and in 1803 had become wholly dominated by loyalist forces. This dominance also seems to have had the effect of pressuring the market for songs and ballads in a way that melded together genres and types of song, and bridged earlier patterns of circulation; it is as if songs were squeezed into circulation by whatever means available. Moreover, a number of these songs – a mix of battle narratives and songs coming from popular entertainments and the loyalist presses – live on as the nineteenth century's inheritance of songs about Nelson. The most popular songs about Nelson in the last half of the nineteenth century seem to have been: 'O'er Nelson's Tomb' *Nelson*, the élite song by Arnold and Braham and 'Old England/Britain's long expected …' *Nelson's Death/Nelson's Monument* (both of which are centred on Nelson's death); 'Come all you gallant seamen that unite in a meeting' *A New Song on the Death of Lord Nelson* and 'The 21st day of October ...' *Brave Nelson* (both battle narratives of Trafalgar); 'Arise, Arise, Britannia's sons arise' *The Battle of the Nile* an élite song about the Nile; and, especially in the 1830s and 1840s, 'The second of August eighteen hundred and one' *The Battle of Boulogne*. Through this legacy, loyalist dominance had an enduring impact on the way Nelson was celebrated in popular public memory in the nineteenth century and, in that sense, is evidence of its more lasting impact on the creation of national unity and national myth.

This success, however, seems to be linked to a broader failure. The picture is a complex one, and it is one about which it is difficult to generalize on the basis of the evidence I have been able to collect thus far, but while there were printings of some of the Nelson ballads throughout the nineteenth century, there are fewer late in the century and little or nothing in the early twentieth century. It also seems that very little of the Nelson material survived in the oral tradition. Interestingly, even in collections of Dibdin's work, except where these aim to be comprehensive, the Nelson songs fare less well than his more generic sailor and soldier songs. Moreover, although the nineteenth century remained alive to some Nelson songs, they generated few new songs, and none that added any depth or colour to the characterization on Nelson.[36] One reason is that the strongly loyalist character of many of the songs sits uncomfortably with popular ballad traditions that take a more objective and critical view of war and its costs; but it may also be that the continuing élite celebration and commemoration of Nelson, combined with the lack of an independent narrative voice in songs from the period, came to act as a deterrent to their continuing salience for popular audiences and ballad singers. The Nelson of the popular songs of his day is the untarnished national hero – there is no ambiguity to exploit, no flaw in the marble and, as a result, no room for some independent purchase on him. That this is so is, I have argued, largely a function of the intensity of the loyalist attempt to dominate and determine the way that people understood and responded to the war and the threat of invasion, but the result is a tradition of singing about Nelson that never gained the objectivity and distance that characterizes so many of the popular ballads that have endured and remain an essential part of a popular cultural memory.

This chapter does little more than scratch the surface of the world of popular song and its relationship to popular politics and cultural and national memory. As should be clear, there is considerably more material than I have been able adequately to discuss here, and I have been able to say only very little about the broader context of song and its place within Georgian political culture and society, despite insisting on the importance of setting this material against that background. Nonetheless, the aim has been to draw attention to material relating to Nelson that has been largely forgotten in the scholarship on him. I have argued that this material should be read against the background of the intense struggle to secure the loyalty of ordinary Britons and to mobilize them against the substantial and serious threats of invasion by Napoleon. The very scale of this activity has led some writers to see the period as a watershed in the building, or forging, of the British nation, but while there is much that it instructive about such a claim, the material I have discussed here suggests more tentative conclusions – confirming the state's ability to ensure a uniformity of expression of sentiment but not wholly to determine that this sentiment was deeply held.

The unalloyed heroism of Nelson that emerges in the songs contrasts strongly with the more nuanced and subtle songs about Bonaparte, Waterloo and the war that appear after 1815, and which suggest a more complex and critical attachment to the country and its enemies than is evident from the Nelson material.[37] In such ballads, Napoleon is represented as a man of passion, as flawed and tragic, but as someone who achieved much and whose standing as a hero is in many respects enhanced by his humanity and his weaknesses. In contrast, in the representation of Nelson in popular songs, there is no flaw. While it is difficult to demonstrate unequivocally that it is the sanitized and untarnished portrayals of Nelson that undermine the chances of survival for songs about him, it is striking both how far they have been lost in traditions of popular song and that this fate has not been shared by some of the later songs about Bonaparte.

Notes

1. I owe thanks to Alvero Herrero who acted as a research assistant in a critical phase of this project, Alexandra Franklin who guided me through the Ballad Collection at the Bodleian, the Department of Politics and International Relations at Oxford for its support, and to Derek McCulloch, Director of *Cafe Mozart*, a group of musicians specializing in the songs and music of the period, for his expertise and access to material covering the more élite songs of the period. The sources of material for this chapter are diverse, but the bulk comes from the Bodleian Library, especially its Curzon and Harding collections and the essential searchable web-based ballads database which is available through the Bodleian's website: <http://www.bodley.ox.ac.uk/ballads/>. I have also drawn on material in the British Library and on the resources of the Cecil Sharp Library (and its enormously helpful librarian) in London. In addition

there are a number of printed sources that are cited whenever they are the source for a particular song.

2. BM Adds MSS 16920, fol 99.
3. See the excellent collection of Irish songs in Terry Moylan, *The Age of Revolution in the Irish Song Tradition: 1776–1815* (Dublin, 2000).
4. All songs are referred to by: First line (tune) *Title*. Where no tune is identified no bracket appears; where the tune is printed with the words '(printed)' appears. This method of reference is not without difficulties, as a number of versions of essentially the same song may have different first lines, but differences in titles are still more common, and it is the standard method. On Freeth, see note 9.
5. Interestingly, when Freeth produced a collection of songs during the Peace of 1803 the Nelson song was not included but an earlier version hymning Russell with the same tune and chorus was reprinted – although it is difficult to be certain, it seems likely that the peace genuinely resulted in a desire to seek a rapprochement with France, leading to a downplaying of recent, more nationalist, songs.
6. See the appendix on the spending of George Rose in Lucille Werkmeister, *The London Daily Press 1772–1792* (Lincoln, NE, 1962).
7. See the discussions in Linda Colley, *Britons: Forging the Nation 1707–1837* (New Haven, 1992); John Cookson, *The British Armed Nation 1793–1815* (Oxford, 1997); Austin Gee, *The British Volunteer Movement 1794–1814* (Oxford, 2003); and the essays on volunteering by Rogers, Newman and Navickas in M. Philp (ed.), *Resisting Napoleon: The British Response to the Threat of Invasion 1798–1815* (Aldershot, forthcoming June 2006).
8. See Mark Philp, Roz Southey, Caroline Jackson-Houlston and Susan Wollenberg, 'Music and Politics 1793–1815', in M. Philp (ed.), *Resisting Napoleon.*
9. See John Horden, *John Freeth (1731–1808) Political Ballad-Writer and Innkeeper* (Oxford, 1993). See pp. 166–7 and 197–8 (the earlier song in praise of Rodney in 1783 is adapted largely wholesale to celebrate Nelson).
10. See G. Cruikshank (ed.), *Songs of the late Charles Dibdin, with a Memoir*, 3rd edn (London, 1852).
11. See especially Gillray's *A Cognocenti contemplating ye beauties of ye antique* (1801), and *Dido, in Despair* (1801). There is a later song, based on a very famous Napoleon ballad, but reworked for Nelson as *The Grand Conversation on Nelson Arose* – that probably first appears in the 1820s, and that does have some lines about the end of the war bringing poverty and hardship, but it is essentially uncritical of Nelson, as is the one song that is preserved on Boulogne (a fragment of which was collected in the oral tradition in Patrick Shuldham-Shaw and Emily B. Lyle (eds), *The Greig and Duncan Folksong Collection* (Aberdeen, 1981), vol. 1, p. 353). While my comments are restricted largely to material published between 1789 and 1815, the lack of criticism holds true throughout the nineteenth century. There are occasional later songs, some printed around the centenary, which are not markedly different from the earlier songs – see for example 'For England love and Beauty' *The Hero of Trafalgar*, composed expressly for the centenary by Sarah Swain 'Poetess Laureate of the West Indies'. In the late 1880s John Parnell also published a long ballad to Nelson ''Tis of a little Norfolk boy' *The Battle of Trafalgar* that adds little, save length, to the loyalist hymning of Nelson 80 years earlier. There

is also, for those interested, a not so clean, twentieth-century ballad (*A Ballad of Good Lord Nelson*) written by Lawrence Durrell that begins, 'The Good Lord Nelson had a swollen gland;/Little of the scripture did he understand;/Till a woman led him to the promised land;/Aboard the Victory O, Victory O.'

12. Indeed, Nelson is used as an example to follow in the campaign in 'Twas on a Thursday morning that from Cadiz we set sail' *Barrosa Plains*: 'Look back to Cape Trafalgar, boys, where Nelson bled before:/the blood that conquered on the sea shall conquer on the shore' (referring to the Battle of Barrosa, 4 March 1811). See Moylan, *The Age of Revolution*, No. 177.

13. For ease of reference songs are referred to by their first line (tune) and *title*. Where the tune is printed '(printed)' is inserted. Those where no tune is named are referred to by only 'first line' and *Title*.

14. There are a considerable number of musical pieces names after Nelson and/or various battles, such as J. Dale's sonata for piano-forte, *Nelson and the Navy*, published in 1798, and a host of dance and folk tunes that develop a Nelson title (such as the *Nelson hornpipe*), although they may well have been earlier tunes renamed.

15. See also the later song, 'The Trumpet sounds, the valiant troops are form'd' *England's Queen and England's Glory* probably written in the late 1840s in which Nelson and the Nile are cited as an exemplar of English heroism.

16. See also Freeth's 'As Englishmen finding our rights are at stake' (Hearts of Oak) *The Sailor's Rouse* (which declares that Nelson is now on his way).

17. See R. Palmer, *Boxing the Compass*, revised and expanded edition (Todmorden, 2001) pp. 184–5.

18. See for example, 'My name, d'ye see, 's Tom Tough ...' *Yo Heave Ho* – which ends with the narrator having lost an eye and a toe, and singing old songs.

19. See, for example, *A new song on the sea engagement 1st June 1794*; *A copy of verses on the glorious victory obtained by Lord Howe, over the enemy, in a long engagement*; *Howe Victorious, or the French Defeated*; *Duncan and Victory*, and so on.

20. In broadside ballad but also in R. Palmer, *Boxing the Compass*.

21. See C.H. Firth, *Naval Songs and Ballads* (London, 1908), pp. 288–9.

22. See W. Roy Mackenzie, *Ballads and Sea Songs from Nova Scotia* (Cambridge, MA, 1928), pp. 203–4.

23. This offers a contrast to Mrs Heman's 1829 poem 'The boy stood on the burning deck' dealing with a boy from *L'Orient*!

24. See Firth, *Naval Songs and Ballads*, pp. 290–5. The alternative version is from a broadside ballad dated 27 January 1855 in the Bodleian collection.

25. See Firth, *Naval Songs and Ballads*, p. 295, but there are also several copies in the Bodleian ballad collection.

26. A fragment of the same song is also recorded in Greig and Duncan. I have taken the verses from a broadside in the Bodleian ballad collection.

27. See J. Ashton, *Modern Street Ballads* (London, 1888), pp. 298–9.

28. MacKenzie, *Ballads and Sea Songs from Nova Scotia*, pp. 203–4.

29. There are several broadside editions, and the song also appears in Ashton, *Modern Street Ballads*, pp. 300–1.

30. See, in the oral tradition, Greig and Duncan, vol. 1, p. 354, and for the street ballad see J. Holloway and J. Black, *Later English Broadside Ballads*, vol. 2 (London, 1975), pp. 174–5.

31. See Palmer, *Boxing the Compass*, pp. 182–3.
32. Firth, *Naval Songs and Ballads*, p. 304.
33. See ibid., pp. 302–4; Ashton, *Modern Street Ballads*, pp. 302–4.
34. See Roy Palmer, *A Ballad History of England* (London, 1979), pp. 88–9. There are also broadside ballads of this song, some beginning 'Britain's long expected great news …'
35. Mackenzie, *Ballads and Sea Songs from Nova Scotia*, pp. 203–4.
36. See above note 11; later songs that mention Nelson include 'O will you buy my images' *Images*; 'All you that are low-spirited I think I won't be wrong' *Sportsmen*; 'The trumpet sound, the valiant troops are form'd' *England's Queen and England's Glory*; 'Oh Britannia! The gem of the ocean' *Nelson's last sigh, or the red, white and blue.*
37. I am thinking of 'It was over that wild beaten track, a friend of bold Bonaparte, Did pace the sands and loft rocks of St. Helena's shore' *The Grand Conversation of Napoleon*; 'By the dangers of the ocean, One morning in the month of June' *Bonny Bunch of Roses O*; 'One night sad and languid I lay on my bed' *Napoleon*; 'I am Napoleon Bonaparte the conqueror of nations' *Napoleon Bonaparte*; 'Bony is gone from the wars of all fighting' *Napoleon on the Isle of St Helena*; 'Napoleon is no more, the French him did adore' *Napoleon the Brave*; 'Attention pay both young and old, unto these lines I will unfold, *Napoleon's Remains*; 'Arrah Muther, but times is hard' *Boney's the boy for kicking up a row*; and etcetera.

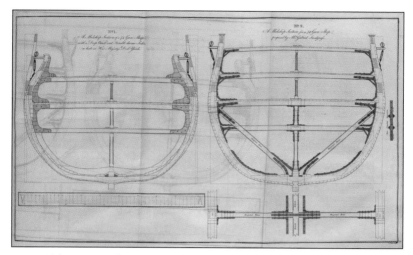

1. A Midship section for a 74–gun ship, proposed by Mr Gabriel Snodgrass.

VISCOUNT MELVILLE.

2. Print of Viscount Melville, First Lord of the Admiralty, 15 May 1804 to 2 May 1805, responsible for crucial decisions on the British fleet before Trafalgar.

3. James Gillray, *The Death of ADMIRAL-LORD-NELSON - in the moment of Victory!*

4. Benjamin West, engr. James Heath, *The Death of Lord Viscount Nelson K.B.*

5. Benjamin West, *The Immortality of Nelson*.

6. James Gillray, *Britannia Victorious. Design for the NAVAL PILLAR*.

7. Richard Westall, *Nelson and the Bear*.

8. Benjamin West, *The Death of Lord Nelson in the Cockpit of the Ship Victory*.

9. Joseph Mallord William Turner, *The Battle of Trafalgar, 21 October 1805.*

10. Philippe-Jacques de Loutherbourg, *Lord Howe's Action, or the Glorious First of June.*

11. 'Twas in Trafalgar's Bay', Turner's 'Trafalgar' explained by a Greenwich Pensioner.

12. Doulton Stoneware, produced for the centenary of the battle of Trafalgar in 1905.

7
The Battle of the Pictures: Painting the History of Trafalgar

Geoffrey Quilley

When news of the Battle of Trafalgar reached Britain, its significance was immediately recognized and seized on by the art world. Proposals were at once solicited and put forward for some form of sculptural or architectural monument to Nelson, the national martyr; and visual responses were produced across a range of genres, from graphic satire by Gillray (see Plate 3) to Benjamin West's extravagant and fictitious 'grand manner' painting (Plate 4). Trafalgar was presented not only as the most critical victory in the naval war against the combined alliance of French and Spanish forces; but it also comprised perhaps the single most appropriate subject hitherto for the pursuit of national artistic excellence. The fact that this also brought with it a considerable potential for, and exploitation of, artistic commercial opportunism was not necessarily contradictory. Since at least the 1750s the function of art had been theorized in terms of its contribution to the improvement of national commerce and industry.[1] Although by 1800 the relationship of art to commerce was severely contested, particularly regarding the lack of public patronage for art, which was seen increasingly as a serious failing of British cultural policy (especially when compared to the French system of state patronage), the terms of this debate in one sense only re-emphasized the interdependence of art and commerce in national culture.

I

One of the most serious criticisms of the lack of state policy and funding for art was that the abandonment of art to market forces could only end up satisfying the limitations of private taste and consumption, which concentrated overwhelmingly on portraiture, at the expense of the highest forms of public art, above all history painting, for which there was by comparison virtually no private market.[2] Hence the potential significance of an event of such enormity as Trafalgar: in its mix of poignancy and glory, individualism and nationalism, centred on the sacrifice of the hero Nelson at the moment of what rapidly became regarded as Britain's greatest naval victory, it fitted all the requirements for the creation of a modern history painting for the commercial maritime nation. This is surely what West was attempting in his epic canvas of 1806, that recapitulated his enormously successful composition, *The Death of Wolfe*, of the early 1770s.

When the painting was exhibited at the Royal Academy to coincide with the publication of Heath's sumptuous print after it (Plate 4), West provided an elaborate apology for his departure from the facts of Nelson's death, to justify his representation of the fallen admiral as a version of the sacred iconography of the Lamentation over the Dead Christ. To show Nelson's demise according strictly to the facts, he argued, would be to lose its national import, the communication of which was one of the primary functions of history painting.[3] Such a glorious death and victory demanded to be depicted in an epic manner:

> being one of the most distinguished that ever occurred in the annals of Great Britain for heroism and national importance. Mr. West, conceiving that such an event demanded a composition every way appropriate to its dignity and high importance, formed it into an Epic Composition. This enabled him to give it that character and interest which the subject demanded. Availing himself of that character in composition, he laid the heroic Nelson wounded on the quarterdeck.[4]

Not only is Nelson's death shown inaccurately taking place on deck, but he is encircled by an unfeasibly operatic chorus of young, athletic tars – the 'gallant officers and men ... sympathizing with each other in the sufferings of their wounded Friend and expiring Commander'[5] – and illuminated by a providential shaft of light cutting diagonally across the scene, that impresses the sense of this being more a theatrical production than a faithful rendition of historical events. West's explanation of his composition, therefore, was also designed to demonstrate, among other things, that 'history' and 'history painting' were by no means synonymous. Thus his reinvention of the death of Nelson precisely imitated his reinvention, some 40 years previously, of Wolfe's death.

This served a double purpose: on the one hand, it sought openly to repeat a highly successful pictorial strategy, adapting the formal academic demands of history painting to a modern, national iconography; on the other, it also advertised the artist's own esteemed reputation in the eyes of Nelson, referring to the latter's remark on seeing West's *Death of Wolfe* that, should he die in battle, he should like West to paint his memorial in like manner.[6] To an extent, therefore, West's picture is as much about artistic self-promotion as it is about contemporary national history and its representation; and it points up the degree to which art, and particularly the representation of the nation's identity through its history, was itself a battleground.

West's perhaps cynical self-referencing and disregard of the facts of Nelson's death also betray a deep awareness of the commercial potential of the subject, that was more fully exploited in the publication of the engraving of the painting in 1811. It thus contributed unashamedly to feeding an unprecedented, consumer-driven public appetite for memorabilia and monuments of the man who was generally accepted to have been Britain's pre-eminent naval leader. Gillray's *The Death of Admiral Lord Nelson – in the moment of Victory* (Plate 3) also refers to this instantaneous public clamour and 'consumption' of Nelson in the caption to his print, which proposes it, with considerable irony, as a 'Design for the Memorial intended by the City of London to commemorate the Glorious Death of the immortal Nelson'. It plays on the blurring of the boundaries between the public and private spheres, in relation both to Nelson and to monumental art: though advertising itself as a design for a public memorial to Nelson, the figure of Britannia, in a melodramatically exaggerated gesture of grief, assumes the unmistakeable features of Emma, Lady Hamilton adopting one of her 'attitudes', while the disconsolate Hardy has the profile of George III. The prescient proximity of the composition both to West's *Death of Lord Nelson* and to his *Immortality of Nelson* (Plate 5), which was itself proposed as a design for a monument, further underscores the degree to which individual, private, professional self-advancement was interchangeable with public artistic sentiment. Gillray's print itself was published quickly – doubtless also to capitalize on the market for such subjects – in late December 1805, which gives some indication of the speed that proposals for monuments to Nelson were devised and promulgated: like West's sketch for a monument to Nelson, which was intended to incorporate his *Immortality of Nelson* and was exhibited at the Royal Academy in 1807, it was doubtless a response to Lord Hawkesbury's call to the Academy of 10 December 1805 for 'the members of that body to consider the best mode of perpetuating the memory of Lord Nelson'.[7]

In fact, proposals for naval monuments or pillars had been made for some ten years, the most intensive public debate coming in 1799–1800 when a committee led by the Duke of Clarence invited entries to a competition for a suitable memorial. Gillray again contributed graphically with a characteristically trenchant and perhaps partly ironic vision of Britannia atop a bizarre pillar isolated in the middle of the ocean and battered by the elements (Plate 6).

One of the most elaborate proposals came from the artist John Opie, who proposed the construction of an ideal structure, on the plan of the Pantheon in Rome, and like West's design for a monument to Nelson, 'composed of three branches of art which constitute the Academy', painting, sculpture and architecture.[8] The interior would be divided into distinct registers and compartments to provide an extensive didactic programme of painting and sculpture representing Britain's maritime history and present-day glory. In prime position (equivalent to 'on the line' at the Academy exhibition) would be a series of paintings 'of the most brilliant victories and remarkable achievements, judiciously and carefully selected from the naval history of Great Britain, beginning from the remotest periods, and coming gradually down to the present day'.[9] Between every two of these, there should be niches to display full-size sculptures of the naval commanders involved in the actions depicted in the paintings. Below the principal paintings should be 'a smaller set, relative to our trade, commerce, colonization, discoveries, and other subjects connected with, and growing out of, the great power and prosperity of our navy'.[10] Above the whole would be an open-ended series of half-length portraits of secondary figures of naval history, leaving sufficient space for future additions, on the assumption that Britain's maritime prowess will continue: indeed, one of the functions of Opie's pantheon would be to provide exemplary national narratives for future generations to ensure such continuity. Finally, in the centre, below the dome, would be

> a colossal group in marble, representing Neptune doing homage to Britannia; and at the head of the room, a statue of his present majesty, George the Third, in whose reign the British naval power has reached a point of exaltation, which seems to preclude the possibility of its being carried much higher by our successors.[11]

Opie's hierarchical visual order for the pantheon's display of art represented also a systematic visual ordering of national maritime history. What is envisaged in his unfeasibly ambitious scheme is nothing less than a comprehensive, encyclopaedic account *in artistic form* of the naval history of the nation. In its taxonomic hierarchy of subject and medium, it anticipates the ordering principles of classification and categorization that were the intellectual underpinning of the art gallery and museum as they would develop over the course of the nineteenth century; more specifically, it anticipates the nationalistic agenda of the Naval Gallery at Greenwich Hospital as it was conceived by its prime instigator Edward Hawke Locker upon its opening in 1824. Locker's father, William, had already outlined a proposal for a national gallery of marine art in 1795. In the 'Notice' to the 1836 edition of the *Catalogue* to the Gallery Locker explained that his father's original scheme was prompted by the disuse of the Painted Hall at the Hospital, which having been unoccupied for almost a century 'should be appropriated to the service of a National Gallery of Marine Paintings, to commemorate the eminent services of the Royal Navy of England'.[12] He goes on to describe how his own later proposal met with royal approval in the substantial donation of a collection of portraits from the royal collection, and other subsequent royal gifts, including in 1829 Loutherbourg's *Lord Howe's Victory, or the Glorious First of June* and Turner's *Battle of Trafalgar*.

As with Opie's proposal, the collection comprised portraits of principal naval commanders together with 'Representations of their Warlike Achievements', as the title to the catalogue put it, and a major function of the Gallery was, likewise, to ensure that 'the eminent services of the Royal Navy will never lose their interest in the view of those who visit Greenwich Hospital'. The larger purpose, however, was a spiritual one: while the pictures

> serve to rekindle the gratitude of this highly-favoured nation, in whose cause our brave countrymen fought and bled, we may ever remember that far higher debt of gratitude which is due to God, who mercifully guided them through all the perils of the deep, and nerved the arm of every fearless seaman in the day of battle.[13]

In a very real sense, therefore, Locker's objective for the Naval Gallery was that of a naval temple in the manner of Opie, or of Major John Cartwright's extravagant conception of a 'hieronauticon'.[14] In turn, it is not inconceivable that Opie may have been aware of William Locker's 1795 scheme, and that this informed his own idea for a pantheon. Whatever, the overriding issue that concerns me here is how such proposals were predicated on a systematic and taxonomic visual classification of national maritime history that in the 1790s was entirely novel, and marks a significant change in the visual representation of national history. It is against this background of the cultural production of a visual history of the maritime nation, rebounding like a loose cannon across the blurred boundaries of the public and private spheres, that the prolific imagery representing Trafalgar needs to be placed.

This is especially true of the paintings and engravings produced for the first major biography following Nelson's death, Clarke and MacArthur's *Life of Nelson* (1809).[15] The illustrations for this history, produced principally by Richard Westall and Benjamin West once more, isolate key heroic episodes in Nelson's life in the manner of a modern version of the Labours of Hercules. So, his somewhat fictionalized encounter with a polar bear (Plate 7) is transformed into a Nelsonic version of Hercules and the Nemean lion. Consequently, following the formal structure of classical heroic mythology, the visual narrative concludes with Nelson's death (this time in a sentimentally mundane and documentary composition, in contrast to West's earlier epic scenography) (Plate 8) and finally his apotheosis to be received among the gods (Plate 5). West again provided an elaborate commentary on the latter painting at its exhibition in 1807, explaining it in similar terms to Opie's proposal for a naval pantheon. However, as already suggested, the visual similarity, no doubt accidental, between West's composition and Gillray's print *The Death of Admiral Lord Nelson* indicates the ambiguities over the proper public representation of Nelson's death: the similarities and, equally important, the profound differences between these two images points once more to the intractable difficulty at this date of deciding what a visual history of the maritime nation might constitute. In addition, the fact that West's painting finished up not as part of a public monument but as an illustration for Nelson's biography also indicates the problems over the public representation of history through history painting, which was displaced in this instance by its transformation into an image for private consumption, as part of a book.

II

As the comparison between Gillray's and West's images suggests, Trafalgar and its histories were not stable and monolithic. The historical discourse on Trafalgar was mutable and sometimes conflicting; its representations served commercial and ideological, as well as historical, ends. All of which raised the issue of what history of the battle was to be represented visually? In the rest of this chapter I want to examine these issues with reference to what became the most notorious painting of the battle, Turner's massive 1824 canvas *The Battle of Trafalgar* (Plate 9). Commissioned by King George IV as a pendant piece to Loutherbourg's 1795 canvas of *Lord Howe's Action, or the Glorious First of June* (Plate 10), this was not simply commemorative, but was a wide-ranging pictorial essay on the nature of the maritime nation at a critical juncture in its self-definition.

William Lionel Wyllie, in his monograph on Turner published in the Trafalgar centenary year 1905, observed the allegorical significance of Turner's historical subjects. Commenting on the pair of classical subjects *Dido Building Carthage* (1815) and *The Decline of the Carthaginian Empire* (1817), he remarked that

> Turner always meant his pictures of the Carthaginian empire to be typical of Great Britain in its war with France. He intended the fate of the enervated, luxurious citizens to be an awful warning to his countrymen of what might befall them if they gave way to slothfulness and ease; Imperial France, of course, was a personification of old Rome.[16]

In other words, in keeping with the academic tradition of history painting, the classical history of the Carthaginian War was presented artistically as a moral and civic lesson to modern imperial Britain, then emerging from its own epic confrontation with Napoleonic France. Arguably, then, *The Battle of Trafalgar* might answer a similar civic purpose, in being a modern history painting for the maritime nation, and taking its subject, like West's depictions of Wolfe and Nelson, from recent rather than ancient history.

However, it is more complicated. Not least, Wyllie's account of the Carthage paintings raises numerous questions regarding the composition and profile of the country that he claims Turner 'meant' to address. Certainly, *The Battle of Trafalgar* failed miserably – and notoriously – to strike any chord with the naval community, suggesting apart from anything else that there was no homogeneous nation available for modern history painting to address. John Ruskin famously described his encounter with a Pensioner guide at Greenwich Hospital, where both Turner's and Loutherbourg's paintings had been transferred from the royal collection in 1829. Having stopped before the Turner, his guide

> supposing me to be detained by indignant wonder at seeing it in so good a place, assented to my supposed sentiments by muttering in a

low voice: 'Well, sir, it *is* a shame that that thing should be there. We ought to 'a 'ad a Uggins; that's sartain.'[17]

For the Pensioner, the mundane but faithfully accurate rendition of shipping and sailing conditions, epitomized in the work of William Huggins, one of the leading marine artists of the day, was of infinitely more value than Turner's nuanced and poetic transcription of events at Trafalgar. More tellingly, he shows a dismissive disdain for any allowance of poetic licence in the representation of maritime subjects, that was certainly consistent with the visual tradition of marine painting and with the documentary role of the visual arts within the maritime context; conversely, he displays a touching, and perhaps naïve faith in the idea that visual representation could provide an unproblematically objective account of historical events, by which principle Turner's picture must indeed logically be deficient.

On several counts, however, *The Battle of Trafalgar* could be regarded as Turner's most important painting: his largest canvas, it was his only royal commission, and its iconography comprises the most significant episode of contemporary national maritime history, in a grandly ambitious and complex composition. The circumstances surrounding its production and reception are well known, and I shall not rehearse the details here.[18] Its shortcomings were elaborated by the contemporary historian William James in the 1826 edition of his *Naval History of Great Britain*. After explaining its commission as the pair to Loutherbourg's 1795 depiction of *Lord Howe's Action, or the Glorious First of June* hanging in the Council Room of St James's Palace – also a lamentably defective painting in James's view – he launches into Turner's rendition of Trafalgar, which is worth quoting at length.

> The first marine painter of the day undertook the task; and in due time, the large area of canvas, which, to correspond with the other picture, became necessary for this, was covered with all the varied tints which Mr. Turner knows so well how to mingle and combine, to give effect to his pictures and excite the admiration of the beholder.

> Unfortunately for the subject which this splendid picture is meant to represent, scarcely a line of truth, beyond perhaps the broadside view of the Victory's hull, is to be seen upon it. To say what time of the day, or what particular incident in the Victory's proceedings, is meant to be referred to, we do not pretend; for the telegraphic message is going up, which was hoisted at about 11h. 40m. A.M., the mizentopmast

is falling, which went about 1 P.M., a strong light is reflected upon the Victory's bow and sides from the burning Achille, which ship did not catch fire until 4h. 30m., nor explode until 5h. 45m. P.M., the foretopmast, or rather, if our memory is correct, the foremast, of the British three-decker is falling, which never fell at all, and the Redoutable is sinking under the bows of the Victory, although the French ship did not sink until the night of the 22nd, and then under the stern of the Swiftsure.

We are sorry to be obliged to add that, with all these glaring falsehoods and palpable inconsistencies upon it, the picture stands, or until very lately did stand, in that room of the king's palace, for which it was originally designed. The principal reason urged for giving to this very costly and highly honoured performance so preposterous a character, is that an adherence to truth would have destroyed the pictorial effect. Here is a ship, shattered in her hull, and stripped of the best part of her sails, pushing into a cluster of enemy's [*sic*] ships without a grazed plank or a torn piece of canvas to fire her first gun. Here is symbolized the first of naval heroes, with chivalric valour, devoting himself to his country's cause; and yet, says an artist of high repute, 'there is a lack of pictorial materials.' We hope some public-spirited individual, if not the State itself, will show whether this is really the case; for it is almost a national disgrace that there should yet be wanted a picture which, in accuracy of representation, no less than in strength and brilliancy of execution, is calculated to illustrate, and to stand as a lasting memorial of one of the greatest sea-battles that has ever been, or perhaps ever will be fought: a battle to the success of which England at this time owes, if not her political existence, her prosperity, happiness, and exalted station.[19]

Clearly, therefore, none of the many more 'truthful' treatments of Trafalgar by marine artists such as Robert Dodd or Nicholas Pocock met James's exacting standards, presumably because they lacked 'strength and brilliancy of execution'. By contrast, Turner's effort fails miserably in terms of the demand for documentary accuracy that James requires. It is important, I think, that he demands such accuracy from both textual and pictorial history, and in this respect he assumes an equivalence between text and image. He is equally scathing of other written accounts of the battle for their inaccuracies and asks:

If a printed misstatement upon an important point of history may be justifiably set right, have we not an equal privilege over a painted misstatement of the same nature; especially when produced under circumstances the most likely of any to inspire a confidence in its accuracy?[20]

If Turner had got it right, he suggests, he would be that much the greater artist. It is such an evaluation that has determined accounts of this painting ever since. The question, however, for the early twenty-first century just as much as the early nineteenth, is: what was or is Trafalgar? Or what is the 'right' Trafalgar?

James's statement raises extremely interesting issues regarding the relation of text to image in the representation of history. It also, of course, closes down other possible readings of Turner's picture. For if Turner's conflation of different chronological events and his licence with the facts of the battle fail to meet the requirements of *history*, as I have suggested they do broadly meet the academic demands of *history painting*. And, as the painted representation of contemporary history from Benjamin West's *Death of Wolfe* on demonstrated, the demands of history and history painting rarely, if ever, coincided. Here, the pyramidal composition, with the iconic broadside ship above a frieze of figures that refers to themes of triumph and sacrifice, not only conforms to academic requirements for pictorial unity, but echoes the format of both monumental sculpture and the emblematic print. The flag signal of 'England expects every man shall do his duty' (the final word 'Duty' is spelt out in the flags streaming down from the mainmast) is complemented by Nelson's motto 'Palmam qui meruit ferat' floating ghost-like in the water below the union flag – 'Let he who merits it take the palm', presumably of victory or of martyrdom: here it refers to both, in the form of the death of Nelson, signified in the falling foremast carrying his personal admiral's flag, and also in the sacrifice of the dead sailor in the foreground, provocatively juxtaposed next to Nelson's motto, who would have been nearly at eye level in the original high hang of the painting at St James's Palace.[21] This recumbent figure, the oblique angle of the group on the boat and in the water, and the raised arms of the figures beyond recall the composition of Géricault's celebrated *Raft of the Medusa*, suggesting Turner's work not only as a counterpart to Loutherbourg's painting, but also as a British equivalent to the transformation of a contemporary maritime event into full-scale grand manner history painting across the Channel.[22]

It is clearly an attempt to transcend the particularities of the battle and turn them into something of general, philosophical and national significance, as history painting was meant to be. In this sense, it may be regarded as an allegory of the maritime nation through reference to the most prestigious and iconic episode of contemporary maritime history. The painting's failure, then, rests in its falling between the incompatibilities of documentary marine painting on the one hand, and history painting on the other. It needs to be remembered also that Turner was responding to the requirement to produce a pendant to Loutherbourg's painting, which is taken account of in numerous compositional and thematic ways, besides sharing identical dimensions. Thus, for example, the falling foremast of the *Victory* that James so disparages in Turner's painting is, besides its symbolic significance, a visual counterpart to the stricken masts and billowing sails of the principal vessels in Loutherbourg's *First of June*. Turner's picture is, therefore, a sophisticated response to the contemporary history of art, both British and French, as well as of the maritime nation. And, as Opie's, Locker's and others' proposals for naval monuments and galleries indicates, the history of maritime art was becoming increasingly closely tied in ideological terms with the history of Britain. Thus James's comparison of Turner's picture with written histories also demonstrates the degree to which the painting was taken to have a resonance with history in general and with the wider significance of historical discourse in the 1820s, particularly regarding the role of maritime history in the construction of the maritime nation. It needs asking, therefore, what was the nature of historical discourse at this moment?

As Stephen Bann has eloquently demonstrated in *The Clothing of Clio*, history as discourse and scholarly practice was undergoing profound change at this period. In place of the self-consciously rhetorical practices of the eighteenth-century writing of history, there developed a historiography that aimed to be transparent and styleless, 'to show only what actually happened'.[23] Bann links this to a wider cultural shift, in poetry, painting, the novel and other forms, towards an emphasis on cognitive values over rhetorical ones, that had its goal in the form of 'life-like representation'. This implied a turn towards accuracy, authenticity and fidelity as the methodological foundations for restoring history, as it were, to life. Part and parcel of this change in the writing of history was also an increasing sensitivity to the historical condition, the historicity of modern culture. He cites Foucault, however, to the effect that such '"awareness of history, the lively curiosity for the documents of traces which time had left behind" was a reaction to an overpowering sense of loss'.[24]

'Life-like representation' was in this sense a form of compensation for, or attempted recuperation of, the distance of the historical past. The urgency at this date to substantiate and authenticate history through, for example, the presentation of increasingly detailed evidence by reference to primary source material was, somehow paradoxically, predicated on its irretrievability:

> The restoration of the life-like is itself postulated as a response to a sense of loss. In other words, the Utopia of life-like representation depends upon, and reacts to, the fact of death. It is a strenuous attempt to recover, by means which must exceed those of convention, a state which is (and must be) recognized as lost.[25]

Bann's analysis is highly suggestive for the potential interpretations of Turner's painting, centred as it is upon the brilliantly ironic juxtaposition of victory and loss. However, my principal concern here is to argue how the painting needs to be understood also in the light of this paradigm shift in historiography. While Bann's study is cosmopolitan in scope and does not investigate the relation of historiography to nationalism, it is surely not coincidental that the historical self-awareness he identifies – the assertion of historicity – developed at the same time as the increasingly urgent articulation of national identity throughout Europe and America, nor that so much historical discourse of this period, whether textual or visual, was directed towards the investigation and construction of a national past and the 'invention of tradition'.[26] *The Battle of Trafalgar* may certainly be considered as part of this proliferation of national history.

III

At precisely the same time that Turner was completing this picture, two major national naval histories were produced, both in five volumes: James's *Naval History of Great Britain*, already cited, the first edition of which was published in 1822–24; and the competing *Naval History of Great Britain* by Edward Pelham Brenton, 1823–25. These are revealing in the different aims and methods they propose for their respective studies and for history in general. While I am not suggesting any direct correspondence between these texts and Turner's picture (though, as already mentioned, James devotes considerable space to it), they are thus also revealing about the expectations of a work of maritime visual history and, implicitly, about the painting's failure as such a work.

James, who criticized Brenton's supposed innaccuracies severely in the expanded second edition of his book of 1826, was nonetheless highly self-conscious of being a simple historian pitted against Brenton's status as a naval professional, with 'the experience of a post-captain of 20 years standing', and the consequent access to other naval officers for the collection and corroboration of his data.[27] Indeed, being a non-naval man, he feels duty-bound to point out Brenton's errors:

> for who is there, when a naval occurrence is related differently by an unprofessional and a professional writer, that will not pin his faith upon the latter?[28]

He goes on to justify the superiority of his own work on the grounds not only of its greater accuracy, but also of its depth of research, while Brenton's is a case of style over substance. Readers who prefer Brenton's style should

> reflect how much easier it is for a writer, who skims over the surfaces of things and finds little or nothing to start at, to construct well-turned periods, than a writer, who dips deeply into his subject, and stops every now and then to investigate a disputed fact.[29]

James's book, therefore, certainly conforms to the historiographical shift towards 'life-like representation', in Bann's terms. He asserts his objectivity, his reference to foreign (mainly French) sources as well as English ones, and is consistently methodical in his relation of naval events and battles. He is aware of the novelty of attempting to give 'a plain narrative of facts', particularly in a naval history, and is sensitive to the possible accusation of appearing thereby insufficiently patriotic, but is concerned to demonstrate that

> a man may write an impartial naval history, and yet belong to the country the most conspicuous in it. I have my feelings, nevertheless; and, while I esteem the brave of every nation, I glory in recounting the exploits and celebrating the renown of the brave Englishman.[30]

It is particularly significant, therefore, that James denounces Turner's painting as being at the centre of a 'national disgrace' regarding the painted representation of Trafalgar, with the implication that Turner's lack of concern for the 'plain narrative of facts' is somehow disloyal. For James, instead, the 'life-like representation' of history has a nationalistic value, in being indirectly linked via this iconic battle with the nation's 'prosperity, happiness, and exalted station'.

Brenton is equally assertive of his patriotic intent as a writer, but sees the national value of his history in rather different terms. Rather than eliding the authorial voice into a transparent presentation of 'facts', he is openly interpretive and his methodology reflective. His intention is:

> to point out, after giving the history of events the causes of failure and success, with a view to the future benefit of the service and the country.[31]

His book, he hopes, will be of greatest benefit to the 'young and inexperienced officer', who may learn from the lessons of the past,

> thus rendering, as it should do, the page of history conducive to the good of his country, and beneficial to the human race.[32]

In these terms he sees British naval history as a divinely-sanctioned teleology, unfolding the progressive benefits of British maritime imperial power to a dutifully grateful world:

> The most distant nations are hourly reaping the benefit of the philanthropic endeavours of our countrymen to spread and communicate the blessings which we enjoy. The abolition of the slave-trade by the British legislature is the greatest triumph which freedom and civilization ever gained over avarice and barbarity. The empire has reaped, and will continue to reap, the fruits of the generous sacrifice, and the name of Britain and Wilberforce will be revered as long as mankind shall retain the records of their ancestors. Arts and civilization are improving the condition of the savage of New Holland and New Zealand; and the Scriptures, by the industry and self-devotion of our missionaries, have been disseminated, not only in these islands, but over the vast countries of India, Tartary, Persia, and Russia. The power of Britain, therefore, has not been used for the destruction, but for the preservation of the human species.[33]

This is, to say the least, a somewhat rosy account of British imperial history, and it is hardly surprising that Brenton came under fire not just from James but from several other quarters as well for his relaxed attitude to 'facts'.[34] However, he seems to have brushed these attacks aside, in part perhaps because they did not divert from his overall intention in writing history, which was to impart lessons. In this regard, his representation of history, though textual, in significant ways follows more closely the stipulations for history *painting* than those prescribed in the 'life-like representations' of James's meticulous scholarship.

Despite their common grounding in nationalist sentiment and their shared understanding of the national value of maritime history, these authors hardly share the same understanding of the substance of that history: they offer very different accounts of both the battle of the First of June and of Trafalgar. More significantly, they differ completely on the way history should be represented; and this has self-evident implications for its visual representation also, whether in the documentary convention of marine painting or in the adaptation of marine to history painting such as Turner provides. James, again, laments the unreliability for truthful history both of primary sources, even the reports of officers present at an engagement, and also of pictorial representation. He includes no illustrations on the grounds that they would confuse by their inaccuracies: 'Of the scores of engravings of sea-fights that have been published, very few will bear a close investigation.'[35] Rather, these accounts indicate the site of historical discourse at this time to be highly conflicted and conflicting, and suggest that maritime history was itself something of a battleground. In this light, Turner's royal commission to paint the Battle of Trafalgar, pitched among the demands of historical fidelity and authenticity and historical interpretation, between art history (in the form of Loutherbourg) and maritime history, and between 'life-like representation' and history painting, could hardly be other than a failure. But its failure did not simply consist of its deficiencies in the myopic eyes of pedantic, philistine sailors, as the prevailing stereotype, deriving from Ruskin, has it. It has much wider ramifications than that, as I have suggested, to do with the intractability of pinning down the precise significance of Trafalgar and what comprised the history of the maritime nation.

IV

To conclude: in the 1859 preface to a later edition of James's *Naval History* the editor noticed the profound change since James first wrote his history that had been wrought upon the character of maritime warfare by steam power, which he calls the 'most important agent in mechanics that man's ingenuity has yet brought into action'. The introduction of steam had produced a change

> equal to that occasioned by the introduction of gunpowder. History and past experience will cease to be referred to as practical teachers.

The best lessons they can now supply are confined to the examples of skill, courage, and patriotic devotion, never to be surpassed, from which future Nelsons may learn how the battles of that great admiral and his contemporaries were fought and won.[36]

He goes on to suggest what the benefits would have been had steam been available at Trafalgar. Such a passage suggests not only an alternative reading of Turner's *The Fighting Temeraire*, a ship of course involved in the Battle of Trafalgar, which Turner famously showed being towed to her last berth by a steam tug; but it also displays an awareness that the representation of history is contingent upon changes in social, political and technological circumstances. The value of maritime history for the maritime nation is, by this account, substantially changed by the advent of steam, and its practical didactic significance severely reduced. The implication is that the meanings of a visual history, such as Turner's of Trafalgar, are also discursive and variable, offering different values and lessons to different generations, and that the distinction between history and history painting in the representation of the maritime nation is not as easy to make as James and others would have liked to believe.

Notes

1. Hence, for example, the significantly titled Society for the Encouragement of Arts, Manufactures and Commerce, founded in 1754. See also, among numerous contemporary publications, especially David Hume's essays 'Of Refinement in the Arts', 'Of Commerce' and 'Of Luxury': Eugene F. Miller (ed.), *Essays Literary, Moral and Political* (Indianapolis, 1987).
2. An extensive literature has recently developed on this subject. See especially Louise Lippincott, 'Expanding on Portraiture. The Market, the Public, and the Hierarchy of Genres in Eighteenth-Century Britain', in Ann Bermingham and John Brewer (eds), *The Consumption of Culture 1600–1800: Image, Object, Text* (London and New York, 1995), pp. 75–88; John Brewer, '"The Most Polite Age and the Most Vicious." Attitudes Towards Culture as a Commodity, 1660–1800', in ibid., pp. 341–61; John Brewer, *The Pleasures of the Imagination: English Culture in the Eighteenth Century* (London, 1997); John Barrell, *The Political Theory of Painting* (New Haven and London, 1987).
3. See, for example, Sir Joshua Reynolds, edited by Robert R. Wark, *Discourses on Art* (New Haven and London, 1975), 'Discourse VIII'.
4. Algernon Graves, *The Royal Academy of Arts: A Complete Dictionary of Contributors and their Work from its Foundation in 1769 to 1904*, 8 vols (London, 1906), vol. 8, p. 220.
5. Ibid.
6. Helmut von Erffa and Allen Staley, *The Paintings of Benjamin West* (New Haven and London, 1986), p. 222, cat. no. 109. See also Charles Mitchell,

'Benjamin West's *Death of Nelson*', in *Essays in the History of Art Presented to Rudolf Wittkower* (London. 1967), pp. 265–73.

7. Graves, *Royal Academy*, vol. 8, p. 218. West's oil sketch for the monument is now in the collection of the Yale Center for British Art, New Haven.
8. Graves, *Royal Academy*, vol. 8, pp. 218–19.
9. John Opie, *Lectures on Painting delivered at the Royal Academy of Arts: with a Letter on the Proposal for a Public Memorial of the Naval Glory of Great Britain* (London, 1809), p. 174.
10. Ibid., p. 175.
11. Ibid.
12. [Edward Hawke Locker], *Catalogue of the Portraits of Distinguished Naval Commanders, and Representations of their Warlike Achievements, Exhibited in the Naval Gallery of Greenwich Hospital* (London, 1836), p. 4.
13. Ibid.
14. Major John Cartwright, *The Trident; or, the National Policy of Naval Celebration: Describing a Hieronauticon or Naval Temple, with its Appendages, Proposing a Periodical Celebration of Naval Games, and ... the Granting of Triumphs* (London, 1802). See also Alison Yarrington, *Commemoration of the Hero 1800–1864: Monuments to the British Victors of the Napoleonic Wars* (New York and London, 1988).
15. James Stanier Clarke and John MacArthur, *The Life of Admiral Lord Nelson KB* (London, 1809).
16. W.L. Wyllie, *J.M.W. Turner* (London, 1905), pp. 71–2.
17. John Ruskin, *The Harbours of England* (London, 1856), p. 16.
18. See especially Martin Butlin and Evelyn Joll, *The Paintings of J.M.W. Turner*, revised edition (New Haven and London, 1984), pp. 155–7, cat. no. 252.
19. William James, *The Naval History of Great Britain, from the Declaration of War by France, in February 1793; to the Accession of George IV, in January 1820*, 6 vols (2nd edn, London, 1826), vol. 3, pp. 473–4.
20. Ibid., p. 472.
21. My thanks to Gwen Yarker for this observation.
22. It is virtually inconceivable that Turner did not see Géricault's painting when it was exhibited in London in 1821: see Lee Johnson, 'The "Raft of the Medusa" in Great Britain', *Burlington Magazine* 96 (1954): 249–54.
23. Stephen Bann, *The Clothing of Clio: A study of the Representation of History in Nineteenth-Century Britain and France* (Cambridge, 1984), p. 8 and ff.
24. Ibid., p. 14.
25. Ibid., p. 15.
26. See particularly, Eric Hobsbawm and Terence Ranger (eds), *The Invention of Tradition* (Cambridge, 1983).
27. James, *Naval History* (1826), vol. 1, p. xxxvi.
28. Ibid., xxxv.
29. Ibid., xxxvii.
30. James, *Naval History* (1822–4), vol. 3 (1823), p. x.
31. Edward Pelham Brenton, *The Naval History of Great Britain, from the Year MDCCLXXXIII to MDCCCXXII*, 5 vols (London, 1823–25), vol. 1, p. viii.
32. Ibid.
33. Ibid., p. xiii.

34. See, in particular, *Statement of a Correspondence which has taken place between Admiral Sir George Montagu, G.C.B., and Capt. Edward Pelham Brenton, subsequent to the publication of Sir George Montagu's Refutation of the 'Incorrect Statements, and Injurious Insinuations, contained in Captain Brenton's Naval History'* (London, 1823); and [John Colpoys], *A Letter to Vice-Admiral Sir Thomas Byam Martin, K.C.B. containing an Account of the Mutiny of the Fleet at Spithead, in the Year 1797, in correction of that given in Captain Brenton's Naval History of the last War* (London, 1825).

35. James, *Naval History* (1822–24), vol. 1, p. xxxiii.

36. James, *The Naval History of Great Britain … A New Edition*, 6 vols (London, 1859), vol. 1, pp. vii–viii.

8
Commemorating Trafalgar: Public Celebration and National Identity[1]

Marianne Czisnik

Since the famous day of 21 October 1805 the battle of Trafalgar has been commemorated in Britain, particularly on its anniversaries. Such commemorations reached a peak in the 15 years leading up to the centenary of the great battle. This chapter will first give an overview of the development of these commemorations until c. 1890; it will then examine the outburst of interest in the battle of Trafalgar at the end of the nineteenth century and finally consider what became of the invented tradition of Trafalgar Day in the course of the twentieth century. The development of the commemoration of Trafalgar was linked to the development of the commemoration of its greatest hero, Nelson. Both went out of and back into fashion in parallel movements throughout the nineteenth century. The years 1805 to 1808 saw an intense grief for Nelson together with a glorification of Trafalgar. The impact of the event on the British public was so strong that it lent itself to being exploited commercially and politically for propagandistic purposes.

I

One commercial form of commemoration of the battle of Trafalgar was the panorama. The new art form of panorama, developed at the end of the eighteenth century, was particularly suited to representations of battles. These representations, however, sometimes reflected more the excitement of the event than historical accuracy. While the well-established panorama in Leicester Square offered a depiction of the battle of Trafalgar, a competitor combined in a 'Grand Nautical Moving

Spectacle of the Naumachia' the different 'Splendid Victories achieved by Lord Nelson, with the Elements and Ships in Motion ... depicting the Havock and Destruction which took place, with all the majestic Horrors which characterised those great Events.'[2]

Other commercial ventures preferred a more intimate kind of commemoration, inspired particularly by the preparations for Nelson's funeral and the elaborate event itself (including the lying-in-state in Greenwich, processions by water and by land, and the interment in St Paul's Cathedral in London).[3] One of these businesses was 'Mrs. Salmon's Wax Work', which included a scene of the death of Nelson in its exhibition. Madame Tussaud's waxworks produced their first Nelson figure at about the same time and they carried Nelson's waxen image across the country on travelling exhibitions. Westminster Abbey, too, commissioned a wax figure of Nelson. The abbey took this step in order to compete with St Paul's Cathedral in attractiveness. The abbey was suffering severe financial losses at this time, whereas St Paul's Cathedral attracted curious visitors first with its preparations for Nelson's funeral and then with his grave. The work that wax portraitist Catherine Andras produced for the abbey pleased not only Lady Hamilton, but also helped the abbey's 'tourist revenue' to recover.[4]

In the main, patriotic references to Nelson were isolated examples and did not add up to a formal commemoration. The College of Arms planned the creation of an 'order of merit to be conferred on 21 October' (the day of the battle of Trafalgar) and hoped to initiate an 'annual ritual' of 'pageantry to St. Paul's', but nothing came of this proposal.[5] It was the navy which most endeavoured to keep the spirit of Nelson alive and to conjure it up in the moment of battle. The Admiralty let it be known, in the same month in which they had received the news of Trafalgar, that they had decided to lay 'down a first-rate man of war ... to be named after' Nelson. According to *The Times* they thereby paid 'the highest tribute in their power'.[6] Officers who had served under Nelson spurred their men on by reminding them of Nelson. On entering into the battle of San Domingo, in 1806, a band played 'God save the King!' and 'Nelson of the Nile' and Captain Keats 'brought out a portrait of Nelson, which he hung on the mizzen stay, where it remained throughout the battle untouched by the enemy's shot, though dashed with the blood and brains of a seaman who was killed close beside it'. In the approach to the battle of Lissa, in 1811, Captain Hoste appealed to his crews with the signal 'Remember Nelson'.[7]

As the Napoleonic Wars wore on, however, and Trafalgar did not appear to have had much impact on its course, the public's interest in the event diminished accordingly. Although the commemoration was briefly revived at the end of the war in 1815, together with the jubilations accorded to the victory at Waterloo, Trafalgar was soon neglected in public memory. This neglect was probably reinforced by Nelson's fall from grace, which was caused by the publication of some of his letters to Lady Hamilton in 1814.[8] There was not much chance to appreciate Trafalgar itself in greater depth either, since a lack of tactical study did not allow contemporaries any better understanding of the event.[9] Trafalgar was thus reduced in the public estimation to a dashing hero's lucky success.

Only within the Royal Navy was the memory of Trafalgar kept alive, mostly by veterans of the battle. As time passed and no other naval engagement managed to surpass Trafalgar in importance, the battle started to become an important part of the identity of the Royal Navy. But as the last participants of the battle began to pass away and members of the rising generation were wondering how to follow Nelson, Trafalgar started to figure more prominently in the national consciousness. J.M.W. Turner sensed the spirit of the time and anticipated a whole movement when he painted his watercolour of 'Yarmouth Sands' in 1830. The painting shows the Nelson monument at Yarmouth towering over a beach, on which sailors arrange improvised ship models into battle formation, while women and boys look on 'absorbing the Nelson legend'.[10] In Turner's wake variously reproduced paintings show survivors of Trafalgar with a portrait of Nelson, or Greenwich Pensioners celebrating Trafalgar and discussing its plan (see Plate 11).[11]

The desire for recognition of the importance of the Royal Navy was therefore often connected with claiming the importance of Trafalgar. This naval interest in commemorating Trafalgar and Nelson found its expression most notably in the years after 1839, when a subscription was started for the erection of a monument to Nelson on the newly named Trafalgar Square in London. This project was in great part initiated by veterans of Trafalgar and their families as well as friends of Nelson's, most notably Captain, now Admiral, Hardy.[12] The erection of the column caused a rise in production of material artefacts in the 1840s that focused particularly on Nelson as the hero of Trafalgar.[13] The song 'Death of Nelson' by Braham, first performed in 1811, was revived. It gained such popularity that it was adapted in the 1860s and 1870s for a soap advertisement about *The Death of King Dirt* and a political parody *'Twas in Trafalgar Square*, which criticized police intervention against a demonstration in Trafalgar Square.[14] The emergence of the serious study of naval history from the 1880s onwards gave the commemoration of Trafalgar a new direction. In their scholarly approach historians further pursued the connection of Trafalgar and Nelson and used both as focal points of their study and thus of the representation of the Royal Navy's past.

This combination of Trafalgar and Nelson was also used for propagandist effect in 'The Royal Naval Exhibition, 1891', which attracted a wide public audience. This exhibition was probably the largest ever display of paintings, prints and relics of Trafalgar and Nelson. Aiming to bring the importance of the Royal Navy before the public, the organizers 'restricted [their display] to purely national objects'.[15] Although the exhibition covered several centuries of naval history and included contemporary matters, it had a particular focus on Trafalgar and Nelson. Apart from the huge 'Nelson Gallery', it provided a model of the *Victory* and a 'Panorama of the Battle of Trafalgar'. In the full size reproduction of the *Victory* visitors could contemplate a waxen re-creation of Nelson's death scene on the orlop deck, produced by Mr Tussaud. The Trafalgar panorama, a 'private speculation' by a German, gave its visitors a supposedly historically accurate impression of the battle as seen from *Victory*'s quarterdeck. Those who entered the 'polygonal building' looked 'straight ahead towards the bow, and there, in the middle of the quarterdeck, you observe the great scene on account of which the picture was painted. You look upon Lord Nelson at the moment that he has fallen mortally wounded.'[16] In the Nelson Gallery of the Royal Naval Exhibition, which displayed pictures and relics, quantity appears to have counted for more than quality. Though eminent specialists sat on the 'Arts Committee' and tried to find authentic pieces, they included some items of doubtful authenticity. A sword which Nelson supposedly wore at Trafalgar was on display, whereas, in fact, he did not wear a sword on that occasion. Pieces of furniture were so numerous that they prompted a contemporary to comment: 'It is simply a physical impossibility that [Nelson's cabin on board the *Victory*] should have contained all the "favourite chairs", "arm-chairs", "chairs and beds combined", and "folding bedsteads" here exhibited as having been used by Nelson at sea.'[17]

II

At the end of the nineteenth century, political organizations went beyond exhibitions in seeking to exploit the significance of the battle of Trafalgar for the country's national identity. The first of a series of associations to do so was the Primrose League (founded in 1884), which propagated Conservative ideas in a pleasant social setting. In its different 'habitations' evening entertainments were organized, at which songs, such as Braham's 'Death of Nelson', were played and 'magic lanterns and *tableaux vivants*

... displayed a series of images of imperial splendour such as ... Nelson on the Victory'.[18] Women, children and all social classes were included and their different interests catered for. A 'Question Paper set for Juveniles' in 1900 contained questions such as: 'Give a brief account of the great naval battle of Trafalgar, and the death of Lord Nelson.'[19] While the battle of Trafalgar and Nelson figured merely as one of many elements of national identity within the patriotic repertoire of the Primrose League, their commemoration took centre stage within the propagandist efforts of the Navy League. This association, bearing a portrait of Nelson in its crest, was founded at the end of 1894 as a pressure group promoting the interests of the navy. Similar to some other leagues, it attempted to further national strength against a perceived external danger. More specifically it argued for the strengthening of the Royal Navy by a variety of means, such as building dreadnoughts and ensuring the supply of a rising generation of British sailors.[20] Like the Primrose League, the Navy League also tried to attract members from all strata of society, from both sexes (a 'Ladies' branch' was founded as early as 1895) and particularly from the younger generation (whole schools were enlisted as members).[21] Anne Summers observes that the Navy League and other 'Leagues grew continuously in numbers and vigour despite their inability to influence government policy; it is arguable, therefore, that for many of their members they fulfilled functions quite other than those outlined in their official literature'.[22]

One of the greatest non-political attractions of the Navy League was the celebration of Trafalgar Day (21 October). In 1895, following the suggestion of the navalist and journalist Arnold White, the Navy League laid a wreath to the memory of Nelson at the base of Nelson's monument in Trafalgar Square on Trafalgar Day. Supported by Arnold White's letter to the press about this 'national demonstration', the event attracted some attention in the newspapers.[23] This was the beginning of a tradition. Until then there appears never to have been any regular habit of celebrating Trafalgar Day outside the Royal Navy, although it had been suggested on the day of Nelson's funeral that the date should be entered 'on the ever-open and wide-spread folios of the British Calendar ... to the remembrance of all ranks' and the anniversary was deliberately chosen as the date for several Nelson-related or generally commemorative events.[24] When the Navy League celebrated Trafalgar Day more lavishly in the following year, investing £50, instead of £10, in the decoration of Nelson's column with wreaths and garlands of evergreens, its members were surprised by the impact of their own celebration. In the *Navy League Journal* they called it a 'triumphant success', partly because it was celebrated in different parts of the country, but mostly because of the demonstration in Trafalgar Square itself:

> It was as if the people had arisen to answer those who say: 'They do not care ...' The hundreds of thousands who for six days from morning till night defiled before the column have shown the unsuspected strength of feeling latent in British hearts. They have shown that Britons do care, that they have not forgotten, that they are still capable of devotion and self-sacrifice. Trafalgar – the very name, with its stirring associations, is a trumpet-call to the nation to do its duty. ... Some, of course, came only to look. But the great mass of the people in the Square were pilgrims, rather than mere spectators. And those who were mere spectators must have learnt much from their gazings. They would realize that the British Navy still regards Nelson as its chosen hero.

The Navy League managed to sell 'an immense mass of literature' on the occasion, but did not otherwise profit materially from the success.[25] The Executive Committee called a 'special meeting' on 22 October 1896 in order to 'consider what steps should be taken to reap the benefits of the demonstration on Trafalgar Day'.[26] They decided to enlarge their League, including its *Journal*. In the meantime private businessmen used the opportunity to make money by selling fake reprints of *The Times* of 7 November 1805 with the news of the battle of Trafalgar and Nelson's death in it.[27]

Gerald Jordan assumes that the Navy League had two aims: to attempt 'to create a popular cult of the admiral and revive interest in the navy', but this overstates the Navy League's interest in Nelson since the admiral was merely a propaganda tool to enlist support for a stronger navy in terms of ships and recruits.[28] The Navy League would readily have dropped any reference to Nelson, had he not served their League's purpose. The Executive Committee twice discussed giving up the Trafalgar Day celebrations, in 1900 and in 1906.[29] On the first occasion, they lowered their investment in the decoration of Nelson's column from £100 in the previous three years to a mere £20,[30] without any impact on the popularity of the event. *The Times* remarked that, though the meagre decoration 'caused some disappointment to many in the large crowds', 'it in no way diminished the interest taken in the celebration'. Since the crowds were 'as large as ever', the report concluded: 'the patriotic endeavours of the Navy League to bring about a national celebration of Trafalgar Day have borne fruit'.[31] By then Trafalgar celebrations were held in a great number of towns and cities across Britain; particularly large ones were held in Liverpool.

The Navy League had reason, however, to feel uneasy about the success of its Trafalgar Day celebrations. The early protests from the 'Increased Armaments Protest Committee' did not greatly disturb the Navy League which responded with public statements in the press about its aims, so that the success of the Trafalgar Day celebrations was not affected.[32] The Navy League took French sensibilities much more seriously, however. The *Navy League Journal* printed, next to the overwhelmingly positive response recorded in the British press, those hostile responses to the massive Trafalgar Day celebrations of 1896 printed in nine different French newspapers.[33] In 1897 Arthur Conan Doyle suggested that Trafalgar Day should be exchanged for Nelson's birthday and thus become a less offensive 'Nelson Day'. This caused a heated discussion in *The Times* and Arnold White attacked the suggestion in the *Navy League Journal*.[34] In the end, neither date nor name of the festivity was changed. The discussion, however, did produce J.R. T[hursfield]'s comment that the 'efforts to manufacture a national anniversary ... have done not a little to vulgarize a great and solemn thought'. Defenders of the celebration maintained that 'Captain Mahan has made Nelson live again for the student, but "the man in the street" needs a shorter and sharper reminder'.[35] With the increasing popularity of the celebration of Trafalgar Day public comment on the event appears to have become ever more positive. In 1898 the *Glasgow Herald* stated explicitly 'that whereas last year several men of influence in politics and religion protested against this annual celebration as likely to offend French susceptibilities, on this occasion not a single voice has been raised against the keeping of the anniversary'.[36] In 1900, the year in which the Navy League had so drastically curbed its expenditure on the Trafalgar Day celebrations, its Executive Committee 'decided that they would dedicate one wreath to the French and Spaniards with a suitable inscription'.[37] As a result the Navy League commemorated all French and Spanish dead of the battle, while on the British side only Nelson was commemorated. This does not appear to have troubled anybody, since the practice remained the same until the First World War, when the League started to commemorate the recently dead.[38]

The propagandist use of Trafalgar carried with it a constant financial burden for the Navy League. In order to rid itself of this problem the Navy League called for contributions and finally, in 1909, created a special 'Trafalgar Fund'.[39] This fund attracted so many contributions that the Executive Committee was able to invest the money in other projects, mainly their newly created 'Boys' Naval Brigades' (the predecessors of the

Sea Cadets). After three years the League itself borrowed the considerable amount of £300 from the Trafalgar Fund; and this while it was still spending only about £50 on each of the annual Trafalgar Day celebrations from 1901 (except the celebrations for the centenary in 1905, for which it was ready to spend £200).[40] Since so many people were ready to invest in the 'Trafalgar Fund', rather than the Navy League itself, it appears that many were more attracted to the commemoration of Trafalgar and Nelson than to the political ideas of the Navy League. Indeed, the *Manchester Guardian* commented that 'a little more ancestor worship would do us as a nation no harm ... [and it] regretted that the public Nelson celebrations should have depended so much on an organisation identified in the public mind with indiscreet and often unintelligent advocacy of increased naval expenditure'.[41]

III

The public celebration of Nelson reached a peak with the centenary of Nelson's most famous battle, Trafalgar Day 1905, for which the Navy League had arranged a short 'semi-religious' ceremony. Though only a part of the ceremony was overtly religious (the reading of a prayer), the whole event was hugely indebted to Christian symbolism of the saviour, reminiscent of Easter, including the notion of death and 'resurrection'. A journalist of *The Times* described the scene in Trafalgar Square, which was filled with a 'sea of people':

> In silence all waited while the hands of St Martin's clock crept round to half-past 2, ... At the first sound of the chime of the half-hour the flags at the four corners [of Nelson's monument], Union Jack, White Ensign, Red and Blue Ensigns, were solemnly lowered to half-mast, all men uncovering their heads, while the band of the Queen's Westminsters played the 'Death of Nelson'. As the music died away Bishop Welldon read the prayer 'To the memory of Nelson' – the preposition perhaps, might have been more prudently chosen ... the bugles sounded the reveille ... and, as the stirring call was blown slow and loud, the flags went up again. The ritual ended with the singing of the National Anthem ... followed by cheers which rang and echoed and thundered around the square.[42]

The *Navy League Journal* made the Easter-like allusion even clearer when commenting on the end of the short ceremony: 'The bitterness of death was overpast. The prayer was answered, and God had given us the victory.'[43] Other organizations all over Britain and the empire joined the Navy League in contributing their own festivities to the centenary of Trafalgar. The massive commemorations included church services, concerts (regularly including Braham's 'The Death of Nelson'), dinners and, in Liverpool, even a public procession led by the Lord Mayor.[44] 'Mssrs. Metzler published 25,000 copies of five songs, patriotic in their nature' for the event, postcards were produced for and of the different events across Britain, journals published articles and pictures of Nelson or Trafalgar and the souvenir industry profited from all these celebrations (Plate 12).[45]

Jordan, nevertheless, maintains that the centenary of Trafalgar was a 'failure'. He measures this 'failure' mostly by the Navy League's inability to achieve its main objectives, to 'revive interest in the navy', to include the working classes in their membership and to 'inculcate bourgeois values'.[46] Moreover, Jordan maintains that Nelson was converted into an upper-class figure, 'a serious, staid, and aloof muscular Christian', and thus divorced from the working classes. He seeks to maintain his view by asserting that '[f]or most of them [the working classes] the Nelson message was simply irrelevant in the daily struggle for survival'. This claim ignores the presence of so many members of the working classes at the Trafalgar Day celebrations. Jordan assumes that the masses who crowded Trafalgar Square were there as mere spectators, like crowds who attended football matches, rather than being genuinely interested in honouring Nelson's memory.[47] He denies the working classes the ability to express their own tastes, opinions and allegiances. It is admittedly difficult to assess the motivations of the assembled masses at these commemorations and one must not assume that their views were the same as those who organized these events. Nonetheless, the desire of the assembled spectators actively to participate (by silently waiting, taking off their hats, cheering) clearly indicates that the event had some kind of meaning for them. Perhaps admiration for Nelson and a desire for national unity explain why the Navy League's celebrations attracted more people than did the League's political ideas.

Jordan also claims that the centenary celebration on Trafalgar Square 'was marked by Admiralty disapproval and the absence of any official naval contingent'.[48] The lack of official support, however, should not be interpreted as proof of Admiralty disapproval of the event. The then First Lord of the Admiralty, John Arbuthnot Fisher, certainly approved of it. He made his admiration for Nelson and his appreciation of Trafalgar Day public, when he insisted on being installed as First Lord of the Admiralty, in 1904, not earlier than 'on Trafalgar Day!' The significance of this choice was well understood at the time, when a cartoon in the *Daily Mirror* showed Fisher about to enter the Admiralty and Nelson about to climb down from his column, commenting: 'I was on my way down to lend them a hand myself, but if Jacky Fisher's taking on the job there's no need for me to be nervous. I'll get back on my pedestal.'[49] Fisher contributed a preface about Nelson to a book that Arnold White, the initiator of the Trafalgar Day celebrations, wrote for the centenary with E. Hallam Moorhouse.[50] Fisher had also learned years before how to use journalistic pressure, particularly that exerted by Arnold White, in order to achieve his political aims.[51] Though clearly interested in exploiting Trafalgar and Nelson, Fisher, as in his earlier propagandist co-operations with White, appears to have preferred to give the impression that the Admiralty reacted to popular pressure rather than making propaganda itself.

The Trafalgar celebrations became ever more focused on Nelson and detached from current issues of naval policy. Among the few who voiced any doubts about or even criticism of the Trafalgar Day celebrations was the reputable author of naval works, F.T. Jane, who claimed there was 'Too Much Nelson'. He argued, 'I deplore and am opposed to the Nelson cult', because 'victories of the future are not to be won by dwelling on the glories of a dead past'. He went on: 'The theory that the British sailor will fight any better because "England expects every man to do his duty" is printed on the handsteering wheel and around the ward-room hatchway is pure and unadulterated moonshine.'[52] The Navy League appeared unimpressed by such criticism and began to personalize its celebrations even more by referring to the 'Nelson Centenary' and 'Nelson Day', instead of Trafalgar Day.[53]

As the names of Trafalgar and Nelson were developing into a trademark of national identity, they also started to attract commercial users. With the growth of brand marketing and imagery in newspapers, Nelson was beginning to be used to sell the usual products of early advertising: soap, washing powder and pills 'for all derangements of the Stomach'. Sometimes only Nelson's portrait was used. In other cases some reference to his name or to his fame or to 'England expects' was made, as in: 'Nelson the Hero of Trafalgar and Pears Soap Have Become the Most Familiar Names in the English Language' or 'England expects that every man this day will do his duty and take Beecham's Pills'.[54]

IV

The commemoration of Trafalgar on 21 October was maintained through the years of the First World War, though now usually combined with some references to recent events, such as: 'I rely with confidence upon the loyal and united efforts of all my subjects. The King.'[55] Although celebrations of Trafalgar Day have lost prominence more recently, some remnants of the tradition, invented by the Navy League, have survived. Hundreds of Sea Cadets (successors to the members of the Boys' Naval Brigades and the only remnant of the now defunct Navy League) still parade in Trafalgar Square every 21 October. At these events wreaths are laid, bands of male and female cadets play, a short service is held and Nelson's last prayer is read. In Portsmouth, the Sea Cadets and the Royal Navy join in a commemoration and take part in a traditional 'Seafarers' Service' at Portsmouth Cathedral. In Edinburgh, Nelson's signal is hoisted every 21 October (unless it is a Sunday) on the local Nelson Monument, overlooking great parts of the city. Trafalgar Dinners are held by different clubs and societies all over Britain, and these always include a toast to 'The Immortal Memory'.[56]

It is difficult to say when specific Trafalgar-related traditions within the navy originated and how they have been observed over the last 200 years. The tradition of giving a toast to 'The Immortal Memory' on Trafalgar Day in officers' messes appears to have been observed continuously since Nelson's death and the wording of the toast can be traced back to November 1805.[57] Ordinary sailors (not only in Britain) are said to commemorate Nelson, most of them unknowingly, in their dress. The three white stripes on their blue collar are supposedly there to commemorate Nelson's victories at the Nile, Copenhagen and Trafalgar. The black silk handkerchief draped round the opening of the sailor's jumper, over his chest, was originally worn around the neck and it is said that the men were ordered for Nelson's funeral 'to drape the handkerchief round the V-opening of the jumper, and tie it with a small tape at the bottom, to keep it in its place'. Admiral Kerr commented in 1932: 'The order was never rescinded, and the men continue to mourn Nelson and all that he stood for, week after week, month after month, and year after year, until it has become a permanent memorial to the best-loved leader that any navy has produced.'[58]

Trafalgar has remained in the public memory thanks in great part to the traditions invented in the later nineteenth century. The recent commemorations of the bicentenary have shown how much public interest there still is in the battle of Trafalgar. In the political sphere, since the Second World War, Trafalgar has rarely been used to represent the navy or notions of national identity, however.[59] It appears that, as when the Navy League tried to exploit the commemoration of Trafalgar for its purposes, the memory of the battle has gained such a broad significance in terms of national unity that it will not easily convert into a specific political message.

Notes

1. This chapter is taken from my doctoral thesis 'Admiral Nelson. Image and Icon' (University of Edinburgh, 2004), which I wrote under the supervision of Professor H.T. Dickinson. Parts of this chapter have been used in chapter 8 of my book *Horatio Nelson: A Controversial Hero* (London, 2005) and in 'The Navy League's Invention of Trafalgar Day', *Trafalgar Chronicle* 15 (2005): 217–29. I am grateful to Dr Frances Dow for her comments.
2. Richard D. Altick, *The Shows of London* (Cambridge, MA, and London, 1978), pp. 97, 136.
3. For the impact of the funeral of Nelson see my *Horatio Nelson* (London, 2005), pp. 3–14.
4. Altick, *Shows of London*, p. 436.
5. Timothy Jenks, 'Contesting the Hero: The Funeral of Admiral Lord Nelson', *Journal of British Studies* 39 (2000): 422–53, at 433.
6. *The Times*, 27 November 1805.
7. Entries of Richard Goodwin Keats and William Hoste in Leslie Stephen and Sidney Lee (eds), *The Dictionary of National Biography. Founded in 1882 by George Smith ... From the Earliest Times to 1900*, 22 vols (Oxford, 1885–1901, reprint 1959–1960), vol. 9, 1297, and vol. 10, 1178 (both contributions are by John Knox Laughton); I am grateful to Jane Knight for alerting me to the note about Captain Keats.
8. Czisnik, *Horatio Nelson*, pp. 63–6, 108.
9. Ibid., pp. 39–40.
10. Judy Egerton, *Turner. The Fighting Temeraire. With a Technical Examination of the Painting by Martin Wyld and Ashok Roy* (series: 'Making and Meaning'; London: National Gallery Publications, 1995), p. 71.
11. Pieter van der Merwe (ed.), *Nelson, An Illustrated History* (London, 1995), p. 58 (Watercolour by S.P. Denning, after John Burnet's oil of Greenwich Pensioners on Trafalgar Day 1835, painted for the Duke of Wellington, showing among others Nelson's former servant, Tom Allen, who shows a picture of Nelson); Lily Lambert McCarthy, *Remembering Nelson* ([Portsmouth]: privately published in the United Kingdom, 1995), pp. 142–3 (no. 133, print with 'Greenwich Pensioners. Commemorating the Battle of Trafalgar' assembled around a plan of the battle, 1836); *The Graphic*, 1 March 1879 (print showing surviving officers of the battle of Trafalgar with death scene and portrait of Nelson in the background).
12. Rodney Mace, *Trafalgar Square: Emblem of Empire* (London, 1976), p. 57.
13. Czisnik, *Horatio Nelson*, p. 116.
14. The original 'The Death of Nelson' was first published as Finale to the 2nd Act of: 'The Americans, A Comic Opera, in Three Acts, Performing with Universal Applause at the Theatre Royal Lyceum. Written by S. Arnold Esq. The Music Composed by M.P. King & Mr. Braham' (London, [1811]) [hereafter: Arnold/ Braham]; 'The Death of King Dirt. And Triumph of "Borax", Health & Beauty. *A Cosmetic Revolution* since The Death of Nelson. Arranged To the Original Air

by "AAG". For The Patent Borax Company' (Birmingham, [c. 1880]) [hereafter: Borax]; Geoffrey Thorn, "Twas in Trafalgar Square. Humorous Parody on "The Death of Nelson"' (London, [1888]).

15. [Anon.], *Official Catalogue and Guide [to the Royal Naval Exhibition]* (London, 1891), p. xxxiv.

16. [Anon.], *Royal Naval Exhibition 1891. The Illustrated Handbook and Souvenir* (London, 1891), pp. 30–2.

17. Ibid., p. 11.

18. Martin Pugh, *The Tories and the People 1880–1935* (Oxford, 1985), pp. 27, 29 (quoting a report about 'a typical evening in January 1888'); Martin Pugh, *The Making of Modern British Politics, 1867–1939* (Oxford, 1993), p. 56.

19. Pugh, *Tories and the People*, p. 214.

20. W. Mark Hamilton, 'The "New Navalism" and the British Navy League, 1895–1914', *Mariner's Mirror* 64 (1978): 37–44, at 37–8; Anne Summers, 'The Character of Edwardian Nationalism: Three Popular Leagues', in P. Kennedy and A. Nicholls (eds), *Nationalist and Racialist Movements in Britain and Germany before 1914* (London, 1981), pp. 68–87, at 73.

21. Hamilton, '"New Navalism"', pp. 39–42; Summers, 'Character of Edwardian Nationalism', pp. 69, 76; *Navy League Journal* 1, no. 6 (December 1895).

22. Summers, 'Character of Edwardian Nationalism', p. 84.

23. Sea Cadet Corps [hereafter: SCC], Minutes of the Executive Committee of the Navy League, vol. B, p. 111 (13 July 1896).

24. *The Times*, 9 January 1806; The laying of the foundation stone to the Nelson monument in Edinburgh in 1806, the opening to the public of the Nelson monument in Dublin in 1809 and Queen Victoria's visit to the *Victory* in 1844 are examples of such events.

25. *Navy League Journal* 1, no. 17 (November 1896): 1 (I, 131).

26. SCC, Minutes of the Executive Committee of the Navy League, vol. B, pp. 111 (£10 in 1895), 126 (£50 in 1896), 140 ('special meeting').

27. *The Times*, 24 October 1896 (p. 9).

28. Gerald Jordan, 'Admiral Nelson and the Concept of Patriotism: The Trafalgar Centenary, 1905', in William B. Cogar (ed.), *Naval History: The Seventh Symposium of the US Academy* (Wilmington, DE, 1988), pp. 143–55, at p. 143.

29. SCC, Minutes of the Executive Committee of the Navy League, vol. F, p. 3 (17 September 1900), vol. L/12, p. 4 (8 October 1906).

30. SCC, Minutes of the Executive Committee of the Navy League, vol. C, pp. 81 (£100 voted for 1897-decorations), 99 (only £90 spent in 1897); vol. D, p. 111 (£100 voted for 1898-decorations); vol. E, p. 100 (£100 voted for 1899-decorations); vol. F, p. 7 (£20 voted for 1900-decorations).

31. *The Times*, 22 October 1900 (p. 8).

32. SCC, Minutes of the Executive Committee of the Navy League, vol. B, p. 149 (26 October 1896).

33. *Navy League Journal* 1, no. 17 (November 1896): 7 (1, p. 137); a tenth French newspaper quoted, *Le Temps*, appears to have remained fairly neutral on the issue.

34. *The Times*, 20 October 1897 (p. 12, first letter from A. Conan Doyle); 22 October 1897 (p. 8, critical response from Admiral R.V. Hamilton); 23 October 1897

(p. 11, second letter from A. Conan Doyle and letter from Norwood Young in support of Doyle); 25 October 1897 (p. 7, response from J.R. T[hursfield] against Doyle); 27 October 1897 (p. 11, response from a member of the 'Ladies' Grand Council, Primrose League); *Navy League Journal* 1, no. 29 (November 1897): 2 (1, p. 268, Arnold White's examples of French naval armament which were obviously regarded as 'insensibilities' towards Britain).

35. *The Times*, 25 October 1897, p. 7; 'J.R.T.' was attacked (in three letters) as well as defended (in one letter) for this remark: *The Times*, 26 (p. 6) and 27 (p. 11, quoted passage) October 1897.
36. Quoted in *Navy League Journal* 3 (November 1898): 166.
37. SCC, Minutes of the Executive Committee of the Navy League, vol. F, pp. 7–8 (24 September 1900); the dedication of the wreath in the end read: 'Respect and Homage To the memory of the gallant sailors of France and Spain, who fell fighting at Trafalgar, October 21, 1805' (*Navy League Journal* 5, November 1900: 180).
38. The vast majority of wreaths were dedicated to the memory of Nelson, sometimes together with the memory of an ancestor of those who had contributed the wreath, on a few occasions only to such an ancestor; among the dozens, if not hundreds of inscriptions of wreaths, I have found only one which included British sailors: 'In memory of those who fought and those who fell at the glorious battle of Trafalgar ...' (*Navy League Journal* 5, November 1900: 181).
39. *Navy League Journal* 6 (September 1901): 160 (first call for contributions); SCC, Minutes of the Executive Committee of the Navy League, vol. O/15, p. 20 (first mention of the 'Trafalgar Day Special Fund', which is referred to in the minutes with various names).
40. SCC, Minutes of the Executive Committee of the Navy League, vol. P/17, pp. 60, 73, 75 and vol. [Q]/17a, p. 103 (means from the Trafalgar Fund used for branches of the Boys' Naval Brigades); vol. [Q]/17a, p. 125 (loan from Trafalgar Fund for Navy League); the amounts for the Trafalgar Day celebrations can be found in: vol. F, p. 137 (£50 for 1901), vol. G, p. 154 (£50 for 1902), vol. H, p. 143 (£50 for 1903), vol. I/9, p. 6 (£50 for 1904), vol. J/10, p. 85 (£200 for 1905 voted), vol. J/10, pp. 92–3 (final amount for 1905 settled, but not stated), vol. L/12, p. 129 (£50 for 1906), [I have not found the amounts for the years 1907–11] vol. R/18, p. 83 (£55 for 1913).
41. Jordan, 'Admiral Nelson and the Concept of Patriotism', p. 150, quoting from the *Manchester Guardian*, 23 October 1905.
42. *The Times*, 23 October 1905, p. 10; *Navy League Journal* 10 (November 1905): 273, estimated that '20,000 men and women and children were in the square, whilst it may be observed that it was estimated that the queue formed on Sunday, the 22nd, of the people wishing to see the Nelson column was from one to three miles in length. It took an hour and twenty minutes to pass from one end round the column, and it was estimated that rather more than seven thousand people per hour passed a given point.'
43. *Navy League Journal* 10 (November 1905): 273–4; at the 'Patriotic Concert at the Royal Horticultural Hall', also organized by the Navy League, the resurrection motif was again used: 'Nelson lives' (ibid., 280).

44. *The Times*, 23 October 1905 (pp. 5, 10–12); another organization that showed particular eagerness to celebrate the day was the 'British and Foreign Sailors' Society', which opened a 'Nelson Centenary Memorial Fund' for sailors' homes abroad and which organized a concert in the Royal Albert Hall on Trafalgar Day 1905 (*The Times*, 12 August, 14 September, 11, 13, 14, 19, 20, 23 October 1905).

45. *The Times*, 14 October 1905, p. 6; illustrations of such postcards can be found in: David Shannon, *Horatio Nelson 1758–1805. A Catalogue of Picture Postcards* (The Nelson Society, 1987), pp. 23 (nos A–D), 24 (nos A and B), 29 (no. A); *Pearson's Magazine*, October 1905 (entirely dedicated to Nelson and Trafalgar); for the production of material artefacts see chapter 13.

46. Jordan, 'Admiral Nelson and the Concept of Patriotism', pp. 143–5; similarly: pp. 147–8.

47. Ibid., pp. 149, 153–4.

48. Ibid., p. 151.

49. Arthur Marder (ed.), *'Fear God and Dread Nought'. The Correspondence of Admiral of the Fleet Lord Fisher of Kilverstone*, 3 vols (London, 1952, 1956, 1959), vol. i, p. 320.

50. Arnold White and E. Hallam Moorhouse, *Nelson and the Twentieth Century* (London, 1905), pp. vii–xiii. The authors were legally barred from disclosing Fisher's name (ibid., p. v), but Fisher himself included a hint as to who he was in the remark: 'By a pure chance (but a delightful one!) from the place where this is now being written [his office in the Admiralty] one can see nothing else but the figure of Nelson on his column in Trafalgar Square' (ibid., p. vii). Even a German reviewer was aware of Fisher's authorship: [Anon., 'v. U.'], 'Die englische Marine 1805 und 1905', *Marine-Rundschau* (1906): 339–43. One of Fisher's letters to A. White proves his authorship: Marder, *'Fear God and Dread Nought'*, vol. ii, p. 62.

51. Ruddock F. Mackay, *Fisher of Kilverstone* (Oxford, 1973), pp. 242–3, 254.

52. White and Moorhouse, *Nelson and the Twentieth Century*, pp. 295–7, where F.T. Jane was given a chance to argue his case.

53. *Navy League Journal* 11 (1906): 19; 13 (1908): 328; David Shannon, 'The Nelson Day Celebrations of 1928', *The Nelson Dispatch* 3 (1989): 148–51, at 151 – the author attributes the change to consideration for the French, partners in the *entente cordiale* since 1904.

54. The Pears' Soap advertisement, published in newspapers in 1897, bears a portrait of Nelson and a depiction of Nelson's column (in Trafalgar Square); Borax; the advertisement for Beecham's Pills (see *Nelson Dispatch* 3, 1990: 175) included a portrait of Nelson and the version of 'England expects' from Arnold/Braham; by the way: the authentic flag code for 'England expects that every man will do his duty' was only re-discovered after the centenary celebrations: [Anon.], *Nelson's Signal at the Battle of Trafalgar* ([London], 4 July 1908).

55. British Film Institute: *Trafalgar Square Celebrations* (1915).

56. [Anon.], 'A Great and Glorious Victory', *Country Life* (25 October 2001): 60–1; 'Trafalgar Day' flyer of the 'Sea Cadet Corps'; David Howarth and Stephen Howarth, *Nelson: The Immortal Memory* (London, 1988), pp. 359, 366.

57. The tradition to observe Trafalgar Day in the Royal Navy is mentioned by Friedrich Althaus, *Admiral Nelson*, in Rudolf von Gottschall (ed.), *Der Neue Plutarch. Biographien hervorragender Charaktere der Geschichte, Literatur und Kunst. Achter Theil* (Leipzig, 1880), pp. 137–288, p. 288, in 1880. The toast was first drunk at the Lord Mayor's Dinner in London in November 1805 (see *The Times*, 11 November 1805).

58. Mark Kerr, *The Sailor's Nelson* (London, 1932), pp. 9–10.

59. An exception from this rule appears to be the 'Trafalgar Club' of the British National Party.

9
The Magic of Trafalgar:
The Nineteenth-Century Legacy

Andrew Lambert

Throughout the nineteenth century the British ignored the reality of Trafalgar, as a subject for study and reflection, preferring to concentrate on the mythic status of the battle in the national memory. The prevalence of this mythic interpretation was most obvious in the hyperbole with which the Victorians surrounded an event they claimed had played a critical role in saving civilization and defeating Napoleon, or even the smaller untruth that it ended Napoleon's invasion plans.[1] Trafalgar did none of these things, but for more than a century no-one questioned that it had. It was as if a conspiracy of silence had descended over the battle, one in which every Briton was complicit. As that ardent navalist Wilhelm II recognized, Trafalgar was a magical event. Even as the fighting died away the events of 21 October were being transformed into the stuff of legend. Trafalgar escaped the fate of so many naval battles: reduced to squalid, contested calculations of numbers and names, arguments and blame. Instead it would embody the very essence of British power for the next hundred years, a central element in national life and culture, a totem given countless public re-statements, from Trafalgar Square to the House of Lords. Furthermore Trafalgar was at once the definitive, and the last battle of its type. There would be no more full scale sailing battle fleet actions between first class nations. Nor would there be any serious prospect of a fleet battle involving the Royal Navy for the next hundred years – what sane man would dare to take on the sublime?

The magic of Trafalgar was purchased at the highest price; it cost Britain the life of her national hero, the iconic talisman who had

155

sustained national resistance to Continental tyranny, and redefined the very concept of being British. By the manner and context of his death, passing into immortality at the very moment of victory, Nelson provided the final ingredient that made Trafalgar magical. Together man and battle transcended mere matters of fact to become iconic, the very definition of success. Nelson and Trafalgar gave the Royal Navy a unique status, closer to religion than reason, one that would be contested, but could not be countermanded. This totemic status was responsible for a sustained failure to examine Trafalgar as history, a failure that reflected the unspoken desires of a nation. However, this left the Royal Navy of the early twentieth century precious little time to recover the realities behind their icon, and while it went to war in 1914 in ships that bore the proud names of those that fought at Trafalgar, the operational and tactical systems in place were the negation of Nelson's career.[2]

I

To harness and use the magic of Trafalgar the British had to be creative. To refine and enhance reality Collingwood was careful to prevent any hint of controversy reaching the public, despite the less than stellar performance of some captains. The myth that another 'Band of Brothers' had fought the battle was implied, and accepted without question by a shocked and stunned nation. As he composed his matchless despatch Collingwood was using the English language to transmit the ideals that his friend had fought and died for, unsullied by petty recriminations or jealousies, this perfect battle would be a critical national asset in the days that followed. The magical Trafalgar would survive the nineteenth century, because it was quickly incorporated into the national mythos of the emerging British state. In the process Nelson was greatly diminished, his sublime genius reduced to unreflective courage, and no attempt was made to comprehend the wider context, or the tactical insight of his final battle. Only in the 1880s did historical scholarship even begin to address the battle as an event, and consider the methods employed. Despite that, otherwise sane men continued to spout nonsense about a central event in their recent history. Because Trafalgar had achieved a magical status incompatible with the prosaic calculation of ships and men, it was necessary to find better results than the capture or destruction of 19 enemy ships if Trafalgar was to be useful. Little wonder we have found new ways of examining the battle for the bicentenary.[3]

In one respect the source of the confusion is obvious: by 1805 Horatio Nelson was already a national icon, a talisman of victory and god-like source of comfort. Consequently his death did not elevate him to the pantheon, as had been the case with Wolfe, instead it elevated the occasion of his death to the realms of magic and myth. It remained there because the occasion was of itself sublime; melding triumph and tragedy, grandeur and genius with the wider consequences of British success in the naval campaign of 1805. This hyperbolic Trafalgar then survived the nineteenth century as a simplified short hand for larger processes, and more complex events. The truth it conveyed was real, but not literal. In life Nelson had achieved divine status among his people, he was the new saviour, and his death was necessarily linked to their redemption from danger and sin. The most obvious results of his death were a century of unchallenged naval mastery, and domination of the global economy.

While Collingwood's matchless despatch began the process others who knew Nelson and served the state sustained the impulse. No sooner had the news arrived in Britain than George Canning, the last statesman to talk with Nelson, turned it to account in his ten-page poem 'Ulm and Trafalgar'. He followed the lead of his mentor Prime Minister William Pitt in using the destruction of Napoleon's fleet as a counter-point to the humiliating failure of the Austrian army. Canning used literary gifts and classical learning, of which he was inordinately proud, to serve the Pittite political cause. Anxious to sustain British defiance in the face of catastrophe it was hardly surprising that Canning strayed into hyperbole or, given the national mood, that his unattributed stanzas were a success.[4] For Canning the 'dear bought glories of Trafalgar's day' flowed with 'radiant glory from thy trophied tomb', to 'grace and guard thy country's martial fame', as 'a mighty beacon', 'to shine and save through ages yet unborn!'[5] The impact of Canning's piece is evident from Southey's decision to use eight lines on the title page of his biography, initially unaware of the author's name. Wittingly or otherwise Canning had set the tone for a century of Trafalgar commentary, while Southey reinforced the trend with his sublime, yet highly mannered Nelson biography.[6] Canning was well aware of the impact that his words would produce. Throughout his post-war career at the Foreign Office he relied on naval might to sustain the national deterrent, citing the 'dormant thunder' of the reserve fleet as the right arm of the state.[7]

Canning's lead was echoed across the century; between 1805 and 1905 the British Library catalogue records 174 works published under the title word Trafalgar, though not one of the English titles could be described a serious examination of the battle. The only book by a reputable scholar, Professor John Laughton's *The Story of Trafalgar* of 1890 was, as the title suggests, a popular work designed to reinforce the legend with some snippets of new research. In particular Laughton repeated the myth about ending the invasion threat.[8] He closed the booklet with a ringing call to his countrymen to remember Trafalgar as an example of obedience, duty, loyalty and devotion, applied with skill, and even genius by a tightly knit fellowship.[9] The other 173 works included poetry, songs, sermons, and a design for the Trafalgar Square waterworks, but not one Briton dissected the event which alone rendered the name so powerful for other literary and artistic forms. The exception to this catalogue of trifles came from another country, rather closer to the battlefield.

Frenchmen who had grown up in the glory days of Bonaparte's empire found the years that followed Waterloo a sad spectacle, lacking drama, glory and heroes. Adolphe Thiers, the most industrious historian of the era, used his 22-volume account of the years between the Revolution and Waterloo to regenerate Napoleonic glory. That he had been Prime Minister, and was dismissed by a king anxious to avoid a war with Britain in 1840, lent Thiers' work on the consulate and empire a powerful anti-British bias. The success of his works, ten editions of the history of the Revolution had appeared by 1848, and translation into many languages made it a standard reference. In the process Thiers invented a number of stories to laud his hero. He alleged, without a scrap of evidence, that Nelson had been 'decoyed' to the West Indies, outsmarted by Bonaparte. This nonsense appeared in English in 1845, quickly generating an invasion scarce. When the relevant sixth volume was translated into Spanish, Thiers' criticism of the performance of the Spanish fleet at Trafalgar caused outrage. On the eve of the first reconstruction since Trafalgar the Spanish Navy could not afford to let such comments pass unanswered. Two books, the first full-length accounts of Trafalgar in any language, and a series of articles appeared within two years, supported by the Naval Ministry. All were critical of the role of the French alliance in the glorious, but catastrophic defeat. Furthermore the Spanish Navy began to commemorate the heroes of the battle, naming ships for Gravina and his companions, names that have endured in the Spanish Navy as a testament to the finest hour of the old Navy.[10] Would that the Royal Navy took a similar view (many of the latest frigates seem to be named for Charles II's bastard sons!).

The Spanish response to Thiers demonstrated a simple truth: a controversial present generates a contested past. The British relied on a naval arms race, many of the new ships being named for Nelson and his battles, rather than a historical counter-offensive. They were content with their mythic Trafalgar, and did not wish to disturb the symbolism of the event. Trafalgar was not a fit subject for careful investigation – it was best left as the sublime example of naval power.

II

Nelson inflicted a blow on the navies of France and Spain that they would never forget, and from which they could never recover. Trafalgar, as the battle was named by George III, crushed the naval power of the enemy, with total losses of more than 20 ships. It also destroyed their morale. The Spanish and French had, in the main, fought like heroes, and yet they had been annihilated. Trafalgar was the coda to Nelson's achievement. He had already destroyed Napoleon's maritime strategy and invasion plans by pursuing Villeneuve to the West Indies and back. Trafalgar destroyed the naval power that alone gave credence to Napoleon's invasion threat. Britain's command of the sea had been placed beyond doubt. British trade and empire were safe to prosper and expand, creating wealth and funding the war. It was time to translate naval power into strategic success. However, the fruits of Trafalgar would take a decade to harvest. Napoleon dominated Europe and set up the Continental System in 1806 – an economic blockade, excluding British trade from Europe. Yet his power had been circumscribed, his ultimate fate mapped out. Britain would survive Austerlitz, and because she controlled the sea, she could block every attempt by Napoleon to escape the bounds of Europe, and the tyranny and extortion that alone kept his regime in power. Finally the tension snapped, Spain revolted, then Russia.

Having destroyed the French fleet the Royal Navy was reconfigured for a new war. With the residue of French seapower tightly blockaded in Brest, Toulon and Antwerp British task forces seized the last remnants of the French and Dutch overseas empires, boosting trade and ending the threat to shipping. Insurance rates fell. British cruisers shifted to the offensive, offshore islands and convoys were swept up, coastal towns attacked and the Spanish rising against the French sustained and reinforced. As Napoleon observed, while a prisoner on board HMS *Bellerophon* in 1815: 'If it had not been for you English, I should have been Emperor of the East. But wherever there is water to float a ship, we are sure to find you in our way.'[11] While Napoleon had been beaten by European armies, by Russia, Prussia and Austria, with the support of the British, Spanish and Portuguese effort in the Iberian Peninsula, this was only possible because Britain never gave up the conflict, never allowed Napoleon the opportunity to consolidate his power and rebuild the continent in his own image. Trafalgar was the beginning of his end. It was also the ideal reference for any diplomatic démarche – if this battle had brought down Napoleon, who could stand against such power?

Trafalgar could be used to make other points: Lord Byron not only modelled his image on the heroic ideal provided by Nelson, and employed the same portraitist, he also used Nelson to define the heroic in his masterpiece *Don Juan*.

> Nelson was Britannia's god of war,
> And still should be so, but the tide is turn'd;
> There's no more to be said of Trafalgar,
> 'Tis with our hero quietly inurn'd;[12]

Another man to recognize the magic was George, Prince of Wales, later the Prince Regent and King George IV. Having met Nelson briefly during his final days in England the Prince took control of the official biography, to establish his connection with the glory of the national hero, and the greatest human being he ever met. George also collected memorabilia and artefacts for display in Carlton House to convey the impression that he, rather than any naval or military men, had been the real architect of Napoleon's downfall. In the 1820s George commissioned J.M.W. Turner to paint the Battle, and the resulting picture, a majestic monumental artistic response to the defining moment in modern history, hung briefly at Carlton. In his opium-fuelled delusions George completely missed both the magic of event, and the power of Turner's picture (see Plate 9). Unable to comprehend the meaning of genius, either at sea or in oils, and tiring of the carping comments of narrow minded sea officers, who found the treatment too stylized, George despatched the picture down to the Naval Hospital at Greenwich in 1829. Turner would return to the theme again in 1839 with the *Fighting Temeraire* which established his own immortality.

Understandably the state was anxious to carry the magic of Trafalgar forward into the post-war world. Although the House of Commons had discussed a national Nelson monument in 1816, it was only in 1835 that the newly cleared space at the north end of Whitehall was named Trafalgar Square. Then the Duke of Wellington and Thomas Hardy helped to collect money for the Nelson memorial that would give the square a focal point. William Railton's design employed a column modelled on those in the Augustan Temple of Mars Ultor (Mars the Avenger, or he who has the last word). By using this architectural quotation from a temple built at the heart of Imperial Rome to celebrate the deification of Julius Caesar, linking him with the god of war, the avenging of his murder and the establishment of an Imperial regime that would last forever, the Nelson monument was loaded with meaning. At Trafalgar Nelson had become the national god of war, and the nation had avenged his death by defeating Napoleon. Curiously enough while everyone associates Trafalgar Square with national celebration, very few understand the original purpose. By the 1840s it was clear that Trafalgar had established Britain's naval mastery for all time: Nelson and an Augustan column provided the ultimate expression of global maritime power. The column and statue were in place by November 1843, 24 years later Landseer's bronze lions completed the design.

The unequivocal meaning of the monument and the universal language in which it was conveyed may explain the vehemence with which some French commentators responded to Trafalgar Square. The impact of the column was, and remains, immense. Hitler saw it as the 'symbol of British naval might and world domination': he planned to take it back to Berlin if his invasion project had been more successful than Bonaparte's. However, British naval might – represented by the fleet flagship HMS *Nelson* – was far more than a symbol, and he did not make the attempt. Aside from the usual delays attending any great national project, the slow process of deciding on the nature of the Trafalgar monument reflected a deeper truth. There was little need for so much effort when the command of the sea was not in doubt. The French and Russian navies posed no threat while a host of Nelson's legatees were on hand to sustain the reality that underpinned the magic. This living legacy reinforced the magic: there were companions of Nelson, Trafalgar heroes, ready for war. While men like Cockburn, Hardy, Codrington and William Parker led the fleet, as they did into the 1850s, who could doubt that a new Trafalgar would be enacted on any fleet foolish enough to pose a challenge? Similar confidence flowed through the political leadership until 1865 when Lord Palmerston, the last Prime Minister to have met Nelson, died. Yet the magic required updating, the symbols renewing.

III

In the 1840s, steam power, a revived French Navy, and the passing of many Trafalgar heroes inspired a restatement of the story. The key events were simple enough, HMS *Victory* was transformed into a shrine, the new HMS *Trafalgar* was launched, the column was completed, Nelson's correspondence was published and the battle was chosen as a key image for the new Houses of Parliament. In 1807 the Royal Navy ordered its first HMS *Trafalgar*, a relatively insignificant three-decked second rate ship. By 1818 it was clear that the name was too important to be wasted. The undersized, obsolescent vessel was renamed *Camperdown*, and a far larger 120-gun first rate *Trafalgar* was ordered. The new ship was built slowly, keeping time with the development of Trafalgar Square until the nation had need of such a potent talisman. After the Syrian Crisis of 1840 – where a fleet commanded by one of Nelson's captains, and including the Trafalgar ships HMS *Revenge* and HMS *Implacable* (which had fought under French colours on 21 October 1805 as the *Duguay-Trouin*) had demolished Egyptian rule in Syria, humiliating France in the process – the old rivalry resumed; with new weapons.

On 22 June 1841 Prince Albert and the Queen attended the launch of the new first rate HMS *Trafalgar* at Woolwich. At the Queen's request Lady Bridport, Nelson's niece, conducted the ceremony before a vast crowd on land and water, estimated to be almost half a million. The explanation for this sudden upsurge of enthusiasm, other first rates had been launched without crowds or patriotic frenzy, was clear enough. France was being saucy, and if the crisis of 1840 had ended without a cross-Channel war, it was still necessary to remind Paris who ruled the ocean. To reinforce the point a new round of warship construction revived many of the key names from Nelson's career, especially Trafalgar. It seemed that every ship in the fleet was in some way connected with the hero, his battles, ships and companions.[13] Albert was suitably impressed by the launch; it was, as he told his father, 'the most imposing sight which I can remember'.[14] Nor did his interest in the heroic past end there. On Trafalgar Day 1844 Albert boarded HMS *Victory*, and was taken to all the key sites by his guide, the Queen. Those present, who included Trafalgar veteran Captain Moubray, noted that Her Majesty had been 'visibly affected' by the occasion.[15] The Royal couple would pass the ship on numerous occasions, as they travelled to their favourite residence Osbourne House on the Isle of Wight. If Albert appeared less affected by the old shrine ship he had not missed the point. His growing identification with the British past included a strong, and for him novel, appreciation of naval history.

The new Parliament buildings were just beginning to rise from the ruins left by the destruction of much of the old Palace of Westminster in 1834. Here was a project close to the Prince's heart, a vast gothic building celebrating the Germanic origins of British democracy. The artistic model he followed was a royal residence in Munich, decorated with scenes from the *Niebelungenlied*, notably the death of Siegfried. The mix of history and magic in the growing German identity was most powerfully expressed in the vast Arminius statue, which the Prince was pleased to support.[16] In 1841 a Committee of the House of Commons declared that the new building provided an ideal opportunity to promote British Fine Arts. Incoming Prime Minister Sir Robert Peel, anxious to secure the support of the Prince to counter-act the whiggish sympathies of the Queen, quickly set up a Royal Fine Arts Commission to oversee the interior decoration of the building with Albert in the chair. The Commission, which had a remit to commission fresco paintings from British artists, offered Albert another opportunity to create tradition. Artists were invited to submit designs, and the best were rewarded and selected for commission.[17] None chose modern subjects. Perhaps the recent past was too problematic for a taste increasingly literal. Allegorical art is most effective when the story being used is simple, and well-known. Even when the Commission selected designs almost all of the history pictures dealt with ancient or medieval subjects.[18]

By 1847 the subjects for the frescos and statuary had been fixed, and Albert ensured that his favourite artist took up the challenge. The Irish romantic Daniel Maclise was given the immense task of capturing Waterloo and Trafalgar for the Royal Gallery.[19] They would be vast pictures, 45 feet long and 12 feet deep, accompanied by 16 smaller pictures of British valour. These military scenes would serve the same patriotic and uplifting function as the magnificent Armada tapestries, destroyed with the old House of Lords. There was going to be a lot of death about, the prominence of heroic sacrifice reflected contemporary attitudes, the emergence of a new chivalry.[20] Nelson was, once again, the central figure. He would be re-invented as an example to future generations, although one wonders what sort of 'sacrifice' the House of Lords was going to be called upon to make. However, it would be many years before Maclise started work on Trafalgar.

In 1852 the British government decided that the new Commander in Chief of the Mediterranean Fleet should not fly his flag in HMS *Waterloo*, to avoid upsetting French sensitivities, but his fleet could include the *Trafalgar*. Two years later, when Britain went to war with Russia France was an ally. While the Russians were suitably impressed by the Royal Navy, and did not come to sea, the French Navy spent the war trying to prove they were at least as good as the British. But the simple fact was that the magic of Trafalgar was only one part of the Royal Navy's superiority; it was sustained by superior seamanship, discipline, initiative and confidence.[21]

IV

Although British strategic planning in the nineteenth century was dominated by the threat from France, Britain fought but one major war, allied to France, against Russia. However, it was a limited war, waged thousands of miles from home, without any of the intensity or danger that had filled the years between 1793 and 1805.[22] Just as in Nelson's day the Russians refused to meet the Royal Navy at sea, only too well aware that they were outmatched by the quality of British ships, officers and above all seamen. Without a great sea battle naval heroics were confined to the odd shore bombardment, and service in the land batteries besieging Sevastopol.

Only one Admiral appeared to satisfy the public need for a hero, Sir Edmund Lyons. Lyons began his career in Nelson's fleet off Toulon in 1804, and secured rapid promotion through connections and courage. He took up diplomatic service in the 1830s, only rejoining the navy in late 1853, on the eve of war. A slight grey-haired figure, Lyons always fancied he resembled Nelson, and managed to convince a good number of his contemporaries that this resemblance reflected something more. The idea, once Lyons had suggested it, was widely taken up. With the 'Life of Nelson' ever to hand Lyons took every chance to play the hero. His posturing certainly impressed the editor of *The Times*, who watched the allied armies disembark in the Crimea in September 1854. For Delane: 'The real commander is Lyons,' he wrote, 'who is just another Nelson, full of energy and activity.' Delane also hoped he would disobey his superiors, citing the incident at Copenhagen as the example to follow.[23] The idea that Nelson was merely energetic, active and insubordinate reflected a limited understanding of the man and his legacy that was all too common in the period.

While he lapped up the newspaper adulation, which appeared with suspicious frequency, Lyons was no genius. His results were unremarkable. Although the Commander in Chief had ordered him to keep his ships safe during a diversionary attack on the Russian batteries at Sevastopol on 17 October 1854, Lyons did the exact opposite. Leading his squadron into a close range action he ensured the ships were badly damaged, and achieved nothing. While his cool conduct under fire excited the admiration of the newspaper correspondents, whom he had carefully cultivated in violation of Admiralty Standing Orders,[24] Lyons lacked the vision, insight or reflection to make use of the opportunities that arose. Any merit in the work of the Royal Navy in the Black Sea belonged to other men, those who planned and conducted the work, not to Lyons, who merely struck a pose. After a year of increasing insubordination, writing home to his political masters behind the back of his Commander in Chief, Lyons was rewarded with the supreme command. By shifting any blame for the supply problems that affected the army onto his subordinates, and leading a few minor operations, Lyons was still in place when the war ended, and was the only naval officer to be ennobled for his role. The

Barony was hardly merited; Nelson received the same for the Nile. Lyons did not live long to enjoy the honour, dying in 1858. This prompted *The Times* to observe that 'he was so like Nelson, the hero whom more than all others we regard with a sort of personal attachment ... Not only in appearance but also in reality there was something of Nelson in Lord Lyons.' In truth the real similarities were restricted to personal failings; Lyons was inordinately vain. He also lacked any talent for the higher direction of war beyond a fluency in French, which alone of his talents Nelson might have envied.[25] A better judge of the man, Foreign Secretary Earl Clarendon, saw little to praise: 'I think him singularly deficient in judgement, he is moreover irritable & one of the vainest men I ever knew.'[26] Lyons was interred in St Paul's, immortalized in stone, and largely forgotten. He was, in truth, a cardboard cut-out Nelson, only fit to fool the enemy at a distance.

This did not matter at the time, for mid Victorian Britain never faced the challenge of total war. The rivalry of the Second Bonapartist Empire, unlike the First, was dismissed with a pair of arms races. Consequently there was little need to reflect on the meaning of Trafalgar, or to develop fresh examples of naval magic. The Crimean War was a paltry affair by the standards set half a century before, and the biggest debates concerned the class from which the heroes were to be drawn, leading to the institution of a classless bravery award, the Victoria Cross. This comfortable world could not last forever; Trafalgar would be needed when the external environment darkened. The only question was what form the new image would take.

With the war over it was time to complete those peaceful projects set aside for the duration, notably the Houses of Parliament. As patron of the artists, and arbiter of taste and subject, Albert brought a great deal of death to the building, but the deaths were uplifting images of heroism and sacrifice, for the new culture of service. Maclise's inclusive *Waterloo* was completed in December 1861. In the same month Albert died of an unromantic complaint occasioned by the medieval drains of Windsor. With one big wall already covered Maclise began to design *Trafalgar: The Death of Nelson*. For this his research was meticulous, as befits the taste of the time, and included the famous bullet-holed coat that his patron had purchased, along with visits to the *Victory* and samples of ropes, fittings and other gear. The composition included over 70 life-sized figures, placed on the upper deck of *Victory* with the fallen Nelson, in the arms of Hardy at the focal centre. There is no glory or triumphalism here. The price of success is represented life sized, and disturbingly powerful.[27] Maclise's picture reflects a new mood; while the hero falls, mortally wounded, at the core of the image, he is surrounded by death and mutilation. The sacrifice is far more democratic than had been allowed hitherto. This Nelson is not a god, just one of many men to die that day.[28] Trafalgar was re-created as a national event, with the death of the hero as the main incident, but the sacrifice of all is honoured.

Trafalgar took nearly two years to execute, completing just as the great project to embellish the Houses of Parliament with mythic images collapsed. Albert 'had been the directing mind and without his determined support the enterprise would probably have ended sooner'.[29] Maclise's *Trafalgar* was universally praised, a masterpiece of narrative art in the high romantic style.[30] The *Art Journal* concluded: 'We are a maritime power, but it is the only picture which we yet possess entirely worthy of our naval history.'[31] Yet such judgements reflect a triumph of literalism over meaning. In pursuit of a chivalric ideal Maclise missed the magic that made Trafalgar central to the British identity. Britain needed its gods, and failing a heroic monarchy, the divine mantle had fallen on the man who placed the capstone on naval mastery, and made the world safe for British trade. Perhaps without realizing it Albert was seeking to dethrone Nelson, to make way for the newly restored monarchy to put the Royal firmly ahead of the Navy.

By the time Maclise's picture had been completed the sense of urgency that had marked much of Albert's naval interest had passed. The naval challenge of the Second Empire had collapsed, although it had provided the opportunity for some neat touches. In 1861 a massive new ironclad battleship was named HMS *Northumberland* – in memory of the old 74 that had taken Napoleon into exile in 1815! She was followed by HMS *Bellerophon*, although such powerful symbolism proved unnecessary: Napoleon III came to England as an exile on a scheduled passenger steamer in 1871. As a long-term resident of London, Louis Napoleon may have taken a slightly more measured view of his host's national hero than his countrymen. In 1859, with the arms race in full spate, social commentator Hippolyte Taine walked through the streets of London. Determined to be displeased by what he saw he found the smoke begrimed buildings and thick fog depressing. When he reached Trafalgar Square he could not bring himself to give the space its name, reserving his vitriol for the heroic figure far above him: 'That hideous Nelson, planted upon his column like a rat impaled on the end of a stick!'[32]

After 1865 Trafalgar was pensioned off; it had no place amidst the economic booms and internal reforms that dominated the next two decades. But this was only a temporary release. The era of Gladstonian economy, defence cuts, tax cuts and attempts to limit the size and cost of the empire came to a shuddering halt in the mid 1880s. In pursuit of domestic agendas, notably extending the franchise, the 'Grand Old Man' had lost sight of the new realities of the age. The masses depended for their daily bread on free access to the sea. Those who made public policy were increasingly aware of economic competition, of tariff barriers against British trade, and the rising tide of imperial conquest. Populist journalist William Stead, editor of the influential *Pall Mall Gazette*, using confidential figures supplied by Captain John Fisher RN, started a campaign to highlight 'The Truth about the Navy'. From mid March 1885 Stead kept up a steady barrage of weekly revelations, revelations that seriously embarrassed the government. In search of allies Stead sent his first editorial to the Poet Laureate, Alfred, Lord Tennyson. Suitably roused Tennyson produced a simple but emotive popular appeal, which appeared in *The Times* and the *Pall Mall Gazette* on 23 April.[33] In 'The Fleet' Tennyson left no-one in any doubt about where he stood. Gladstonian finance had gone too far, it was time to reinforce the defences of the country and the coaling stations that held Britain's global empire of trade together. While it did not require a poet's sensibility to employ Nelson as the exemplar of English greatness, or the polar opposite of Gladstone, dismissively reduced to the familiar 'you', the genius lay in the completeness of the image. 'The Fleet of England is her all in all, and in her Fleet her fate.' Behind the naval concerns lay a deeper fear, of hungry masses, political change and social chaos.[34]

There can be little doubt that the 'The Fleet' summed up the national mood, or that Gladstone was listening. Within weeks a supplementary naval estimate, the 'Northbrook Programme' had been placed before Parliament, and passed into law. Among the new ships built to meet the renewed French challenge were the *Nile* and *Trafalgar*, menacing ironclad leviathans, the very acme of naval might.

V

In 1891 the naval revival reached a new level of popularity with the Royal Naval Exhibition at the Chelsea Hospital. In a grand spectacle designed to demonstrate 'the relation between Britannia's naval expenditure and naval responsibilities' Nelson was the central figure, and a full sized mock-up of the *Victory* the dominant image, complete with a suitably located 'Death of Nelson' waxwork by Madame Tussaud's, based on Arthur Devis's picture. Between 2 May and 24 October some 2,352,000 visitors attended, inspecting everything from Nelson artefacts, many with the flimsiest of provenance, to modern ships, guns, engines and boilers. There was a large circular panorama of Trafalgar, a modern mock naval battle on the lake and a massive catalogue, the historical part written by Professor John Knox Laughton, the historian who pioneered the academic study of Nelson. Crowds entered under a suitably Nelsonian motto, taken from the Articles of War, 'The Navy, whereon under the good providence of God, the wealth, safety and strength of the Kingdom do chiefly depend.' A smaller travelling version of the show then toured the major cities, gradually selling off artefacts and curios.

Nelson was the patron saint of the Navy League, founded in 1894 to press for a bigger and better organized navy. The purpose of the League was to inform the people about the importance of naval supremacy on which the British empire depended for trade, food and survival. Suitably informed, the people would support expenditure required for an adequate navy. The chief fund-raisers for the League were City firms, involved in trade, banking and investment, through the London Chamber of Commerce. League advertising went for the jugular, linking a great figure with their message. 'Nelson's life and death, it was foreseen, might be utilised to personify British Sea Power to the children, if not to the veterans of British democracy throughout the world.'[35] The League also made full use of Trafalgar Square, celebrating Trafalgar Day in 1896 with a massive turnout that emphasized national concern for naval strength. Similar events occurred in other major British cities, and across the empire. Liberal opinion formers were outraged, and expressed an astonishing level of concern that the French might be offended by ostentatious celebrations. George Bernard Shaw even suggested it would be better to pull down Nelson's column.[36] He did not trouble himself to think why the French should be offended by Trafalgar, and its public celebration. In truth the French were acutely conscious of the sustained and repeated insults that British naval power had forced them to swallow ever since 1805.

Trafalgar ended the nineteenth century on a high note. In 1898 Britain and France almost went to war over the headwaters of the Nile, and the Fashoda Crisis provided a final opportunity to assess the magic of Trafalgar. The Royal Navy responded to the crisis, as they had to most nineteenth-century international disagreements, by preparing to bombard the nearest hostile naval base. The obvious target was Cherbourg, and the French hurriedly moved their fleet to Brest and backed down, convinced the arrogant British would be only too pleased to finish what they had begun at Trafalgar.[37] The latest naval budgets, propelled by Stead and Fisher's alarmist campaign, had purchased victory in the struggle for empire and trade without war. As the Kaiser observed: 'The Poor French, they have not read their Mahan!'[38] However, while enjoying his little joke Wilhelm took no heed of the underlying power that the French had recognized. Trafalgar remained both a definitive magical symbol *and* a convenient short hand for the most powerful force in global politics. When Wilhelm decided to challenge Britain for command of the seas he put his country on a collision course with the magic of Trafalgar, and relied on logical political calculation to counter the sublime. Two years after Fashoda the German Admirals concluded that the British fleet had the power to steam past all their fortifications, enter the River Elbe and sink their fleet.[39]

The Victorian era in which the magic of Trafalgar had held undisputed sway over the world's oceans came to an end in 1901, and the old Queen was carried in state into Portsmouth harbour, past the ship of memories, by now a rather tired old vessel, occasionally battered by her more modern successors, and increasingly hard to maintain.

While the largest rival fleet was still that of France, now allied to a resurgent Russia Trafalgar was an ideal national symbol. Yet a sudden shift in Britain's international position crippled the commemoration of the centenary of Trafalgar. In 1904 Britain signed an entente with France. This agreement settled the squabbles of the past 30 years, and allowed the two nations to co-operate in the face of growing German power. The Foreign Office was so concerned to avoid upsetting French sensitivities that official celebrations were effectively stifled, and the Admiralty ordered the fleet not to make any special display. The Navy Records Society had planned a speech to commemorate the event, but the Admiralty considered that a public lecture on some aspect of Nelson's career was acceptable, but it was 'important that … the address should not include anything which might wound the susceptibilities of France or of any other foreign nation'.[40] Lord Charles Beresford, commanding in the Mediterranean, was similarly instructed to avoid triumphalist display. Beresford ignored the order and reviewed 3,000 men on the parade square at Malta. The event was handled with becoming dignity, and reflected more on the loss of the hero than on the victory.[41]

Quite who came up with the absurd idea that we should forget our past merely to avoid upsetting the sensitivities of our current friends is unknown, but such feeble, apologetic nonsense did not show the country in a particularly favourable light. Trafalgar is a matter of fact and record, the outcome is not contested. Certainly contemporary French attitudes to the past were unrestrained by any such considerations. The popular Bonaparte biography of pre-1914, Frédéric Masson's *Napoléon et sa famille*, stretched across 13 anti-democratic, militarist and violently anti-British volumes. In a telling passage in volume 8 of 1906 Masson blamed Britain for the defeat of Bonaparte, and with him of the dream of a united Europe.[42] Throughout the nineteenth century the link between interpretations of Bonaparte and attitudes toward Britain were obvious. From Thiers in the 1830s those who yearned for the glory of the First Empire and strong military leadership took up a line that culminated in the Dreyfus Affair. As an angel of chaos, a man who destroyed everything he touched, Bonaparte proved a deeply divisive symbol in French politics, and, as Louis-Philippe and Louis-Napoleon had discovered, proved too powerful a weapon for mere mortals to wield. By contrast Nelson, who had given his life to uphold king, church and country, was an ideal heroic exemplar.

The apologetic tone adopted by the government left the centenary of Trafalgar to be marked by relatively unimpressive events: there was nothing of the national need so evident in 1805, or in 1914. Much of the press had taken the entente line although there was a widespread belief that the day should be made a national holiday. There was a Navy League wreath-laying ceremony in Trafalgar Square, and an exhibition of relics at the Royal United Services Institution on Whitehall. New books appeared, although none of any significance. The nation was still content to attribute Trafalgar to 'character' and get by on myths and make-believe. It was courage and self-sacrifice that the late Victorians and Edwardians found so ennobling about Nelson. His devotion to 'duty' chimed with the service ethic of the age, his Christian values were modernized to suit current tastes, disposing of declarations that Emma was his wife before God. Even the cautious Laughton gave way to hyperbole in the fervid atmosphere of the 1905 commemorations, portraying Nelson as the redeemer, saving Europe by his sacrifice. It helped that he was a popular hero, above class or clique, without a significant political role, and of course the sea was Britain's element.[43]

Yet Trafalgar was not without serious students, its lessons were not entirely lost. As far back as 1871 a certain Commander Fisher had demonstrated a sound grasp of the Trafalgar memorandum and how it would be applied to steamships. He learnt to appreciate naval history and great admirals when he worked with Admiral Sir Geoffrey Phipps-Hornby, the master of fleet tactics who bridged the worlds of scholarship and seamanship in the 1870s and 1880s. Fisher knew Mahan's works, chose 21 October 1904 as the ideal day to take up the office of First Sea Lord and cited Nelson as the example for new measures wherever possible. That his first Commander in Chief had been Sir William Parker, the last of Nelson's captains, made him something of a living link with Nelson.[44] The fleet he built while serving as First Sea Lord, 1904–10, revived every

Trafalgar-related name on the Navy List – even his iconic new battleship HMS *Dreadnought* bore a Trafalgar name. Fisher expected these ships would have to fight a new Trafalgar, but picked out John Jellicoe to be his Nelson.[45] It must have been obvious to Fisher that Jellicoe was quite unlike Nelson, afflicted by uncertainty, doubt and caution that were alien to the mind of his supposed model.[46] Unfortunately Churchill took Fisher's advice in 1914.

The nineteenth century had produced no naval heroes worthy of a statue in Trafalgar Square. It remained to be seen if there would be any in the twentieth. During the nineteenth century Nelson recovered his place as the chief secular deity of the state, whenever the security of the British Isles, the empire and above all the trade routes that linked them together was questioned. But it was not until the century ended that the 'magic' of Trafalgar was linked to serious attempts to understand his intellectual legacy, and turn his genius to account. Only in the new century would historical scholarship and naval doctrine combine to rethink the man and his final battle, recovering their meaning from the wilderness of popular obsession with character and morality; but the work was far from complete in 1914.[47] The first book-length treatment of the battle, Julian Corbett's 1910 *The Campaign of Trafalgar*, was based on a lecture course delivered to the Naval War Course, and the Army Staff College at Camberley. Corbett, the pre-eminent naval historian, educator and theorist, produced a book worthy of the battle and the hero.[48]

VI

Across the nineteenth century Trafalgar remained a mythic event, which was recalled or ignored in response to the current state of the French Navy. In the 1820s, between the early 1840s and the mid 1860s, and again from the late 1880s Trafalgar was a major presence in British culture. In other times it slipped into the background, not forgotten, but not necessary, or compelling. The place of history, myth and magic in national life has always reflected the contemporary context. History addresses current agendas; it should seek to explain how we arrived at this time and place, rather than simply revisit older studies concerned to explain how our ancestors saw their past. The development of modern historical methods in the nineteenth century was intimately connected with the creation of national myth. Historians in Imperial Germany affected to see in Prussian military success the completion of a pre-ordained purpose, writing their histories to support this contemporary agenda, imposing a linear inevitability on the chaos of the past that separated Arminius from

Bismarck.[49] This prompted a typically explosive response from Friedrich Nietzsche who stressed: 'You can explain the past only by what is most powerful in the present.'[50] We must remember that History is both a record and a process, and that the process is the more important of the two. How we think is more important than what we know. How far Trafalgar lives in the realm of magic and how far in history is a question that will occupy us all for years to come – but we must always leave a space for the magic.

Notes

1. C.F. Behrman, *Victorian Myths of the Sea* (Athens, OH, 1977), pp. 104–5 etc.
2. A. Gordon, *The Rules of the Game* (London, 1996).
3. For example, M. Duffy, 'All Was Hushed Up: The Secret Trafalgar', *Mariner's Mirror* 91, 2 (June 2005): 216–40.
4. W. Hinde, *George Canning* (London, 1973), pp. 138–9.
5. For a full transcript of the verse see: J. Bagot, *George Canning and his Friends*, 2 vols (London, 1909), vol. I, pp. 415–19.
6. See G. Callender (ed.), *Southey's Life of Nelson* (London, 1922) for a serious assessment of the text.
7. H. Temperley, *The Foreign Policy of Canning: 1822–1827* (London, 1925), pp. 119–20.
8. A.D. Lambert, *The Foundations of Naval History: Sir John Laughton, the Royal Navy and the Historical Profession* (London, 1998).
9. J.K. Laughton, *The Story of Trafalgar* (London, 1890), p. 40.
10. I am indebted to my friend Carlos Alfaro for information on the Spanish response to Thiers. See: M. de Marliani, *Combate de Trafalgar* (Madrid, 1850); J. Ferrer de Couto, *Combatate Naval de Trafalgar* (Madrid, 1851).
11. Sir F.L. Maitland, *The Surrender of Napoleon, being the Narrative of the surrender of Buonaparte, and of his residence on board HMS Bellerophon* (London, 1826 and 1904), p. 26.
12. T.G. Steffan and W.W. Pratt, *Byron's Don Juan; Volume II* (Austin, TX, 1957), 1st canto, 4th verse, p. 23.
13. A.D. Lambert, *The Last Sailing Battle Fleet: Maintaining Naval Mastery 1815–1850* (London, 1991). John Fisher would do the same during his tenure as First Sea Lord, 1904–10.
14. T. Martin, *Life of the Prince Consort* (London, 1875–80), I, p. 115.
15. K. Fenwick, *HMS Victory* (London, 1959), p. 348.
16. S. Schama, *Landscape and Memory* (London, 1995), pp. 100–20.
17. T.S.R. Boase, *English Art, 1800–1870* (Oxford, 1959), pp. 214–15. R. Cook, *The Palace of Westminster* (London, 1987), pp. 109–11.
18. Cook, *Palace of Westminster*, p. 266.
19. N. Weston, *Daniel Maclise: Irish Artist in Victorian London* (Dublin, 2001).
20. M. Girouard, *The Return to Camelot: Chivalry and the English Gentleman* (Yale, 1981).

21. J. Codman, *An American Transport in the Crimean War* (New York, n.d.), pp. 192–3 is the key passage.
22. A.D. Lambert, *The Crimean War: British Grand Strategy against Russia 1853–1856* (Manchester, 1990).
23. Delane to A.I. Dasent 13.9.1854: Delane MSS Volume 5, f. 90. News International Archive.
24. This led to a major row with the First Sea Lord in late 1855. Lambert, *Crimean War*, p. 264.
25. S. Eardley-Wilmot, *Life of Vice Admiral Lord Lyons* (London, 1898), pp. 415–19.
26. Lambert, *Crimean War*, p. 329.
27. The two large pictures are considered disturbing by Westminster security staff. Weston, *Daniel Maclise*, p. 251.
28. Ibid., p. 243.
29. Boase, *English Art, 1800–1870*, p. 215.
30. Ibid., p. 218.
31. Quoted in Weston, *Daniel Maclise*, at p. 249.
32. H. Taine, *Notes on England* (London, 1995), p. 9.
33. Tennyson to Stead, 14.3.1885: in C.Y. Lang and E.F. Shannon, *The Letters of Alfred, Lord Tennyson Volume III* (Oxford, 1990), pp. 311–12.
34. V. Pitt, *Tennyson Laureate* (London, 1962), pp. 163–4.
35. League Pamphlet cited in A.J. Marder, *The Anatomy of British Sea Power: Naval Policy 1880–1905* (London, 1940), p. 52.
36. See ibid., pp. 44–61.
37. T. Ropp, *The Development of a Modern Navy, 1871–1904*, ed. S. Roberts (Annapolis, 1989), p. 261. R.C. Hood, *Royal Republicans: French Naval Dynasties between the World Wars* (Baton Rouge, 1981), pp. 7–16. Marder, *Anatomy of British Seapower*, pp. 550–67.
38. P.M. Kennedy, *The Rise and Fall of British Naval Mastery* (London, 1976), p. 206.
39. I.N. Lambi, *The German Navy and Power Politics 1862–1914* (London, 1984), pp. 158, 215.
40. William Graham-Greene (Secretary to the Admiralty) to John Laughton 18.12.1904: A. Lambert (ed.), *Letters and Papers of Professor Sir John Knox Laughton 1830–1915* (Aldershot, 2002), p. 228.
41. Lord C. Beresford, *Memoirs* (London, 1916), pp. 513–14.
42. P. Geyl, *Napoleon: For and Against* (London, 1949), p. 206.
43. Behrman, *Victorian Myths of the Sea*, pp. 93–107.
44. R. Mackay, *Fisher of Kilverstone* (Oxford, 1973), pp. 3, 88, 140, 180, 287–9, 365, 385.
45. Fisher to Arthur Balfour (ex Prime Minister) 23.10.1910: ibid., p. 428.
46. Fisher to Churchill 26.10.1911, 30.12.1911 and 31.7.1914: R.S. Churchill (ed.), *Churchill. Companion Volume II* (London, 1969), part II, pp. 1299, 1366; and part III, p. 1965. He repeated the point to opposition Leader Balfour on 31.7.1914; M. Gilbert, *Churchill Vol. III* (London, 1971), p. 16.
47. A.T. Mahan, *The Influence of Sea Power Upon the French Revolution and Empire 1793–1815*, 2 vols (London, 1892). Mahan used Trafalgar as the pivot point of his second *Sea Power* book, the first volume focused on securing command of

the sea, the second dealt with the consequences of unchallenged command secured at Trafalgar.

48. J.S. Corbett, *The Campaign of Trafalgar* (London, 1910).

49. See Anselm Kiefer's painting *The Ways or Worldly Wisdom – Arminius's Battle of 1978–80*, Art Institute of Chicago. P.S. Wells, *The Battle that Stopped Rome: Emperor Augustus, Arminius, and the Slaughter of the Legions in the Teutoburg Forest* (New York, 2003), see esp. ch. 2.

50. F. Nietzsche, *The Use and Abuse of History* (1873), trans. A. Collins (Indianapolis, 1976), p. 40.

10
Trafalgar in World History: From the Armada to the Second World War

Paul Kennedy

I wish to offer some thoughts, long pondered upon, concerning Trafalgar and its possible place in European and world history. It is of course a hopelessly ambitious theme, and I float it only to provoke thought, dissent and correction. In the first instance I simply mean to add a gloss, here or there, to the insights of that broad array of scholars of Nelson, Trafalgar and the late-Georgian Royal Navy who have emerged during the past 30 years. If I pay little direct reference to their works in this chapter, it is because I am writing in another dimension. Yet I cannot but express my awe, and my great glee, at the revival of the study of British maritime and naval history over the past quarter of a century. When I was composing *The Rise and Fall of British Naval Mastery* some 30-odd years ago, Marder and Roskill were going, or gone; and naval history had virtually disappeared from the British and North American scene, except such as was taught in the service academies. In those days it would have been inconceivable to have been a contributor to a book such as this, on a subject such as this.

I

It may seem as though my title has a certain Victorian or Edwardian mustiness to it. It has echoes of Ranke's essay on 'Die Grossen Maechte' (The Great Powers), perhaps too of Mackinder's 'The Geographical Pivot of History', bold writings which focused upon *la longue durée* of History well before Braudel. The obvious and most direct precursor to my chapter, methodologically, is that offered by the quintessential mid-Victorian, Sir Edward Creasy, who, during his spare time as a barrister at the Temple Chambers composed, in 1851, his classic book *Fifteen Decisive Battles of the World* – quite a title.

Now Creasy was smart enough to admit that different historians would have different lists and rankings of their most important battles, and all would have plausible reasons why *their* shortlist should be preferred to others. What interested him were the general criteria for getting onto the shortlist to begin with. There are some battles, he argued, which, 'independent of the moral worth of the combatants', claim our attention on account of their enduring importance. Like any fellow Benthamite, he thought the effect of such battles could be measured 'by reason of their practical influence on our own social and political condition'. Those struggles have an abiding and actual interest, he added, because 'they have helped to make us what we are'. Finally, they cause us to speculate on 'what might have been' had they ended differently. This was, of course, a very Whiggish and Western history; indeed, all of the 15 decisive battles chosen by Creasy occurred in the West, or the North. It was the perspective of one for whom the defeat of Napoleon's France was the culmination of world history.

Still, Creasy's definition for what constitutes a decisive battle in History seems to me a fair criterion for any assessment of Trafalgar. Where does it stand in the history of the world, what was its influence, how does it relate to where we are today, and what might have happened had it gone the other way? If we come forward another half-century from Creasy, to the centennial of Trafalgar in 1905, the change of mood would be notable. There were, to be sure, the obvious tributes and memorializations. To many a politician and editor, not to mention the leaders of the Navy League, it was a cause for celebration, and for stirring speeches about the importance and role of the Royal Navy in British History. Fair enough. But there was another debate going on that was less celebratory, and much more concerned. Would the Trafalgar effect still last? Would Britannia still rule the waves?

I take for my text here – in addition to Creasy's work – an incredibly significant article written and published in 1905 by the great editor of the *Observer*, J.L. Garvin, journalist, imperialist, navalist, and political economist. Garvin's article was included in a collection of pieces composed by renowned British imperial thinkers and then edited by G.S. Goldman; the book was entitled *The Empire and the Century*, and designed deliberately to appear at the centennial of Trafalgar. It happened to overlap the Russo-Japanese War, and the Battle of Tsushima. It was only a few years after the Spanish-American War, and the rise of the US Navy. It was a mere five years after Tirpitz's Second Naval Law, which doubled the size of the German battlefleet. The world was in a flux. Great Powers were rising and falling.

The essays in *The Empire and the Century* reflect this world of flux. All are weighty articles but none is as significant as Garvin's. He entitled it 'The Maintenance of Empire', a topic which obsessed himself and many of his contemporaries, especially the followers of Joseph Chamberlain. And the essay begins with a remarkable sentence: 'Will the Empire which is Celebrating the Centenary of Trafalgar still Exist in One Hundred Years' Time?' Let me repeat that line. 'Will the Empire that is Celebrating the Centenary of Trafalgar still Exist in One Hundred Years' Time?' The author looked back to 1805, and forward to 2005, and then attempted his answer.

Garvin's reply, supported by impressive data about the economic and military and naval rise of the United States and Germany, was that it would *not*, unless there was an astonishing and radical integration of Britain, its Dominions and its Colonies. If that change, that is, Imperial Federation, did not occur, sheer material heft would force Great Britain – and the Royal Navy – from the centre of the stage. The island nation, which had maintained itself, usually alone, against all vicissitudes from the age of Elizabeth I to the Napoleonic era; the nation which had become the greatest and largest imperial and maritime state in all of History, it too would find its own time had come, not quite at one with Nineveh and Tyre (to use Kipling's words), but much reduced nonetheless.

I focus upon Garvin's grim observations, *not* to throw cold water upon our current testimonials to the 200th anniversary of the Battle of Trafalgar, but to put Trafalgar in its longer-term historical context. What I wish to do is to examine the possibility that this 1805 battle off the south-west coast of Spain was what Hegel might have termed 'a world-historical moment'. And, further, to consider whether it was the apotheosis of Britain's place in world affairs.

To those of us who teach international history and modern European military and naval history, it is not difficult to offer the context for Trafalgar. But if a Martian spaceship had visited the Earth in 1815 or, in Creasy's time, in 1851, those Martians would have been hard pressed to explain to their headquarters back home why a small group of islands off the north-west coast of Europe – islands, as Orwell once put it, that were chiefly reliant upon barley, herrings and potatoes, why *they* dominated the oceans of the world. Why was it not the Philippines?

Why not Madagascar? Why not Taiwan? Why were the trade routes not controlled by a great state based in Central Asia, Halford Mackinder's fabled 'Heartland', or by China? Why no Chinese gunboats patrolling the Thames, the Rhine and the Hudson? And why do we rarely ask such questions ourselves?

II

The larger context, clearly, has to refer to the rise of the West in relation to the rest of the world. This is no place for a detailed recital of what can be found in Toynbee and McNeill, or in E.L. Jones' *The European Miracle* and Geoffrey Parker's *The Military Revolution*. Europe's growth from about 1450 on was the result of many factors. The explosion of scientific knowledge was a primary one, although it must be admitted that many of the advances made in mathematics, astronomy, chemistry and nautics during the Renaissance and the Scientific Revolution itself were imports, direct or indirect, from the East. Perhaps it would be better to say that Europe organized the assembly, dissemination and application of knowledge better than anyone else. The Reformation, far from slowing things down by inducing sectarian bloodshed, merely quickened the pace of acquisitiveness, exploitation, and acute fear of being left behind.

The fact that during the sixteenth century there had arisen a select number of sovereign, ambitious nation-states, each with a national centre, bureaucracy and taxation system, is also a key part of the explanation. Their sheer competitiveness helped to drive the Military Revolution, both on land and at sea; one only has to read about the reforms enacted by Maurice of Orange, John Hawkins and Gustavus Adolphus, to see testimony of that. To succeed – or, in the case of the Dutch Republics and Elizabethan England, to survive – one simply had to be better. And it is no coincidence that, for all nations bordering the sea, the state organization of naval force came to play a leading part in their Darwinian struggles. Each of them felt, to paraphrase Palmerston, that they had no permanent allies and no permanent enemies; just permanent interests. It therefore behoved them to have permanent, standing forces.

But these lengthy, inter-state contests could not be confined to Europe itself; they spread out, to the western hemisphere and to parts of Asia, in the wake of the early explorers and conquistadors. They were encouraged by their awareness that they had fighting platforms, in their long-range, gunned, sailing-ships, that could not be opposed by local craft; the latter were simply blown out of the water. These adventurers were driven, so they claimed at the time, by the ideological and religious desire to convert the heathen, outflank the Turk, and destroy the wily schemes of the Catholics – or the Protestants (whichever viewpoint you took). They were most clearly driven by the passionate desire for wealth, be it Eastern spices, Peruvian silver, Caribbean sugar, or North American furs.

However one orders the motives, the fact is that Europe exploded into the outer world, from the time of Henry the Navigator, through the sixteenth, seventeenth and eighteenth centuries, and would still expand all the way up to 1919. The European states thus fought in two theatres, or in pursuit of two aims: the first was the struggle for mastery on the Continent, or to deny that mastery to another; and the second was the struggle for mastery of the oceans. And, as the range and ambitions of their struggles expanded, the rest of the world trembled. But, with the exception of the Russian drive through Siberia and the American push across Appalachia, this expansion came by sea. It was built upon, and sustained by sea power. From the great battles of the Anglo-Dutch Wars, to the campaigns at the Nile and at Trafalgar itself, to the imposition of the Pax Britannica, here was the underlying cause. Captain Mahan's various works on 'the influence of sea power upon History' may strike us as quaint and old-fashioned today – as quaint as Creasy. But the reason that he is known so well is because he said something that his contemporaries and later generations realized, instinctively, was true. Command of the sea counted. For an island nation, it counted above all else.

Within this larger context of the rise of the organized fighting and trading states of the West, the pre-eminence of Britain and its Royal Navy can more easily be understood – and measured. To be sure, there is considerable new, and very respectable literature about British maritime power during the seventeenth and eighteenth centuries, and even at the time of Trafalgar itself, which points to an amendment of the progressive Mahanian tale: that the British lead was often precarious; that its financial system shuddered, close to a halt, at various times; that the administration of the fleet was poor on so many occasions; that the government's strategy in some of the conflicts lovingly described by Mahan was inept and confused. In sum, this was a nation which often was damned lucky to survive. All such amendments can indeed be taken on board, but without significant change to the overall explanation of Britain's maritime mastery and the defeat of Napoleon's naval ambitions.

For the incontrovertible facts are these. By being an offshore island, Britain had a massive – just impossibly massive – geopolitical advantage over all of its European rivals. Because England and Wales had merged under Henry Tudor, and merged again with Scotland under James I, and because they had ferociously subdued their Irish neighbours, they were strategically intact, a fortress girt around by a moat, as Shakespeare put it. They could be part of the continent of Europe, or separate from it; basically, it was their choice, so long as they kept a powerful navy.

The British also had a strong political constitution, relative to other countries. They had fought a dire civil war in the 1640s, but it was nothing like the religious wars that tore apart France and Germany, and divided the Low Countries. They escaped the excesses and internal confusions of Spain, Italy and Russia. The great compromises between the King and Parliament after 1660 and 1688 gave Britain a political structure that the late J.H. Plumb termed 'adamantine in its nature'. It could be rocked, but not overthrown, even by the 1715 and 1745 Jacobite rebellions, even by the South Sea Bubble, even by the mutiny at the Nore in 1797. The system held. It was underpinned by a merger of interests of the landed and urban élites. It was girded by the Bank of England, the London stock market, the county banks, the parliamentary vote on the estimates, and the pledge to repay all government debts. Little wonder that Dutch, Swiss and even French investors preferred British bonds to their own!

It is now easy to fit the navy of Nelson's day into this picture. Of course he himself was unique, in my view the greatest fighting admiral of all time; and it is wonderful that recent writing has begun to explore his magic, both during his life and in the later impacts he made, upon his service and upon his nation. His actions at Cape St Vincent, the Nile and Trafalgar still make me shake my head in awe. But Nelson's genius, and the Trafalgar victory, had to rest upon strong foundations. This is why I invoked Hegel. Few people read the Prussian philosopher these days, and the English-language translations are even more incomprehensible than the original German. But Hegel has an interesting set of ideas upon what he terms 'world-historical figures'. By this he means persons – Alexander, Julius Caesar, William the Conqueror, surely he would have included Churchill – who achieve great things, yes, of course, because of their individual character and genius, but *also* because they were in conjunction with certain broader trends and structures.

This is where I place Lord Nelson. His tactical, operational and strategical skills have no equivalent, but he had to pace the decks of HMS *Victory* every day, and HMS *Victory* and the rest of the battlefleet were built upon solid foundations, even in a swaying sea. That battlefleet rested upon a strong government structure, notwithstanding the political intrigues of the day. It rested upon the booming trades to the Americas, the West and East Indies. It rested upon the new industrial production, though

Professor Crouzet is wise to caution us not to exaggerate. It rested upon the best naval administration in the world, though again Professor Knight is wise to offer caution on that point. It rested upon the best credit system in the world (a historical reminder which our contemporary Number One power, with its catastrophic deficits, might take more seriously to heart). It rested upon the largest industry that the world had ever seen – the British shipbuilding industry of the early nineteenth century. It rested, not just upon the line-of-battleships that Nelson and his dear friend Collingwood took into the middle of the Franco-Spanish fleet, but upon the hundreds and hundreds of frigates and sloops and despatch-vessels that served in the Royal Navy and secured its maritime dominance.

Ultimately, it rested upon good organization – a vital element, whether one is thinking about navies, or businesses, or History departments. The British were simply better organized than the rest. That may sound like the old Flanders and Swann ditty – 'The English, the English, the English, are best', but in terms of organizing fighting force at sea it simply was the case. Now, give those strengths to someone like Nelson, and the combination is irresistible. It had of course been seen before, this combination of the fighting admiral and the back-up organization, as evidenced by two of my favourite admirals, Blake and Anson. They, together with another dozen at least, going back to the Elizabethans, had left the nation with Kipling's Heritage.

The story thereafter is a little triste, and then recovers. Admirals and captains of the post-Trafalgar generations revered that victory and hoped to repeat it in their own time. Alas, none of them could do it, in part because none of them were Nelson, in larger degree because the geopolitical circumstances had changed. The naval campaigns of the Crimean War were local and spasmodic. The First World War in the North Sea had the potential for a second Trafalgar and every British naval officer thought about it. But the newer technologies, indecisive actions, and then the Skaggerak mists, conspired against that. Even when Germany surrendered, and its fleet sank itself at Scapa Flow, few Britons felt it had been a good war for the Navy.

The Second World War at sea was better, much more respectable. Those who were junior officers at Jutland were now of flag rank, and determined not to turn away from enemy torpedoes or shells. Their Prime Minister wanted aggressive, Nelsonic action, sometimes alarmingly so, as one reads in Michael Simpson's fine study of Admiral Cunningham. The island-nation was on its own again, save for the distant Dominions. As in Elizabeth and Pitt's time, it was fighting for survival. To survive in those years, of course it also needed air power; but above all it required command of the sea-lanes. If it lost those, it would fall. But it did not. One imagines that if Nelson had been brought back to join Force H in Gibraltar, or Cunningham's Mediterranean Fleet off Crete, he would have smiled. Rightly so.

III

Two further thoughts about Trafalgar by way of conclusion. In many ways, the effort of the relatively small British nation around 1800 or 1805 is astonishing. How could it put out such immense naval power *and* be holding on to India, *and* its many other distant possessions, *and* be within a few years of despatching Wellington's army into the Peninsula? This was a society and a system that was being strained to the limit, strategically, materially, fiscally, and psychologically. Trafalgar, although attended by the tragic news of Nelson's death, eased those strains.

It did not, of course, lead to the immediate downfall of Napoleon. Far from it. Within a short while he would be ravaging central and eastern Europe once again, and the Royal Navy could do little there. Still, the Emperor had been stopped at sea, and the island-nation would be able to continue to supply monies, munitions and eventually an army to aid its European allies in the defeat of French expansionism. There were many years of fighting to go, but one has the sense that more peoples than the British recognized that epic encounters had occurred off Cape St Vincent, the Nile and finally off Trafalgar, and that Nelson *was* something special – just look at the peals of joy in Haydn's great work 'The Nelson Mass'. That an Austrian living in Hungary could devote a Catholic sung Mass to a British Protestant Admiral from north Norfolk who had just won a battle off Egypt is noteworthy indeed.

My final thought is this. Looking over the long sweep of naval and strategic history from Elizabeth to Churchill, and even to today, the British were always punching above their weight. This is a point worth further discussion, and some contention, but surely it is true. The Royal Navy was outnumbered against the Armada, in the Trafalgar campaign, and hopelessly vulnerable to German air power off Norway and Crete, Japanese naval and air power off Malaya, battered with severe losses on the Malta and Murmansk convoys, and came close to losing the Battle of the Atlantic in both world wars. This is *not* a concluding line of patriotic hyperbole. But the track record is impressive. It just happened to be good in adversity.

Its apogee was in Nelson's victory at Trafalgar, followed by Wellington's astonishing 15-victories-without-defeat campaign in Spain, but the whole history of the naval and military impact of this small state upon the world suggests that some favourable conjunction was present here. A number of creative statesmen and officials had put together a really strong infrastructure, which was complemented, fortuitously, by the emergence of a long line of resourceful wartime leaders who, relying upon that infrastructure, could turn it into effect, both on land and upon the seas. And, of all those wartime leaders, Nelson, as usual, was in the van. It is in this way that we should regard the larger meaning of the Battle of Trafalgar in world history.

Index

Compiled by Sue Carlton